Dead Reckonings

Dead Reckonings

Ideas, Interests, and Politics in the "Information Age"

John Kurt Jacobsen

HUMANITIES PRESS
NEW JERSEY

First published in 1997 by
Humanities Press International, Inc.,
165 First Avenue, Atlantic Highlands, New Jersey 07716

© 1997 by John Kurt Jacobsen

Library of Congress Cataloging-in-Publication Data

Jacobsen, John Kurt, 1949–
    Dead reckonings : ideas, interests, and politics in the
 "information age" / John Kurt Jacobsen.
        p.   cm.
    Includes index.
    ISBN 0–391–04007–3 (cloth : alk. paper).—ISBN 0–391–04030–8
(pbk. : alk. paper)
    1. Policy sciences.   2. Ideology.   3. Mass media—Political
aspects.   I. Title.
H97.J33   1997
320'.6—dc20   96–26894
                                                                CIP

Printed in the United States of America

10 9 8 7 6 5 4 3 2 1

For Mac and Skylla

Contents

Introduction: Ideology and Interests in a New Fin-de-siècle   ix

PART I. THEORETICAL ORIENTATIONS

1. Science and Democracy, or Who's Afraid of Paul Feyerabend?   3
   (*coauthor: Roger Gilman*)
2. Much Ado About Ideas: The Cognitive Factor
   in Economic Policy   25

PART II. INVESTIGATIONS

3. Safeguards and Profits: Civilian Nuclear Exports,
   Neo-marxism, and the Statist Approach   53
   (*coauthor: Claus Hofhansel*)
4. Peripheral Postindustrialism: Ideology,
   High Technology, and Development   82
5. The Political Economy of High Technology   123
6. Technology and the Politics of Trade Policy   148
7. Is Peace a Rational Choice in Ulster?   165
8. Are All Politics Domestic?: Rethinking
   The National-International Connection   188

PART III. POSTSCRIPTS: POLITICIZATION AND HISTORICAL IMAGERY

9. Television, Ideology, and the Korean War   215
10. *Schindler's List*, American Culture,
    and the Politics of the Holocaust   224

Index   233

Introduction: Ideology and Interests in a New *Fin-de-Siècle*

Dead Reckonings investigates how scientific (and some pseudo-scientific) ideas interact with material circumstances and social ideologies to influence the way in which actors define their interests and devise strategies to achieve political goals. I analyze predicaments that arise when public authorities strive to fashion policy strategies that will augment their own power and at the same time cope competently with tough challenges posed by technological change, economic dislocation, ethnic conflict, and media representation. It is probably fair to say that the critical concepts guiding this book stem from a simple cynical observation: that is, that powerful actors always work to interpret and accordingly distort any action, cause or need so as to buttress their favored agenda. In democracies, for all their shortfalls and shortcomings, the "stories" that governing groups assiduously spin about the course of events are contested by rivals (usually wielding fewer resources) who diagnose and portray this same "data" quite differently in their own effort to win crucial support from the wider citizenry. Hence, politics. I hasten to say that I hope that readers will find that this scholastic application of cynicism is only the beginning of wisdom, not its end.

Part I, Theoretical Orientations, kicks off with a defense of the "anarchist theory of knowledge" advanced so controversially over several decades by Paul Feyerabend. This opening sally argues that his deeply misunderstood model (or anti-model, as the case may be) is a valuable device for investigating perennial issues in the study of science and technology, such as its social purposes and political guidance. Feyerabend's perspective informs the critical approach taken through ensuing chapters even if, in some cases, only implicitly. I suspect, however, that some readers will be disinclined to plumb what may seem to be arcane debates in the philosophy of science. So I urge these readers to use the second chapter as their starting point, which shifts from the metatheoretical realm to debates raging in the 1990s in U.S. political science over the most useful applications of "ideas-oriented approaches," particularly in the analysis of economic policymaking.

The six chapters comprising Part II probe (1) the prudent supervision of the export of nuclear fuels and facilities; (2) the socioeconomic impact of foreign high-technology investments on host states; (3) the difficulties of reconciling the microelectronics revolution with social needs in advanced industrial societies; (4) the role that technology as an "independent variable" plays in the politics of trade policy, especially in the United States; (5) the prospect of "peace as a rational choice" in the vexing but hopeful Northern Irish case and (6) a radical (some International Relations specialists will say retrograde) reconsideration of the "national-international connection" in political science and its implications for the maintenance of the porous border between the subdisciplines of international relations and comparative politics.

Part III shifts ground to offer a pair of short and hopefully sharp "postscripts" on political culture and the media. Chapter 9 details the travails of two historians who scripted a public television documentary intended as a thorough assessment of new evidence about the origins and conduct of the Korean War. Blatant ideological biases and outright interference erupted in this volatile mass media realm where professional research standards, commercial concerns and public opinion clash and where something has to give. Chapter 10, originally written for a European (specifically German) audience, assesses the impact of *Schindler's List* upon especially American audiences. In this delicate analytical foray into popular culture, Hollywood narrative, and Steven Spielberg's cinematic style I tease out troublesome latent attitudes and messages, trace their origins, and appraise their ideological impact.

Several strong thematic threads bind these disparate topics together. Parts I and II address contemporary debates on economic policy and technological change, examine how counter-elites and/or the mass public tries to gain or improve access to decision making, sift out how "ideas" and interests come to blend in each policy arena, and draw a set of "lessons" for both analysts and activists. Part III applies these theoretical concerns to ideological influences in television and cinema. This volume is intended primarily for social scientists but I hope it will be of some interest to nonspecialists interested in current debates on development issues, economic policy, the politics of science, and the portrayal of controversial political events in the media.

THEMES

Why the title? Dead reckonings are navigational procedures that attempt "to locate something in space or in time (as a goal, a target, a historical event) by deduction, unaided by direct observation or direct evidence; broadly: *guesswork.*"[1] This definition seems to sum up candidly the state of theoretical work in the social sciences. Social scientists certainly try as best they can to build models based on observations and data that are more or less verifiable. But, as the opening chapter argues, causal insights derived from theory-laden observations are bound to be imperfect and so always should be regarded as tentative and context-bound. In social science there are no definitive conclusions; there are only arguments of varying persuasiveness about the use of theory, evidence, and research tools. The continuous confrontation of rival theories, and of these theories with new evidence will continue, as it should in a vibrant field, to generate new analyses. This modest volume criticizes and in turn contributes to this inescapably flawed but absorbing enterprise.

The technical meaning of "dead reckoning" takes us a step further in explaining the book's purposes. That definition is, "the determination without aid of celestial observations of the position of a ship or aircraft deduced from the record of the courses sailed or flown, the distance made, and the known or estimated drift." The nautical language seems apt because in periods of rapid change social scientists usually are very much "at sea." This certainly was the case in the 1960s when the complacent "end of ideologies" thesis was scuttled and is so again in a post–cold war era that, beneath the triumphalism of western elites and frothy philosophizing about an "end of history," is really quite precarious. Boundary markers and judgments based on past behavior do not hold up or else—much the same thing—our confidence in the relevance of these old borders wanes. Hopefully the dead reckonings herein correct for the roll and pitch of historical "drift" better than the works at which I take aim.

The dominant theme is the role of ideas in guiding political action. In the social sciences the time for "ideas" has come around again (the last revival occurred in the mid-1960s) because of growing discontent among scholars over the inadequacy of rational choice and of interest-based models for explaining policy choices. Many social scientists attempt to fill in explanatory gaps of the reigning models by resorting to ideational factors either as a supplement or as a potential basis for a new paradigm. This is an exciting enterprise even if some variants of it do seem stubbornly intent on reinventing chariot wheels.

I address what scholars have come to call the "social construction" of political phenomena, such as the "perceived degree of threat" (in which our ideas about opponents' motives can matter as much as—sometimes more than—behavior when we assign a meaning to their actions). This is a reasonable and revealing enterprise, but the vital task in each instance is to identify the impact of ideas upon policy without downplaying or ignoring the tangible influences of market forces, global trends, and potent elites and organizations. Many analysts conceptualize "ideas" as if they were a force in exactly the way that "interests" are conceived. As noted in Chapter 2 too many scholars, after announcing their acute awareness of the pitfalls involved in assessing the power of ideas, and even after carefully enumerating these pitfalls, fall headlong into idealist traps anyway.

By way of remedy I argue that Antonio Gramsci offers the most supple framework for coming deftly to grips with the task of sifting ideational elements in the formation of political interests. (I do not assert that this tack is the *only* remedy.) In this tricky intellectual terrain "cultural studies" practitioners prove to be the most adroit scholars although even some among them, as Feyerabend warns regarding the tendency of brash new theories to turn into incipient orthodoxies, show signs of becoming shufflers of slick concepts very much like the rational choice theorists they abhor. I hope I am wrong about this dismaying trend.

THE CONTENTS

Chapter 1 explores the dialectical character of the philosophy of science of Paul Feyerabend and highlights the vibrant challenge he offers to scientists, social scientists and, indeed, all citizens. I and coauthor Roger Gilman compare Feyerabend's work with that of the Frankfurt School in order to point out important affinities between such extremely unlikely comrades. The Herculean task is to overcome the distortions which Feyerabend's colorful writings have suffered so that his strengths can be appreciated and so that questionable aspects of his work may be addressed clearly and fairly. A comparison between the prescriptive aspects of Jurgen Habermas's philosophy and those of Feyerabend is, we believe, especially instructive.

Chapter 2 scours social science literature on economic policy where a resurgent interest in the role of ideas for explaining choices got under way in the 1990s. Most of these new, if far from unprecedented, works analyze the interpenetration of interests and ideas so as to plumb the variability of interest-formation, and to consider the needed degree of public influence over economic policy. The bold thesis that ideas have a force all their own (independent of all interests) is misguided. This chapter spells out the flaws and difficulties of recent ideational approaches, such as the fad for "epistemic community" analysis, and introduces a means of conceptualizing the efficacy of ideas so that analysts need not, in the act of acknowledging ideational influences, make the mistake of fetishizing them.

Chapter 3 contrasts structural marxist theories of the state with "statist" approaches (particularly Stephen Krasner's sophisticated version) in explaining the policy decisions regarding control of civilian nuclear facilities and fuel. During periods of harmony between the interests of "state managers" and powerful private actors, scholars find little to choose between these two models. In moments of "policy crisis" however, a structural marxist model is, I and coauthor Claus Hofhansel argue, a far more illuminating guide as to how international agents and pressures affect the calculus of domestic policymakers. This highly sensitive issue-area recently brought the United States to the brink—or a convincingly contrived brink—of war with North

Korea. The core case is a study of the passage and aftermath of the 1978 Non-Proliferation Act (NPT).

Statist and marxian approaches both incorporate ideology as an important factor in their explanatory dynamics. The touted difference between "peaceful" and military uses of the atom, for example, was a purely conceptual barrier—a figment of a skewed political imagination—yet one which, while it seemed credible, was employed in the struggle among competing interests within the "strategic field" of state institutions so as to fortify their arguments for their agendas. This chapter offers a Gramscian study of short-run, incremental policy struggles—that is, political battles falling well short of systemic crises.

Chapter 4 applies this approach to a case study by examining how, in the course of what I term "policy struggles," external pressures are converted by domestic agents into programmatic messages to potential allies as to the best policy response. The central case is the Irish Republic which is situated intriguingly between the First World (whose political institutions it adopted) and the Third World (whose economic characteristics it resembles). The Irish have pursued, since the mid-1970s, a high technology development path based on enticing foreign investors. The chapter is a cautionary study of the political limits of an export-led development approach and a tempered application of Gramsci's insights to the analysis of middle-range policy where marxism is ordinarily thought to offer scant insight.

Just as Chapter 4 investigates technology choices and consequences in developing countries, Chapter 5 addresses these issues in advanced industrial nations. I scrutinize the ballyhooed "microelectronics revolution" and the politics of policy choices in the United States, Western Europe (primarily Britain and France), and Japan. Ideology helps set the terms of debate: the notion of the "autonomy" of technology is an advantageous asset for groups promoting the current rightward policy momentum. The chapter evaluates debates in the scholarly realms over the depiction of automation as a "job-killer."

The key quandary policymakers face is the "microchip dilemma": that is, in a competitive global economy rapid adoption of high-technology processes erodes jobs while slow adoption guarantees greater losses in the long run. I argue that the quantity and the quality of employment are the result of *political* choices rather than of irresistible dynamics imposed by technology or the market. Political processes shape technical innovation; automation is the cumulative result of alterable patterns of the distribution of wealth, power, and knowledge in a society.

Chapter 6 examines the use of a concept of technology as an "independent variable" influencing the choices made in trade relations among advanced industrial countries. The narrow notion of an "irresistible" and "unidirectional" technology interacts with the likewise ideologically-charged notion of free trade to promote particular interest-ridden economic programs. Although regionalization arrangements are all the rage, I argue that especially the advanced industrial states still wield a considerable degree of power in an economic game whose domestic component demands that they promote competitive goals in ways that achieve some semblance of balance with wider concerns for a fair distribution of costs and benefits.

Chapter 7 addresses the Northern Irish conflict that, despite what one hopes was a brief burst of violence in February 1996, has been undergoing a fits-and-starts process toward a political resolution. I consider, in a suitably wary manner, the cultivation of conditions under which peace can become a rational choice for all warring parties. Ideologies, interpretations, and impressions are literally life-or-death matters in that long "low-intensity" conflict. This exercise takes a skeptical stance regarding the application of rational models of conflict management, but that is not to say these models—when applied with humility—are without value.

Chapter 8 reviews tentative efforts in political science to span the theoretical divide between the fields of comparative politics and Realist-oriented international relations. I take the rather unusual step of incorporating contributions by British scholars who have treated this integrative task more interestingly and rigorously than do counterparts in the *mainstream* wing of U.S. IR. (Indeed, one ornery U.S. reader of an earlier version of this chapter decided that I must be a "Brit.") I contend that "all politics are domestic" in nature, if not in origin, and that historical sociological approaches offer the most promising ways to bridge the cross-disciplinary gap between IR and comparative politics.

Chapter 9 investigates the plight of two historians whose scripts for a British-American coproduction of a Korean War documentary were distorted, they complain, for ideological reasons by television producers. This essay examines competing versions of the disputed events and details what were probably inherent difficulties in disseminating historical research in a highly charged ideological atmosphere. Although there was an effort by a right-wing "watchdog" group to alter materials to suit their own biases, it appears that it was the producers' intuitive sense of what they believed the American public would be willing and able to comprehend about the war that seems to have determined the content.

Chapter 10 ventures into the politics of popular culture, specifically cinema. I trace the narrative strategy, cultural impact and political implications of Steven Spielberg's *Schindler's List*. Political phenomena, as cultural studies analysts never tire of demonstrating, can be found in the strangest places, such as advertisements, cinemas, and shopping malls. This essay is a fitting note on which to conclude inasmuch as critics ranging from the Frankfurt School scholars to Hannah Arendt to Feyerabend long have fretted that an untempered search for final answers in science tends to lead, even if unwittingly, to a sinister search for final solutions, too.

There are so many people to thank for constructive criticism that listing them would run for pages and pages—and still inadvertently omit valued friends, colleagues, and seers. One ought to try to acknowledge debts anyway. So I alphabetically want to thank Alba Alexander, Helmuth Berking, Steve Bronner, Dr. Noel Browne, Jim Caporaso, Bruce Cumings, Raymond Duvall, John Freeman, David Garrow, Ira Katznelson, Ed Klark, Steve Krasner, Joel Krieger, Bill Leahy, Emmet Larkin, Charles Lipson, Desmond and Skylla MacNamara, Robert Melville, Brendan O'Leary, Adam Przeworski, Paul Ricouer, Lloyd and Susanne Rudolph, Phillipe Schmitter, Mary Schmuttenmaer, Sabine Schweinitz, Duncan Snidal, Brian Trench, Daniel Verdier, Michael Wallerstein, Jack and Nell Wendler, James Wickham, Kent Worcester and all those anonymous referees. I also am grateful to Cindy Kaufman-Nixon at Humanities Press for her efficient and gracious help through the production process.

Most of the work comprising Parts I and II was presented at the Program in International Politics, Economics, and Security at the University of Chicago and benefited from the lively, generous, and exacting critiques routinely dispensed there. Finally, I acknowledge permission to use chapters which appeared earlier in article form in *Nature, Society and Thought, World Politics, the International Political Economy Yearbook, New Politics, British Journal of Political Science, International Studies Quarterly, New Political Science, The Bulletin of Concerned Asian Scholars, Brown Journal of World Affairs* and *Comparative Politics.*

Note

1. *Webster's Third International Dictionary* (New York: R. C. Merriam Publishers, 1964) p. 580.

PART I
THEORETICAL
ORIENTATIONS

1

Science and Democracy, or Who's Afraid of Paul Feyerabend?

Since publication of his flamboyant treatise, *Against Method*, critics across the ideological spectrum have denounced Paul Feyerabend's "anarcho-dadaist" argument.[1] Feyerabend observed, not without glee, that right-wingers vilified him as a fan of totalitarian China while certain scholars on the Left blithely labeled him a "class peripheral parasite."[2] Many readers, he explained, mistook his slogan "anything goes" as a formula for disciplinary diarrhea when all he prescribed for science was an occasional counterinductive enema! This chapter argues that Feyerabend (despite his own disavowal) is best understood as a "marxist outlaw," that his critique of science is grasped most clearly in comparison with the neo-marxist critique by the Frankfurt School and that his work is an extremely useful aid for examining the politics of science policy.[3]

A common classical criterion for classifying studies of science is whether they claim that "social conditions influence only the behavior of scientists and scientific activity or that they also influence the basic concepts and the logical structure of science."[4] Feyerabend argues that both forms of influence always occur and in a reciprocal way.[5] He was in complete accord with Max Horkheimer that in "genuinely critical thought, explanation signifies not only a logical process but a concrete one as well," and while "rational knowledge does not controvert the tested findings of science, unlike empiricist philosophy, it refuses to terminate with them."[6] Feyerabend, who died in 1994, was no mere mischief maker; he strived, like the Frankfurt scholars, to illuminate the philosophical basis and social preconditions for the practice of science in a truly rational world.[7]

We treat him as a "marxist outlaw," that is, one who views marxism as a "powerful source of demystification yet is well aware that marxism may become a form of mystification itself."[8] Marxist outlaws resist the reification

3

of marxism; they use the dialectic to study dialectics.[9] This fierce consistency, this universalness of procedure, attracted for Feyerabend silly epithets from some leftists who evidently believed that marxism cannot lead to the same suppression of the presence of the speaker in his speech or of the observer in their observations as does the positivistic version of empiricism (which disguises our "attributions" as "properties" of the worlds and transforms "contingencies" into "necessities").

Feyerabend devised an epistemological strategy that requires science to remain rigorously critical in a way consistent with the goals of the Frankfurt School. Yet his tactics of *internal* subversion differ in disturbing ways from those of critical theorists. The latter favor a fostering of *external* criticism that will lead to reform of the institutionalized "speech situation" in which scientific theories get debated, causing them to be subjected to alternative forms of rationality that thereby nourish democratic activity. This shared emancipatory goal animates both Feyerabend and the Frankfurt School.

Feyerabend has been difficult to appreciate or even to comprehend.[10] His acerbic prose, which tempts even radical scholars to dismiss him, is partly and perhaps mostly to blame.[11] Still, this aversion to Feyerabend seems odd because anyone who has worked outside the mainstream will know precisely what Feyerabend means when he observes that in formal settings an argument "becomes effective only if supported by an appropriate attitude and has no effect when the attitude is missing (and the attitude I am talking about must work *in addition* to the readiness to listen to argument and is independent of an acceptance of the premises of arguments)."[12] Here he addresses a subtle but potent layer of predispositions affecting a scientific community, a layer of predispositions which Jürgen Habermas's institutionalized "speech situation" does not readily confront or remedy.

The predicament that Feyerabend squarely addresses is how one is to act when the deck is stacked, when authorities are anything but welcoming.[13] This chapter demonstrates that Feyerabend's self-description as a dadaist is misleading, the similarities of his and the Frankfurt critique, that both critiques stem from similar motives; and draws out troubling implications of their different prescriptions.[14]

SCIENCE AND DOMINATION

Alvin Gouldner capsulizes the view, shared by Feyerabend and the Frankfurt theorists, that there is an "inevitable politics of science"

> not only in the trivial sense of who gets to be the government's science adviser but in the more profound sense of how diverging views are brought into consensus, when and if they are. This means that the structure of domination will be found at the boundaries and limits of a culture of

rational discourse. The more this is denied or repressed the more difficult
it is to diminish their influence on, and prevent their subversion of the
grammar of discourse.[15]

Feyerabend argues that "modes of conception" in science are heavily dependent upon the "mode of producing" science—that is, on how institutions shape the expression of ideas. This familiar proposition remains fiercely
controversial.[16] In a study of science in the seventeenth century, Robert
Merton stressed the indispensible role played by an ascendant merchant class
who valued technologies as devices to augment wealth and viewed science
as an advantageous solvent upon aristocratic rule.[17] Scientists chose the path
of least resistance:

> Under the conditions of ideological impasse that were reached in England
> in 1640 scientists found themselves in a situation in which it was increas-
> ingly useful to adopt Baconianism as a strategy of survival . . . natural sci-
> ence served as a symbol of a neutral meeting ground. Official support of
> science in France and elsewhere on the continent came from absolutist
> conservative rulers. The insistence on the strict neutrality of science and
> the specificity which made it accessible only to experts was therefore, a
> condition for the freedom of scientific inquiry.[18]

The Royal Society in England prohibited discussion of politics and religion. Lewis Mumford pointed out that a rueful legacy of this prudence was
that it "discouraged the scientist from critically examining his own metaphysical assumptions [and] even fomented the delusion that he had none—
a theme only recently, and reluctantly, opened up."[19] The reductionist and
mechanistic aspects of science actually were derived from religious presuppositions of order (e.g., Newton's God as Divine Watchmaker; Kepler's Music
of the Spheres), but this embarrassing source was obscured by a growing list
of impressive accomplishments—in pursuit of the "technically sweet," as Robert
Oppenheimer phrased it.

Epitomized in Lord Kelvin's exhortation, scientists strove to advance knowledge "one more decimal place" and so substituted an evolutionary optimism
for a realistic analysis of their relationship to the social forms in which experimental activity occurs. This utopian impulse was absorbed into positivism and expressed in its truncated terminology. Feyerabend appraises this
approach in his analysis of science as a *social institution* in the eighteenth and
nineteenth centuries:

> In these years science was a liberating force not because it had found the
> truth or the right method (though this was assumed to be the reason by
> defenders of science), but because it restricted the influence of other ide-
> ologies and gave the individual room for thought . . . The methods and
> achievements of science were subjected to a critical debate. In this situation

it made perfect sense to commit oneself to the cause of science. *The very circumstances in which commitment took place turned it into a liberating force.*[20]

His bottom line is that "no ideology and way of life is so perfect that it cannot be improved by consulting alternatives."[21] There is nothing inherently liberating in science or any ideology. They deteriorate the moment they succeed. Feyerabend contends, like Marx, that facts are constituted by older ideologies whose origins have faded from awareness, and that prejudices are more effectively exposed by contrast than analysis.[22] He urged that old theories be revived in order to flush out presuppositions and other ideological barriers to new knowledge.[23] These barriers, or "silences" as they are dubbed in social theory, are "unarticulated assumptions and unrealized mediations" that ought to be voiced and noted.[24]

Of course, some paradigms will be superior guides for certain purposes of inquiry. The criteria for choosing these paradigms are lodged in both the "universal intent" (as Michael Polanyi termed it) and in the intersubjectively validated norms and procedures of a scientific community. But this depiction of science circles back to the point at which Feyerabend and the critical theorists commence their critiques. "By objectivity of the data," Ian Barbour observes, "we can only mean its reproducibility within a scientific community sharing a common set of assumptions and concepts."[25] The Frankfurt scholars were alert to the political implications. In the heyday of logical positivism Horkheimer lamented

> Because of existing conditions the prevailing practice of science is in fact cut off from important insights and is outdated in form. The judgment on how far the total structure of science and the condition of individual sciences correspond to the knowledge now available is itself a complicated theoretical problem and cannot be decided once and for all.[26]

The abiding problem was Karl Mannheim's paradox; that the principles in light of which knowledge is to be criticized are themselves socially and historically conditioned. Horkheimer implied that this paradox can be defused dialectically, but did not give exact instructions

> [In dialectical theory] the fact that subjective interest in the unfolding of society as a whole changes continuously in history is not regarded as a sign of error, but as an inherent factor of knowledge ... To realize an explicit interest in a future rational society the prerequisite is that the individual abandon the mere recording and prediction of facts, that is, mere calculation; that he learn to look behind the facts; that he distinguish the essential from the superficial without minimizing the importance of either; that he formulate conceptions that are not simple classifications of the given; and that he continually orient all his experiences to definite goals without falsifying them; in short, that he learn to think dialectically.[27]

Feyerabend proposes a set of procedures by which scientists can "think dialectically." Indeed *Against Method* is so saturated with a shrewd Leninist sensibility that it amounts to a *What is To Be Done?* for seditious lab personnel. Regarding Mannheim's paradox, he suggests an approach very much like that of the Frankfurt theorists who posited a utopian "other" as a standard by which to measure the rationality (or barbarity) of the social order.[28]

> We need an external standard of criticism, we need an alternative set of assumptions or, as these assumptions will be quite general, constituting as it were, an entire alternative world, we need a dream-world in order to discover the real world we think we inhabit (and which may actually be another dream-world) . . . We must invent a new conceptual system that suspends or clashes with the most carefully established observational results, confounds the most plausible theoretical principles, and introduces perceptions that cannot form part of the existing conceptual world.[29]

SCIENCE AND SUBVERSION

Feyerabend relates what he called "slightly bowdlerized versions" of historical development to illustrate his point that "given any aim, even the most narrowly 'scientific' one, the non-Method of the anarchist [i.e., proliferation of methods and hypotheses] has a greater chance of succeeding than does any well-defined set of standards, rules or prescriptions."[30] Epistemological anarchism is antimonistic and antiabsolutist. It opposed any single comprehensive, foundational, or exclusive method. Albert Einstein, for example, attested that the facts of experience do not permit scientists to be too much restricted in the construction of their conceptual worlds.[31] Scientists *must* be opportunists.

Significant research always violates methodological rules. Galileo's heliocentrism, Newton's gravitational theory and Bohr's atomic model did not satisfy positivism's criteria for scientific conduct. In Galileo's case Ptolemaic theory not only displayed superior empirical content (though not elegance, simplicity, or consistency) but the only visible means of support of his hypothesis, the telescope, was so primitive an instrument that it could not provide decisive evidence.[32] The church, to put it perversely, had a point. (See Feyerabend's letter on p. 19.)

E. A. Burtt reckoned that "empiricists, had they lived at the time, would have been the first to scoff out of court the new philosophy of science."[33] The triumph of Galileo's view was attributable to rhetorical skills by which he attracted support from a rising commercial class, eluded challenges to his law of circular inertia, and so propagated a view which absurdly claimed that the earth rotates on its axis. If Popper's demand for retaining the theory with greater empirical content had prevailed, Feyerabend argues, worthy challengers like Galileo, Newton, and Bohr would have been smothered on their speculative cribs.[34] Instead, they set up new research programs, assembled new kinds of factual domains, and created new ontologies and methods.[35]

All's fair in science—especially when the rules favor, and resources accrue to, the status quo. Stealth, guile, and cunning may be necessary if a new or revitalized theory is to insinuate itself into the prevailing framework, until the latter is displaced by a cumulative process of subversion. If afforded a "breathing space" a promising theory would have been awarded a margin of safety in relation to powerful rivals.[36] Feyerabend's analysis resonates with Horkheimer's combative lament that "in regard to the essential kind of change at which critical theory aims, there can be no corresponding perception of it until it actually comes about."[37]

Feyerabend's debt to dialectics becomes startlingly clear when one compares him with the non-Frankfurt, marxist Louis Althusser:

> At its moment of constitution, as for physics with Galileo and for the science of evolution of social formations (historical materialism) with Marx, a science always works upon existing concepts, "Vorstellung." . . . It does not work on a purely objective "given," that of pure and absolute facts. On the contrary, its particular labor consists of elaborating its own scientific facts through a critique of ideological facts. To elaborate its own "facts" is simultaneously to elaborate its own "theory" since a scientific fact . . . can only be identified in the field of theoretical practice.[38]

In justifying counterinduction Feyerabend cites marxist formulations of uneven development and of unequal relations, for which guerrilla warfare is prescribed. Galileo is the prototypical hero and the "epistemological illusion" (wherein "the problems and facts of the older theory are distorted so as to fit the new framework") is the strategic vehicle for success.[39] He urges application of the counterinductive (dialectical) method to "forms of life" within which the theory may display its highest degree of utility. Even if the challenger fails, the contest improves the older theory by subjecting it to rigorous critique. "Knowledge so conceived is not a process that converges toward an ideal view," Feyerabend writes, "it is an ever-increasing ocean of alternatives, each of them forcing the others into greater articulation, all of them contributing, via this process of competition, to the development of our faculties."[40]

Is Feyerabend advocating proliferation for the hell of it? Has he crossed the thin line between scientific fecundity and frivolousness, thereby degrading science to relativistic drivel? These accusations are unwarranted because there *is* a dialectical core to his argument and a liberatory motive guides his analysis. He aims at restoring historical tension to one-dimensional reason. His objectives are identical with those of a theorist he derided as "a third rate intellectual." Herbert Marcuse writes:

the given reality has it's own logic and its own truth; the effort to comprehend them as such and to transcend them presupposes a different logic, a contradicting truth. When the historical content enters into the dialectical concept . . . ontological tension between essence and appearance, between "is" and "ought", becomes historical tension, and the "inner negativity" if the object world becomes understood as the work of the historical subject—man in his struggle with nature and society, Reason becomes historical reason. It contradicts the established order of men and things on behalf of existing societal forces that reveal the irrational character of the order—*for "rational" is a mode of thought and action which is geared to reduce ignorance, destruction, brutality and oppression.*[41]

Next we discuss Feyerabend's "rhetoric of relativism," his dialectical link with the critical theorists, and the connection between Feyerabend's procedural tips and the process of democratization.

THE RHETORIC OF RELATIVISM

Feyerabend warns critics regarding the apparently lurid logic of his argument that:

There is no attempt on my part to show "that an extreme form of relativism is valid." I do not try to justify the autonomy of every mood, every caprice, and every individual." I merely argue that the path to relativism has not yet been closed.[42]

The "specter of relativism" motivates much of the misreading of Feyerabend.[43] *Political relativism* affirms that all traditions have equal rights (to protective institutions and laws); *philosophical relativism* asserts that all traditions are equally true. *The first form of relativism is not dependent on the second. Feyerabend avows a belief in political relativism, not philosophical relativism.*[44] His narrow goal is to show that philosophical relativism is not irrational; his broader concern is teasing out the democratic consequences of political relativism. He notes:

People living in a society that does not give their tradition the rights they think it deserves will work towards a change. To effect the change, they will use the most efficient means available. They will use existing laws, if that is going to help their cause; they will "argue rationally" when rational argument is required; they will engage in open debate . . . where the representatives of the status quo have no fixed opinion and no fixed procedure; they will organize an uprising if there seems no other way.[45]

Protective institutions are historically—not just theoretically—based, so discussions of "justice," "rationality," and "freedom" are never utterly abstract. Since different traditions embody different forms of rationality, and since any standard of comparative judgment must be derived from one of the traditions themselves, the exchange between traditions is an "open" exchange, not a "rational" one. The procedure does not engage in comparative evaluation of content by an agreed-upon value, rather, it involves an exchange of incommensurate values. Scientific rationalists are just one group protecting its interest even if they believe this coincides with a universal interest.[46] Note that Feyerabend's prescription "anything goes"—epistemological dadaism—does not consist of thinking or acting without methods.

> I argue for a contextual account. But the contextual rules are not to replace absolute rules; they are to supplement them. My intent is to expand the inventory of rules and also to suggest a new use for all of them. It is this use that characterizes my position and not any particular rule-content.[47]

Feyerabend relies on historical studies that demonstrate how standard methods were suspended by successful scientists and describe the procedures that these scientists substituted. He demonstrates how counterinduction reveals the limits of induction, how proliferation discloses the limits of falsification, and how redefinition reveals the limitations of meaning invariance.

If this is the meaning of "anything goes," then Feyerabend is no dadaist. Dadaists oppose all rules and methods. "Dada," says Hans Richter, "not only has no program, it was against all programs."[48] The power of dada is entirely negative. Surrealists are more aptly invoked because they seek alternative methods rather than to deny the value of rules altogether. *Feyerabend is a surrealist, in the Bretonian tradition of wedding a liberatory motive to the discipline of the arts and sciences.* The "mode of justification" is not suspended; it is expanded to include "modes of discovery," increasing the chance to detect human interests at work in research.

"Surrealism in its first intent," explained Ferdinand Alquie, "may be defined as the denial of everything; always beginning again":

> it endeavors to extend human experience, to interpret it outside the limits and framework of a narrow rationalism ... Rapt hope in the future, interpretation of the marvelous as a sign of a beyond ... concern to lift all prohibitions to attaining "the life of presence, nothing but presence," hope of changing the worlds by liberating desire—such are the motifs which lead Breton to condemn writers who speak of asceticism and dualism and to cherish those who promise reconciliation of man with the world and with himself. ... Revolution is for Breton only one of man's tasks—a task that derives its sense only in light of its end, which must be thought or felt independently of means to attain it.

Prescribing unorthodox means to achieve emancipatory ends, Feyerabend's intention is to make science conscious of the ways in which knowledge is constructed and employed within systems of domination so that the spread of this consciousness will nourish a wider social struggle. *Not only does Feyerabend's tactics increase the latitude for action within scientific communities; the exposure of interests (an increase in proliferation and emancipation) may "spill over" into society and stimulate new alignments between science and social forces.* The Frankfurt School, despite its legendary pessimism, surely would agree with this goal.

Like John Stuart Mill, Feyerabend asserts that proliferation of hypotheses and methods will encourage and fortify the protective institutions of a dynamic democracy. Feyerabend is very careful to explain that protective institutions by themselves cannot guarantee a creative science and vibrant society—rather it is the habit of the proliferation of ideas and methods that will secure (if anything can) these objectives.

FEYERABEND AND CRITICAL THEORY

The goal of Feyerabend's internal critique of science—disclosure of hidden contradictory premises within prevailing theories—overlaps with the goals of the external critique propounded by critical theorists. Both Feyerabend and critical theorists attack ahistorical images of scientific enterprise and point out how asymmetrical power relationships (within and encompassing the scientific community) are disguised. Horkheimer and Theodor Adorno noted that if "truth" of scientific knowledge must be tested by its pragmatic consequences (in Peircean fashion), then it ultimately is evaluated by the technology it produces and so science tends to dwindle into "instrumental" reason. But what counts as "instrumental," as a useful technology, is always tied to a particular set of human interests.

These interests vary as does the power to implement any one set over others. If economic and political institutions (the social formation within which science and its products are evaluated) are controlled by a skewed market of class interests, then scientific knowledge, unconsciously and indirectly, but all the more powerfully promotes the interests of those who dominate the "exchange process."[49]

Horkheimer and Adorno too argue that the Enlightenment view of reason was a truly liberating belief that eventually became a stumbling block.[50] Marcuse attacks Auguste Comte's *Cour de philosophie positive* for heralding science as "the only positive knowledge of reality" and for viewing men and institutions as "neutral objects" governed by "natural necessity."[51] This belief induced "people to take a positive attitude toward the prevailing state of affairs" such that any reform introduced into the society, including the institutions for the creation of knowledge, must be sanctioned by "the machinery of the established order."[52]

This implies that the status quo is always rational—a verdict that critical theorists regard as preposterous. The primacy of "utility" is built into the concept of instrumental reason: people are valuable if they are useful (to whom?); they are useful only if predictable (to whose benefit?); and knowledge is useful only if its applications make people useful, that is, makes them to be predictable means to an end determined by someone else.[53] Ends that serve nonutilitarian values are ignored by positivist science.[54] The utility of activity becomes more important than its social purposes and impact—a chilling trend in the development of epistemology from Kant and Nietzsche to DeSade.

Feyerabend and the critical theorists repudiate this trend as flawed and repugnant. The world of objects is instead a world of *our* objects, of human interpretations. The "given" is mediated by a consciousness full of needs— full of human interests, and conflicts among them—a consciousness that has a specifiable and contingent history, which is the product of a whole social practice, a practice which certainly includes noninstrumental values.

The knowledge process cannot be severed from the historical struggle of humans with nature or with one another—at least not without distortion. Positivist method insists on conferring ontological necessity onto things that are historical and contingent.[55] *What is suppressed is the potentiality of things.* Instrumental reason systematically ignores the alternative meanings that subjects can give to their actions; it ignores alternative ways of organizing social life (including the organization of science); it denies that the act of evaluating is also an intimate part of describing and explaining.

Science becomes ideology when it masks contradictions that work to the advantage of dominant groups. Claiming to represent a "common interest," to deal only in "facts," and that reality is basically harmonious and "natural," is a disguise for inequalities and contradictions. The degree to which a form of knowledge either mystifies or adequately reflects social life must be assessed on a case-by-case basis using a variety of alternative rational methods. An alternative method, no less than the method challenged, inevitably is bound by culture and time. *But this does not imply a radical relativism.* It simply means that neither the objects nor procedures of knowledge are singular and eternal; they are products of activity, not of contemplation.[56]

Only the actual practice of alternative ways of living and knowing can serve as proof of their value; and there is no simple way to evaluate them. Any form of knowledge must exist as a product of some politically and historically bounded method. Horkheimer concludes that only a full-fledged classless society can guarantee the existence of a variety of these practices— a variety Feyerabend zealously promotes. Feyerabend will not wait patiently for the advent of perfectly democratic institutions; he exhorts us to undertake a piecemeal subversion of hegemonic institutions.

DIALECTICS AND DEMOCRACY

Horkheimer and Adorno long ago dismissed Soviet Science as a sorry instance of the triumph of "subjective rationality." Marcuse rued the perversion of dialectical thought by party hacks.[57] Still, Feyerabend finds dialectical materialism is a congenial means for advancing knowledge. Note his admiration for this passage from Lenin's notebooks

> Human Knowledge is not (does not) follow a straight line, but a curve, which endlessly approximates to a series of circles, a spiral . . . The approach of the human mind to a particular thing, the taking of a copy (= a concept) of it is not a simple, immediate act, a dead mirroring but one which includes in it the possibility of transformation, of which man is unaware, of the abstract concept into fantasy . . . It would be stupid to deny the role of fantasy, even in the strictest science.[58]

If "dialectics is a many-sided, living thing," then anything goes. The need for "tenacity was emphasized by those dialectical materialists who objected to extreme 'idealist' flights of fancy," Feyerabend adds. "And the synthesis, finally, is the very essence of dialectical materialism in the forms in which it appears in Engels, Lenin, and Trotsky."[59] Feyerabend refuses to pledge allegiance to dialectical materialism because, like any method, it can become an oppressive orthodoxy. It is absolutely essential to acknowledge that Feyerabend is as concerned that his tactics promote democratic diversity as they are with fostering scientific creativity. In fact, more so.

While dialectical materialism need not smother science, neither does Feyerabend discern a necessary connection between dialectics and the promotion of "human happiness."[60] Hence, he places his bets on proliferation. Science is one among many "traditions," neither good nor bad, as such. Proliferation should counter the manipulation of science into a legitimizing device and he hopes, like Mill, that it will exert an educative impact on citizens outside the labs.[61] Feyerabend is an *iconoclast* in the literal sense that he intends to smash not science, but atavistic images of science. It is astonishing that so many critics consistently overlook his values in their rush to judge him as peddling "a conservative, relativistic position which tolerates everything, including the intolerable."[62]

SCIENCE, DEMOCRACY AND SURREALISM

Feyerabend does not trumpet proliferation for its own sake; rather, he argues that the proliferation is the most compatible principle with advancing the frontiers of knowledge and with enhancing human liberty and happiness. If proliferation conflicted with humane values, he would ditch the former. Criticism is "*dangerous* unless we can show that a society enjoying criticism create greater happiness" and anarchism is "excellent medicine for epistemology," he says. But medicine "is not something one takes all the time."[63]

There are times when one should "give reason a temporary advantage and when it will be wise to defend its rules to the exclusion of all else"—which is politically astute.[64] (One suspects he has in mind conditions ranging from sheer fatigue to resisting fascism.) The criterion for "medicine" is the researchers' judgment that such an action is likely to contribute to "a more enlightened and more liberal form of rationality."[65]

Feyerabend begins, as Mill does, by affirming that the *social consequences* of rationalism are more important than any beliefs, doctrines or practices concerning the acquisition of "truth" or "rationality." The rights of people to arrange their own lives according to their own tradition, is more valuable than any intellectual invention or endeavor. However this is not to say that Feyerabend means by "anything goes" that "everything stays," or that he encourages pursuit of trivial or odious lines of inquiry.[66] Appraising the Shockley-Jensen genetic hypotheses on race in the 1970s, Noam Chomsky raised an objection that is applied frequently to Feyerabend: "Of course, scientific curiosity should be encouraged (though fallacious argument and investigation of silly questions should not), but it is not an absolute value."[67]

Isn't this Feyerabend's point? Would he not reply that proliferation of hypotheses and methods hasten the peeling away of ideological layers that obscure the social motivations for pernicious lines of inquiry? One might dare to hope that a bonus of conflictual interaction might be an improvement in public memory so that the tiresome replay of the Shockley-Jensen charges in the brouhaha over Charles Murray and Richard Hernnstein's *The Bell Curve* would not be greeted with the naiveté it has recently gotten in the U.S. media.[68]

The belief that rational discussion deters naive commitments is drawn from Mill. So, too, is the proviso that pushing views to their limit to increase testability "is a useful *command* only if it does not conflict with important commands elsewhere, such as moral commands."[69] Mill, eager to prick the "deep slumber of decided opinion," drew the line at interfering with the liberty or harming the well-being of others. His key criterion for proceeding with an action was "utility *in the largest sense*, grounded in the permanent interests of man as a progressive being."[70] This affinity with Mill means that Feyerabend is a dadaist only in a very restricted sense. To understand Feyerabend's analogy of dadaism with "anything goes" as a preventive "medicine" for the zealotry of embracing any single method, substitute "Feyerabend" for "Tzara" and "science" where "art" appears in the following:

> the aim of dadaism was to humiliate art, to put it in a subordinate place in the supreme movement measured only in terms of life. The moral and existential was considered to be superior to the merely aesthetic or scientific ... Unlike many Dadaists, Marcel Duchamp was not satisfied with merely iconoclastic or anarchistic gesture, not satisfied with escaping from logic into the symbolic world of the irrational ... he was ... groping

toward a radically new "language" of art that would inherently obey a whole structure of logic *that was yet to be invented.*[71]

Feyerabend is not so frivolous as to say that science is whatever the scientist spits or spills or declares to be so. His motive is not that the individual merely please himself, but an enrichment of human freedom in the kind of rational society envisioned by the critical theorists. A crucial element in this project is the exposure and examination of the influence of social structure on scientific practices. Especially in an intensively competitive high-tech era when scientific resources become more integrated within capitalist production structures, the "hidden substratum" of research must be revealed to the citizenry to secure greater democratic control.[72] This requires the tenacious testing of "what is prevalent."

But the "groping" of a Marcel Duchamp obviously will surpass the grip of lesser talents, and there remains a difference between a "good" dadaist and a "poor" dadaist (though a devout dadaist doubtless would deny it). *The point is that in Feyerabend's work the "context of justification" is not eliminated, as some critics infer, but is expanded to incorporate tests that detect the role of human interests in research.* Many readers assume he is abandoning tests. Quite the contrary.

The power of dada to expose meaninglessness has always surpassed its capacity to restore or create new meaning. Rather than dabble in dada's vacuous villainy, surrealism fastens inquiry to humane ends. Here Feyerabend and the critical theorists fuse in a shared sensibility that is manifested in their investigations of art and science. "The artistic universe is one of illusion, semblance, *schein*," Marcuse argues, "However, this semblance is a resemblance to a reality which exists as the threat and promise of the existing order."[73]

If so, the scope of individuals—their critical capacities and social consciousness—can be "broadened in unraveling of metaphysical and concrete alternatives."[74] Feyerabend recommends a procedure, counterinduction, and avowedly devious tactics by which science can be pried safely out of the surrounding "affirmative culture." The first step in creating an "emancipatory science"—whose design we cannot anticipate—is to make contemporary science conscious of domination, of its historical specificity, of its "insertion" into a mode of production, so that ensuing debates stimulate democratic activity.

When Lenin met zealots who tried to apply marxism to all knowledge domains, he reproached them for "communist conceit." Conversely, scientists promoting their disciplinary modes in politics were reproved for "chemical conceit," "physics conceit" and so on.[75] Why allow an otherwise valuable tool of analysis degenerate into a conceit? As Gouldner notes, marxism exposed "the limits of one form of ideology, that of *idealistic* objectivism; but marxism itself "generated a materialistic objectivism and remains bound by the specific linguistic, nonreflexivity of a materialist ideology. . . ."[76]

Feyerabend places his bets upon "citizen's initiative instead of epistemology" and urges that "duly elected committees of laymen" examine matters like the theory of evolution, medicine, the safety of nuclear reactors, and other issues so that the "last word will not be that of the experts but that of the people immediately concerned."[77] Here he echoes Bakunin: "[B]ecause human science is always and necessarily imperfect... were we to try to force practical life of men ... into strict conformity with the latest data of science we would condemn society as well as individuals to martyrdom on a Procrustean bed."[78] This proliferation should contribute to "politicizing the discussion of the terms and conditions of access to science," which is "the crucial intermediate position between production and application"— and will be explored in following chapters on nuclear power, economic policy, and microtechnology.[79]

However, democratic relativism "will not materialize overnight." What his anti-method exposes is the role of power within the institutional production of knowledge, Feyerabend justifies deceit in unevenly developed milieus—and what milieu is not?—where the rules favor and resources accrue to the status quo. In an uneven milieu, "mutant" concepts will develop only by a cunning political struggle. Deceit is a regrettable and paradoxical necessity because people, as Mill lamented, "are not more zealous for truth than they often are for error."[80] Ideally the practice of "democratic relativism" should approximate the conditions of "communicative competence" Habermas prefers, where scientific dialogue extends effectively to a wider and empowered community. But we do not yet inhabit this world. We note regarding the viability of the Feyerabend's implicit vanguard strategy that

> there may be differences among individuals and groups in their perception of the breakdown (or exhaustion) of the paradigm [of science] due to either location in the scientific community or to differences in their individual sensitivity ... It is possible, therefore, to envisage normative variation leading to as fundamental a change as revolution but issuing from the feelings of frustration and search for innovation by *only a small portion of the community*.[81]

Feyerabend's tactics suit this situation nicely. Once a group pries its view, by hook or crook, into the scientific contest, "what changes, and how, is now either a matter for historical research or for political action carried out by those who participate in the interacting traditions."[82] Nevertheless, deceit remains highly troubling as a tactic because history also repeatedly records how noxious means pervert good ends.

HABERMAS AND FEYERABEND COMPARED

Habermas endorses Max Horkheimer's classic marxist view that the essential problem is not science itself but "the social conditions which hinder the development and are at loggerheads with the rational elements in science."[83] Habermas crafts a view of a science that exposes flaws and interests within instrumental reason in order ultimately to aid citizens in the making of history "with will and consciousness."

Indeed, Albrecht Wellmar describes Habermas's project as a struggle for the critical soul of science."[84] Habermas is as concerned with the perversion of marxism into "strict deterministic explanations and technocratic management" as he is with debunking positivistic science.[85] Scanning the growing interdependence of science, industry, and state power, Habermas concludes that a positivist science is utilized as an ideology to legitimate the prevailing distribution of power (though perhaps with less and less success).[86] "Reflection on the community of investigators would necessarily burst the pragmatist framework" because

> this self-reflection would have to show that the subject of the process of inquiry forms itself on the foundation of an intersubjectivity that . . . extends beyond the transcendental framework of instrumental action.[87]

The insidious influence of instrumental reason skews not only specific class interests but the "general structure of human interests." Habermas shows how cognitive interests confine the possibilities of knowledge and he carefully sets out a variety of motives for inquiry. He favors a cognitive interest in a reflective appropriation of life, without which the interest-bound character of knowledge goes undetected. Habermas argues that we have an interest in generating knowledge that enhances autonomy, where the results are not a means to other ends.

Habermas distinguishes three human cognitive interests: technical, practical, and emancipatory. Each poses a different vantage point from which to constitute reality. Habermas ultimately encourages creation of an "ideal speech situation" in which to evaluate the role these forms of reason should play in social life and public policy. The goal is to "reach a consensus" about the definition and the value of truth, freedom, and justice.[88] For the sake of the progressive values that critical theorists deem an indispensable component of the truly "rational," a constraint-free milieu for debates on science, technology, and public policy must somehow be institutionalized.

Habermas, like Feyerabend, insists that only when there is more than one basis for rationalization of actions is there latitude for human freedom. So, he argues that the burgeoning penchant for modeling social problems in terms of "game theory" is to restrict human values to the computational or strategic and to treat all values misleadingly as "technical" in nature.[89] A concern for exactness and computability is not neutral; it is a preselection of values that lend themselves to the technology of control. One result is to disqualify the judgment of lay people in what really may be a conflict of values (between alternative forms of reason or between priorities of values) by portraying these conflicts as concerning "neutral" procedures or simple cost-benefit tallies.

Habermas addresses a notoriously unresolved tension in Marx's thought. This tension stems from ambiguity in the concept of human "productive action," which is defined both as necessary technical acts of survival, and as free, self-defining acts that actualize species-being. This tension was, in the Soviet case, resolved for a while in favor of dogmatic scientism.[90] The emancipation of subjects was conceptualized as a purely technical problem, which required intensive, or even obsessive, development of society's economic capacity, rather than seen as a process, which requires alerting citizens to what invariably are value judgments. The former breeds elitism; the latter, egalitarianism.

Scientism afflicts societies because there definitely is a systematic relationship between a "knowledge form" and the uses to which it is put.[91] The project of creating an identity for the species is viewed by positivists as an irrational activity. This verdict assumes that the invention of meaning is pursued solely for the sake of material gain or power. But it is only in self-reflection that reason grasps itself as interested in motives of power-augmentation, self-development, or both; only critical reason dissolves unacknowledged barriers or silences. People will experience a "rationality deficit" to the degree they lack freedom to exercise all forms of reason. Habermas, like Feyerabend, calls, in effect, for a theoretical pluralism. Alternatives keep us honest. Now we can look at what Habermas recommends about "praxis."

The dramatically disparate tactics of the pair derive from their analytic strategies. Habermas critiques science by focusing *externally* on social institutional coercion while Feyerabend launched his *immanent* critique by directing attention to exaggerated claims of science regarding its own internal standards and practices. Both critiques imply the need, indeed an imperative, to reform or transform institutions in democratic directions.

For Habermas the locus of struggle is in class and social structure; for Feyerabend the locus is within the scientific community. *Habermas wants first to democratize science, while Feyerabend will go either way, but assumes that the struggle in all likelihood will begin within science, whatever the external political conditions.* Feyerabend's tactics ironically require a vanguard of anarchic scientists. Habermas exhorts a grassroots citizens' movement to arise, and suggests that political tactics are theoretically undecidable—that is, they can only be discovered in the field of practice. (Offering alternatives does not mean one is necessarily oppositional.)[92] Thus, he makes no scandalous noises about employing deceit, yet tacitly must make such a wide allowance for action that he might be "trapped" into endorsing Feyerabend's strategy.[93]

In the absence of a liberatory social movement scientists get no clues from Habermas as to how to behave, how to proceed against stiff opposition. Feyerabend, on the other hand, appoints the scientific community as the key site for subversive activities and dispenses insurgency tips. Far from being caught in a "dead end of dadaism," his concerns are remarkably, if sometimes troublingly, consistent with dialectical materialism and he presents all traditions with an extremely lively and provocative challenge. Is this not "the ruthless criticism of everything existing"?

CONCLUSION

It is a typical irony that the "village atheist" is revealed upon scrutiny to be far more moral in behavior and attitude than those who piously rue him. Feyerabend preaches neither "science for the hell of it": nor does he damn science. Rational standards are neither denied nor ignored; rather the range of testability is expanded to include a scouring of human interests. Though Feyerabend aligns himself with Mill as a polemicist for democracy, we can find no trace of cynicism here (except for theatrical effect)—unless one wished to dub his critical enterprise (which presupposes emancipatory standards and values) as "purposive cynicism." If so, this is the stuff of which critical theory was spun.

Feyerabend decries the tendency "to dwell on what is" while ignoring the serious question of "what should be." This questioning ought to occur under "ideal speech situations." But in their absence he tells us how we might proceed—if we dare. "It is time for philosophers to recognize the calling of their profession," he writes, "to free themselves from an exaggerated concern with the present (and the past) and to start again anticipating the future."[94] This passage may not be Marx's eleventh thesis on Feuerbach but it is not a bad approximation either.

LETTER FROM PAUL FEYERABEND—11/09/91

Just as I was sliding into a position very close to "Hands off Science!" I receive your paper about my past as a "marxist outlaw." If you are right then I was much better than I now think I was. And, indeed, there was a time when having looked at Lenin, Marx, Engels, Lukacs, *plus* Mill, I thought there were ways of keeping science in motion so that its liberating potential would not be lost. I like the connection to Marx, etc., *especially now* when a superficial interpretation of political events has prompted many people to conclude that marxism is dead. Far from it.

I am less sure about the Frankfurt School. I tried to read the one or the other of those guys but I simply could not understand them. What I liked about dadaism was its destruction of false values which was especially valuable around World War I, but I agree that Duchamp is preferable to Tzara who was too self-involved.

Disliking the deep seriousness of much of philosophy I could not (and still cannot) help making jokes here and there. Incidentally, what do you think of my observation that by its action against Galileo the church gave strength to a wider point of view that regarded science as something limited and thereby had a positive effect? At any rate—many thanks for the article!

Best Wishes,
Paul Feyerabend

Notes

1. Paul Feyerabend, *Against Method: Outline of an Anarchistic Theory of Knowledge* (London: New Left Books, 1975).
2. Paul Feyerabend, *Science in a Free Society* (London: Verso, 1978). He refers to the attack by J. Curthoys and W. Suchting in their "Feyerabend's Discourse Against Method: A Marxist Critique" in *Inquiry* (Summer 1977).
3. On the Frankfurt School, see Martin Jay, *The Dialectical Imagination* (Boston: Little, Brown, 1973) and Stephen E. Bronner, *Of Critical Theory and Its' Critics* (Oxford: Basil Blackwell, 1993).
4. Joseph Ben-David, *The Scientist's Role in Society: A Comparative Study* (Englewood Cliffs, NJ: Prentice-Hall, 1971), p. 2.
5. A point most recently reiterated in Feyerabend's *Three Dialogues on Knowledge* (Oxford: Basil Blackwell, 1991).
6. Max Horkheimer, *Critical Theory: Selected Essays* (New York: Seabury Press, 1972), p. 211.
7. Like critical theorists, Feyerabend is concerned "not only with goals already imposed by existent ways of life, but with men and all their potentialities." Horkheimer, ibid., p. 164.
8. Alvin Gouldner, *The Dialectic of Ideology and Technology* (New York: Seabury Press, 1976), p. 21.
9. Feyerabend, *Science in a Free Society*, p. 191.
10. Among the exceptions is Denise Russell's "Anything Goes," *Social Studies in Science* 13, 3 (August 1983). Also see the appreciative eulogy by Sergio Benvenuto, "P. K. Feyerabend (1924–1994) Search for Abundance" *Telos* (Winter 1995) 102. Feyerabend had just completed his autobiography, *Killing Time* (Chicago: University of Chicago Press, 1994).
11. Feyerabend, *Against Method*, p. 21.
12. Feyerabend, *Science in a Free Society*, p. 8.
13. "Once one has experienced the desperation with which clever and conciliatory men of science react to the demand for a change in the pattern of thought,"

Werner Heisenberg reflected, "one can only be amazed that such revolutions in science have actually been possible at all." Heisenberg, *Across the Frontiers* (New York: Harper Torchbooks, 1974), p. 162.

14. Scanning the main currents of Western marxism—Hegelian historicism, marxist humanism, and critical theory—it is critical theory (especially Horkheimer, Adorno, Marcuse, and Habermas) to which he displays greatest affinity. The historicists likewise detect "something problematic in the fact that capitalist society is predisposed to harmonize with the scientific method." Lukacs asserted that positivism's breaking of wholes into parts and reifying them into "social facts" reflected an alienation and reification endemic in capitalism to which historical materialism should serve as "counterpoise." The humanists are inclined (as is Habermas) toward a dualism of sciences: social sciences require a hermaneutical method while physical sciences, in another tidy category, require an epistemic one. Nonetheless, critical theory is the most fruitful comparison. See Georg Lukacs, *History and Class Consciousness* (Cambridge, MA: MIT Press, 1971), p. 7.

15. Alvin H. Gouldner, *Dialectic of Ideology and Technology*, p. 21.

16. Ian Hacking argues that "a philosophy of experimental science cannot allow a theory-dominated philosophy to make the very concept of observation become suspect," In *Representing and Intervening* (Cambridge: Cambridge University Press, 1983). Feyerabend, however, asserts that "observations are not merely *theory-laden* . . . but *fully theoretical*" because "scientists often use theories to restructure abstract matter as well as phenomena . . . and no part of the phenomena is exempt from the possibility of being restructured in this way." In *Reason, Rationalism and Scientific Method*, p. x. The Frankfurt School is nearer Feyerabend regarding the issue of the correspondence between empirical procedures and truth. "An optimistic belief in such a correspondence is perfectly legitimate for any scientist engaged in actual nonphilosophical research but to a philosopher it serves as the delusion of a naive absolutism." Horkheimer, *The Eclipse of Reason* (New York: Seabury Press, 1974), pp. 77–78.

17. Robert Merton, *Science, Technology and Society in the Seventeenth* (New York: Howard Fertig, 1938); also, see Colin Russell, *Science and Social Change in Britain and Europe 1700–1900* (New York: St. Martin's Press, 1983) and James R. Jacob, "The Political Economy of Science in Seventeenth Century England," in Margaret C. Jacob, ed. *The Politics of Western Science 1640–1990* (Atlantic Highlands, NJ: Humanities Press, 1994).

18. Joseph Ben-David, *The Scientist's Role in Society*, pp. 74, 86.

19. Lewis Mumford, *The Myth of the Machine: The Pentagon of Power* (New York: Harcourt Brace, 1970), p. 115.

20. Feyerabend, *Science in a Free Society*, p. 75.

21. Ibid., p. 138.

22. Feyerabend, *Against Method*, Chapter 17; also *Science in a Free Society*, pp. 138, 146.

23. *Science in a Free Society*, p. 138.

24. See Henry Abelove et al., eds., *Visions of History* (New York: Pantheon, 1984), pp. 9–10.

25. Ian Barbour, *Issues in Science and Religion* (New York: Harper & Row, 1966), p. 34.

26. Max Horkheimer, *The Eclipse of Reason* (New York: Seabury Press, 1974), p. 34.

27. Ibid., pp. 162, 181.

28. For Feyerabend's account of motives behind his flamboyant writing style, see Chapter 21 in the 1988 revised edition of *Against Method*; Chapter 12 in *Farewell to Reason* (London: Verso, 1987), and his "Dialogue on Method," in Gerard Radnitzky and Gunnar Anderssen, eds., *The Structure and Development of Science* (Dordrecht, Holland: D. Reidel Publishers, 1983).

29. Feyerabend, *Against Method*, p. 31.

30. Ibid., pp. 41, 47, 204.

31. Quoted in Feyerabend, *Against Method*, p. 18.

32. Ibid., p. 117.

33. E. A. Burtt, *The Metaphysical Foundations of Modern Science* (Garden City, NY: Doubleday Books, 1954), p. 38.

34. See Feyerabend, *Against Method*, p. 204; also see Chapter 9 in *Farewell to Reason*.

35. Feyerabend's examples demonstrate the counterfactual nature of the *critical rationalism* in which, according to Popper, one must "try to falsify a hypothesis by increasing its balance of empirical content and avoid all *ad hoc* hypothetical explanations of empirical phenomenon; and *logical empiricism* in which, according to Carnap, one must "be precise by constructing theories exclusively on instrumental measurements and avoid all vague, nonformalized, and nonoperational concepts."

36. For examples, see Feyerabend, *Science in a Free Society*, Part I, Chapters 5 and 6, and Part II, Chapters 6 and 9. See, as well, *Against Method*, Chapters 1, 3, 4, 6, 8–11, and 13.

37. Horkheimer, *Critical Theory*, pp. 220–221.

38. Louis Althusser, *For Marx* (New York: Vintage, 1970) p. 184.

39. Feyerabend, *Against Method*, p. 178.

40. Feyerabend, *Reason, Rationalism and Scientific Method*, Vol. 1 (Cambridge: Cambridge University Press, 1981), p. 107.

41. Herbert Marcuse, *Eros and Civilization* (New York: Vintage, 1956), p. 112.

42. Feyerabend, *Science in a Free Society*, p. 41.

43. Ibid., p. 82.

44. Feyerabend, *Against Method*, p. 67. Also, his "Notes on Relativism" in *Farewell to Reason*.

45. Feyerabend, *Science in a Free Society*, pp. 84–85.

46. A majority of the scientific community endorses the belief that "science is structured on objective truths apart from human values." In Leonard Cole, *Politics and the Restraint of Science*, p. 164.

47. Feyerabend, *Science in a Free Society*, p. 164.

48. Hans Richter, *Dada: Art and Anti-Art* (New York: McGraw Hill, 1965, p. 13.

49. The enlightenment view is of "a science that is universal" because it is produced by structures of the mind common to all. The knowledge produced when particulars are dominated by the abstract is a means-to-ends (instrumental) form of reason. Its purpose is control of one's passions and will, and of the physical and social worlds. This form of reason inevitably produces a technology of control as the manifestation of its adequacy, or "reasonableness." Place this form of knowledge in the social context of a market economy and you have dynamite.

50. Michel Foucault has analyzed, in contexts ranging from hospitals to prisons, how instrumental reason abets domination. Like the Frankfurt School, he finds the genesis and satisfaction of motives is historical, not universal or timeless. See his, *The Archeology of Knowledge* (New York: 1962); *Madness and Civilization* (New York: Random House, 1965), *The Birth of the Clinic* (New York: Ran-

dom House, 1975), *Discipline and Punishment* (New York: Random House, 1977), and *The History of Sexuality* (New York: Random House, 1978).

51. Marcuse, *Reason and Revolution* (Atlantic Highlands, NJ: Humanities Press, 1960) p. 343.
52. Ibid.
53. See Michel Crozier's comments on predictability and hierarchy in complex organizations, in *The Bureaucratic Phenomenon* (Chicago: University of Chicago Press, 1967).
54. Horkheimer, *Critical Theory*, p. x. See Leszek Kolakowski, *Positive Philosophy* (New York: Penguin, 1972) for an account of versions of positivism.
55. The critical theorists say that their critique of positivism is similar to that of Edmund Husserl. See Marcuse, "On Science and Phenomenology," in *Positivism and Sociology* edited by Anthony Giddens (London: Heinemann, 1974), Max Horkheimer and Theodor Adorno, *Dialectic of Enlightenment* (New York, Herder and Herder, 1972), pp. 25–26. Feyerabend snipes at Husserl in *Farewell to Reason*.
56. Karl Marx, *Collected Works*, Vol. 31 (New York: International Publishers, 1971), pp. 226–227.
57. "In Soviet marxism the function of dialectics," Marcuse writes, "has been transformed from a mode of critical thought into a universal 'world outlook' and universal method with rigidly fixed rules and regulations, and this transformation destroys the dialectic more thoroughly than any revision." *Soviet Marxism* (New York: Vintage, 1961), pp. 121–122.
58. Vladimir I. Lenin, *Philosophical Notebooks*, Vol. 38, of *V. I. Lenin: Collected Works* (Moscow: Progress Publishers, 1972), pp. 372–373.
59. Feyerabend, "Consolations for the Specialist," in Imre Lakatos and Alan Musgrave, eds. *Criticism and the Growth of Knowledge* (Cambridge: Cambridge University Press, 1970), p. 211.
60. Michael Polanyi, *Personal Knowledge* (Chicago: University of Chicago, 1962), pp. 237–246.
61. Decisions about science (not within science), he argues, are better made by active lay people since they are not members of the club committed to science they can better see through the "delicate and refined charades of scientists." *Science in a Free Society*, pp. 87–88 and 96–97.
62. John Krige, *Science, Revolution and Discontinuity* (Atlantic Highlands, NJ: Humanities Press, 1980), p. 215.
63. Feyerabend, *Science in a Free Society*, pp. 96–97.
64. Feyerabend, *Against Method*, p. 22; *Science in a Free Society*, pp. 32 and 186–187; and *Farewell to Reason*, p. 60.
65. Feyerabend, *Against Method*, p. 308.
66. "If 'anything goes', then reason goes too . . ." Feyerabend, *Science in a Free Society*, pp. 39–40.
67. Noam Chomsky, "Psychology and Ideology," in *For Reasons of State* (New York: Vintage, 1973), p. 360.
68. Charles Murray and Richard Hernnstein, *The Bell Curve* (New York: Free Press, 1994). See Adolph Reed Jr.'s caustic review, "Looking Backward," in *The Nation*, 28 November 1994.
69. Feyerabend, *Reason, Rationalism and Scientific Method*, p. 145.
70. John Stuart Mill, *The Essential Works of John Stuart Mill* (New York: Bantam, 1971), p. 264.
71. Kenneth Coutts-Smith, *Dada* (New York: Hutchinson, 1973), p. 18.

72. See David Dickson, *The New Politics of Science* (New York: Pantheon, 1984), p. 310.

73. Marcuse, *Counterrevolution and Revolt* (Boston: Beacon Press, 1972), p. 60.

74. Stephen E. Bronner, "Art and Utopia: The Marcusean Perspective," in *The Politics and Society Reader*, edited by Ira Katznelson, et al. (New York: David McKay, 1975), p. 199.

75. David Joravsky, *Soviet Marxism and Natural Science 1917–1932* (New York: Basic Books, 1961), p. 98. Lenin and Trotsky believed that natural scientists spontaneously practiced dialectical materialism so that nothing short of outright sabotage warranted the Party's intrusion, p. 43. Zhores Medvedev characterized the 1920s as a "golden age" for Soviet scientists, in his *Soviet Science* (New York: Norton, 1978).

76. Gouldner, *Dialectic of Ideology and Technology*, p. 45.

77. Feyerabend, *Against Method*, p. 306, and *Science in a Free Society*, pp. 96–97; and *Problems of Empiricism* (Cambridge: Cambridge University Press, 1981), pp. 25–33.

78. Sam Dogloff, ed., *Bakunin on Anarchy*, (New York: Vintage, 1972), pp. 227–228.

79. Dickson, *The New Politics of Science*, p. 310.

80. Mill, *The Essential Works*, p. 280.

81. Ben-David, *The Scientists' Role in Society*, p. 110.

82. Feyerabend, *Against Method*, p. 136.

83. Horkheimer, *Critical Theory*, p. 6.

84. Albrecht Wellmar, *Critical Theory of Society* (New York: Seabury Press, 1974), p. 53.

85. Habermas, *Toward a Rational Society* (London: Heineman, 1971); *Knowledge and Human Interests* (London: Heinemann, 1971); *Theory and Practice* (London: Heinemann, 1974); *Legitimation Crisis* (London: Heinemann, 1973); and "The Public Sphere" in Armand Mattelart and Seth Siegelaub, eds., *Communication and Class Struggle* (New York: International General, 1979).

86. Habermas, "Science and Technology as Ideology," in *Toward a Rational Society*, pp. 102–195.

87. Habermas, *Knowledge and Human Interests*, p. 139.

88. Habermas, "On Systematically Distorted Communication," in Hans Peter Dreitzel, *Recent Sociology* (New York: Vintage, 1972) and idem. "Toward a Theory of Communicative Competence," in ibid.

89. Habermas, *Knowledge and Human Interests*, pp. 130–142. See, also, Ida Hoos, *Systems Analysis in Public Policy* (Berkeley: University of California Press, 1973).

90. Lysenkoism is an obvious example, although there was no necessary link between Lysenko's Michurinist biology and dialectical materialism—and the latter certainly was not incompatible with chromosomal theory.

91. Habermas, *Knowledge and Human Interests,* p. 47; and *Theory and Practice*, Chapters 1 and 2.

92. See the cautionary essay, "New Age—A Kinder, Gentler Science?" in Andrew Ross, *Strange Weather: Culture, Society and the Technology in the Age of Limits* (London: Verso, 1991).

93. Feyerabend approves of a similar analysis in Habermas, finding it congenially fostering "open exchange." *Farewell to Reason*, p. 29, n. 13.

94. Feyerabend, *Reason, Rationalism and Scientific Method*, p. 103, n. 3.

2

Much Ado About Ideas:
The Cognitive Factor
in Economic Policy

The revival of interest in the role of ideas for explaining policy choices is both startling and predictable. After a long period of indifference, and even hostility toward ideational explanations, the time for "ideas" has come around once again in political science and especially in the field of international relations. It now seems obligatory for every work in international political economy to consider the "material power of ideas" as at least a mediating variable—even if only then to dismiss it.[1]

The last surge of ideas-focused studies occurred in the late 1960s when many scholars challenged what they regarded as the analytical myopia of the "behavioral revolution" in social sciences because so rational and quantitative an enterprise had failed spectacularly to anticipate the social upheavals of that era.[2] A sense of *dejà vu* may affect readers familiar with that period and its preoccupations, and for such observers there may be an irritating air of discovery about some writings in this revival. "Almost any idea that has not been around for a while," Albert Hirschman impishly, but accurately notes, "stands a good chance of being mistaken for an original insight."[3] Arguably, an interest in ideas never vanished, but was simply relegated to the bailiwicks of "reflectivists," neo-marxists and other marginal figures in the discipline.[4]

After domestic turbulence and a costly Asian intervention subsided in the 1970s, interest-based and especially rational choice models held sway and allowed little, if any, weight to ideas which at best were deemed minor intervening variables. The motivation behind the revival of ideas-focused research is twofold: discontent with the inability of rational interest-based models to explain, let alone predict, policy outcomes (except by resorting to a host of auxiliary assumptions), and the evident onset of another era of profound socioeconomic change. The dissolution of the Soviet Union, the

25

imperative to upgrade productive structures, and prospective shifts in trade arrangements all threaten to disrupt incremental patterns of change. It is no surprise that skeptical scholars are searching for analytic approaches that will supplement, or even displace, dominant models.

This chapter examines four volumes by mainstream scholars who argue that ideas exert independent effects upon economic policy choice, as evocatively suggested in remarks by Max Weber on ideas as "switchmen" on history's tracks, and by John Maynard Keynes on the influence of "defunct economists."[5] (Marx, except for one essay in Goldstein and Keohane, is hardly mentioned.)[6] Two volumes are collections: Judith Goldstein and Robert Keohane's *Ideas & Foreign Policy*, which is the product of several conferences on ideas and politics; and guest editor Peter Haas's *International Organization* number on epistemic communities. My discussion is confined to essays that address the impact of ideas upon formal economic policy and thus I omit topics such as the control of arms or pollutants even though these issue areas certainly have an economic dimension. I also examine two book-length studies championing an ideas orientation: Goldstein's study of U.S. trade politics and Kathyrn Sikkink's study of "developmentalism" in Argentina and Brazil.

This essay asks: (1) do the authors prove that ideas ever operate as more than "hooks" (intellectual rationales) for material interests?;[7] (2) under what circumstances are ideas important intervening variables?; (3) and can ideas-oriented approaches usefully expand our concepts of rational analysis and action—beyond toting up relative resource and force levels and accordingly doing what one will to those who suffer what they must? I will argue that the case for the "power of ideas"—that ideas have a force of their own—is not successfully made but that the authors do demonstrate that an "ideas" approach is *always* a valuable supplement to interest-based, rational actor models.[8]

Moreover, the ideas literature draws the attention of students of IR to an aspect of politics downplayed, or downright ignored, in a field which until recently has been inhospitable to domestic level explanations: that is, legitimacy as a political resource.[9] The question of legitimacy directs analytical attention to "feedback loops" (to pick one possible term) between policy makers and mass publics without whose consent no policy is genuinely rational.[10] Parsimony is sacrificed when we burrow beneath elite levels but the sacrifice appears reasonable in exchange for gains in explanatory depth.

In the following sections I examine the case regarding the shortcomings of rational choice and interest-based models, assess the merits of several approaches incorporating ideas into explanations, and, finally, introduce a means of conceptualizing ideas as a malleable factor in power games without quite reducing them to mere hooks. The arduous effort to avoid the "hooks" characterization has forced writers into unnecessarily strained arguments. The theoretical snarl is that the strong case—that the "power of the idea itself explains its acceptance"—first demonstrates that interests are interpenetrated by ideas, but then these ideas must be shown to exert influence untainted by the very interests they have just been shown to interpenetrate. The move is untenable and, in any case, is not required to establish the utility of an ideas-focused approach.

In this political economy-centered study what distinguishes an ideas approach from related research on values, political culture, and psychological factors is that economic ideas are *explicit* programmatic ways of conceiving the organization of production and the distribution of its benefits and burdens.[11] Like all the authors, I treat economic ideas as "shared beliefs" and so exclude idiosyncratic or leader-specific beliefs as explanations.[12] Hence, the assertion that sunspots create fiscal havoc is not an economic idea; that a high Yugoslav official one day decided, and in concert with Tito, other officials and a receptive public went on to try, to realize "Marx's free association of workers" is indeed an economic idea (Halpern in Goldstein and Keohane, p. 108).[13]

Political culture and values approaches, however, do address shared beliefs: particularly, the standards the lay public uses to judge economic choices. So, it is useful to distinguish between (1) what Paul Rohrlich terms "consensual social beliefs," which shape the legitimate *ends* of economic activity and (2) economic ideas, which are the *means* to reach socially approved ends.[14] The two categories are not mutually exclusive and social beliefs need not be literally consensual to form a constraint. Actors always try to alter ends to fit the means they favor (and in Sikkink's analysis of Argentine political economy we encounter a failed attempt).

If markets were believed to be just, then private losers would be no concern of public policy. But the postwar "bargain of embedded liberalism" reconceptualized labor from dispensable factor of production to the key carrier of national prosperity (because "human capital" skills and Keynesian-fed consumption drive modern economies), and state intervention was affirmed to protect the populace against gross market inequities.[15] Hence, a social belief that citizens have a "right to make a living" will clash with a belief in market efficacy when the latter fails to deliver necessary opportunities; social democracies in effect are political systems that negotiate between these economic imperatives. Even "the most cynical view of public opinion," Mary Furner and Barry Supple observe, "grants that, in democracies at least, a lack of public support falling far short of organized opposition can still frustrate government policies."[16] Thus, deceit—or careful packaging of information—is the tribute that elites so often pay to the values they fear the public will act upon if well informed.[17] Instead of advocating upward redistribution of income as a remedy, for example, a conservative party is better advised to hail the "magic of the marketplace" as the proper means of achieving social objectives.

Finally, economic ideas, even if Pareto-optimal, never are "innocent" objective schemes devoid of distributions of gain and pain affecting the sponsors (although most Haas contributors seem to believe an idea is absolutely neutral when championed by an epistemic community).[18] We are dealing with projects articulated by groups who inflect the ideas they adopt—whatever their origin— to serve their own needs. This is *not* to say ideas are entirely manipulable items and mean only what Lewis Carroll's Humpty Dumpty "pays" them to mean. They can go awry, boomerang, or be hijacked by opponents. Witness the myth of American MIA/POWs in Vietnam, an officially encouraged story that rebounded on encouragers and even became an ideological obstacle to the material interests of U.S. business whose lobbying power only recently overcame it.[19] Economic ideas are always contested and never ultimately settled, at least not by argument—as attested by the attack on Keynesianism and "social contracts" in the last decade, and the inklings of a comeback in this one.[20]

RATIONALISM AND ITS DISCONTENTS

The authors launch a collective assault on the "actual softness that hides behind the seeming toughness of rational choice theories which see individuals as calculating interest" (John Hall in Goldstein and Keohane, p. 39). Rational choice sees politics as individuals optimizing under a given set of restraints—but which set of restraints? For economists "and political scientists captivated by their modes of thinking," Goldstein and Keohane charge, "ideas are unimportant or epiphenomena either because agents correctly anticipate the results of their actions or because some selective process ensures that only agents who behave as if they were rational succeed" (p. 4). Interests are given and logically prior to any beliefs held by actors: so ideas get relegated to "unexplained variance."

Ideas may be important "precisely because unique predictions cannot be generated through an examination of interests and strategic interaction (utility functions and payoff matrices); almost all "games with repeated play have multiple equilibria, the ideas held by players are often the key to a games' outcome." (Goldstein and Keohane, p. 17) Wendt, for example, champions "a cognitive, intersubjective conception of science in which identity and interests are endogenous to interaction, rather than the "microeconomic analysis in which identities and interests are exogenously given by structure and process is reduced to interaction within these parameters."[21] Most contributors to the edited volumes try to stake out a "middle ground" between rational choice proponents and the variegated scholars lumped together as reflectivists. (Goldstein and Keohane, p. 6; Haas and Adler, p. 371)[22]

In a world "shrouded in uncertainty," interest maximization tells us very little about particular policy choices. (Goldstein, p. 23) So "many different types of activities can plausibly be construed as preferences structured by the desire to stay in office." (Sikkink, p. 18) The translation of "interest into appropriate policy (and preceding that, preference) is not unproblematic." (Goldstein and Keohane, p. 240) Many game situations yield multiple equilibria, and actors cannot guarantee the consequences of their actions so that it is the "*expected* effects of actions that explains them."(p. 13)[23] Because "preferences and payoffs are seldom obvious, the nature of the game is often obscure, and institutions are not fully responsive to new problems," Peter Haas and Emanuel Adler assert their epistemic approach provides "the necessary prerequisites for rational choice analysis, explaining where alternatives and payoffs come from." (p. 369)[24]

Individual preferences contain an interest-component and a theory-component: the latter is "knowledge of causal relationships," and, accordingly, they are an individual's beliefs "about how a particular arrangement will affect his or her interests. They will be quite sure of their interests but less so about how alternative constitutions will help or hurt them—so the more complex society becomes the more uncertain the individual becomes, hence the greater need for rational discourse."[25] This demand for "rational discourse" may signify to scholars a need either for enhanced rule by specialized elites (or those who make use of them) or else the avid fostering of better informed, more conflictual, and democratic debates between and among policymakers, various elites, and the public.[26] Apart from differing over prescriptive morals drawn from this opaque state of affairs, the authors try to provide evidence about the conditions under which causal connections can be reliably claimed to exist between ideas and policy outcomes.

IDEAS, IDEOLOGIES AND ALL THAT

Goldstein and Keohane divide ideas into *principled beliefs* that specify "criteria for distinguishing right from wrong, and just from unjust," *causal beliefs* which "derive authority from shared consensus of recognized elites," and *world views*. (pp. 8–11) Most economic ideas incorporate all three aspects as in the cases of supply-side "Reaganomics" or Thatcher's "enterprise culture"; trouble will erupt especially when causal beliefs clash with principled beliefs, as amply attested in recent memoirs.[27] Ideas, Goldstein and Keohane say, influence public policy when (1) "the principled or causal beliefs they embody provide road maps that increase actors clarity about goals or ends-means relationships," (2) when they become "focal points that define cooperative solutions or act as coalitional glue" and (3) by becoming embedded in political institutions.

Road maps link "policies to a constellation of interests." One can usually reach a destination by several routes. Although "we" need national health coverage, a competitive economy and a vibrant international trading order, an account of the interests immediately involved is not usually sufficient to explain the content of competing options, let alone the policy outcome. Different constellations of interests can alter not only the route chosen but the destination, the conveyances, and justifications used.[28] Sometimes, as in the old joke, "you can't get there from here" until a coalition sheds and/or acquires different members, unless the original members all alter and align their views in a compatible way. Ideas serve as "focal points" that enable this reordering to be brought about by interested actors or policy entrepreneurs.[29]

Economic ideas are relatively inexpensive ways to gain consent and mobilize support.[30] Persuading players to accept a "definition of the situation" is to control the outcomes because defining the problem will determine the nature and scope of the solution.[31] Ideas unify or divide groups by influencing how they relate their interests to shifting circumstances. They can become "constitutive of interests," and even trigger a change of the context, which is comprised of both intellectual precepts and institutional arrangements and procedures that determine the limits of permissible political action.[32] Hence, we should distinguish not only "between different types of interests, but among different social arrangements that generate different belief systems and different structural possibilities, and which produce a set of socially created definitions that make one of the other goals appear rational and desirable.[33] This context itself can become the high stakes in political contests among groups promoting economic ideas (though few, if any, authors recognize this aspect).[34]

Thomas Kuhn's work is the touchstone for all these depictions of economic ideas, and is worth recounting briefly.[35] A scientific paradigm is an orthodoxy, a directive for, and a constraint on, research; it determines the conceptual terms in which paradigm-workers, or policymakers, interpret reality; it presupposes an ontology, a view of reality, the nature of the phenomena in it, and how it is to be described. A paradigm ("universally recognized achievement that *for a time* provides model problems and solutions") need not, cannot, and never does explain all the facts with which it is confronted. The touchiest implication is that paradigm shifts are inescapably political phenomena. Indeed, other authors argue that on occasions scientists proceed by forms of lobbying and by stealthy tactics to insinuate their candidate into power.[36] Paradigm change occurs when anomalies accumulate to the point of throwing the reigning model into crisis, which can persist until a fully articulated successor ultimately is backed by the community.

This account, however unhappy it may make a few philosophers of science, fully parallels the explanatory dynamics of the economic ideas approaches. Hence, it is no shock that the Chinese, despite the absence of Soviet occupation troops, chose Stalinist political economy; they required a credible and proven framework that balanced their power-retention needs with economic growth. (Halpern in Goldstein and Keohane, p. 98) Likewise, former Soviet bloc regimes recently have rushed to implement a tempting textbook version of free enterprise, which seemed so well-proven and foolproof.[37]

The authors resort to ideas to explain choices made especially under conditions of uncertainty and within margins set by material constraints.[38] Indeed, the influence of ideas is assumed to vary inversely with the degree of uncertainty that actors encounter in a policy realm. While rejecting the suggestion that ideas alone create interests, the authors do argue that material constraints are subject to the ideas that actors have about them. Ideas and interests are "both concepts and therefore are ideas" because "interests are perceived through the lenses of the existing ideologies in various historical settings. (Jackson in Goldstein and Keohane, p. 112)[39] A favorite example is the "multiplier effect," which, when viewed through pre-Keynesian lenses, makes as little sense as claiming that two plus two equals five.

Still, an economic idea must appeal to the self-interest of, and sooner or later prove itself, to the butchers, brewers, and bakers, Adam Smith mentions. Economic ideas always portend new distributional effects that all actors— politicians, organized interests, the mass public—will appraise with whatever capacity available. The accuracy of assessments matter less than the confidence the actors have in their own judgment and in that of authorities. Legitimacy is an important factor in two senses: in respect to what is permissible within the range of standard economic knowledge, and what is deemed legitimate in terms of the public's interests and values.

THE POLITICAL POWER OF (OR BEHIND) IDEAS?

How ideas acquire force, and specifying the conditions under which they do so, was the objective of Peter Hall's volume examining Keynesian policy shifts which, he argues, "did not simply reflect group interests or material conditions"; rather, ideas "had the power to change the perceptions a group had of its own interests, and they made possible new courses of action that changed the material world itself."[40] Congruence between ideas and circumstances is important, and dramatic changes in circumstances, such as war and depression, affect the pertinence of particular ideas. Especially important is the congruence between these ideas and the needs of elites who have to "solve the puzzle of coalition formation."[41]

Contributors examined how ideas affect coalition-building, and how "administrative-political processes" affect the selection of new economic ideas—

"although without the confirmation of sociopolitical forces, innovation would be short lived."[42] What matters most is not cogency—that is, the intrinsic force, logic, and viability of an idea—but that the idea serves to reconcile the interests of elites operating in and around the institutional processes of a given state so that a strengthened or recast coalition emerges to enact it (the idea as "focal point").[43] Apart from Albert Hirschman's essay, and some perfunctory remarks about "moral visions" forging a sense of collective national purpose, Hall's volume comprises not so much a "power of ideas" argument as an eclectic, though effective, blend of elite and institutionalist analyses. The upshot is bromidic; the more powerful the sponsors who appropriate ideas, the more powerful the ideas. Do the authors under review venture any further?

In a meticulous study of U.S. trade politics Judith Goldstein strives to make a case wherein, unlike Hall, the "power of the [economic] idea itself explains its acceptance. (p. 2, fn. 1) Yet Goldstein undermines this bold thesis by consistently retreating into a political sponsorship argument. "Objectively 'optimal' ideas with which leaders can attain their political goals may exist," she writes, "but their adoption is contingent on their being embedded in some politically salient theory or analysis." (p. 2) Salient, that is, to "well-placed" elites. Goldstein may also exaggerate "the puzzle of the 'paradox' of a history of U.S. trade policy that cannot easily be explained by either of the dominant modes of analysis—structural realism and domestic interest group politics." (p. 237) However, neither is this apparent paradox so difficult to explain by interest-based paradigms.[44] There are plausible interest-based explanations that account no less exactingly for policy shifts.

A more defensible claim is that "beliefs about casual connections between interests and policies are at least as important as the nature of the interests themselves," which recalls W. I. Thomas's comment that anything defined as real will be real in its consequences. (p. 237) American trade policy is a story of how the "protectionist vision and its accompanying institutions biased all political activity," yet it is quite rational that U.S. policy moved from a protectionist past to a stance of wanting both free and "fair" trade. This was a matter of shrewd "interpretations" by state and economic elites regarding their own interests and those of whatever groups they needed to appease and recruit to achieve their ends.[45] There is no paradox discernible here—unless it is the familiar one that free trade, like the free market, requires vigorous state intervention in order to work.[46]

This world, according to Goldstein, is "clouded with uncertainty" so that policy entrepreneurs cannot select with any assurance a preferred course. Yet this plight is relatively rare. Whenever policy entrepreneurs appear we certainly are dealing with economic ideas as articulated projects sponsored by advocates who are looking for allies on the basis of shared interests.

When an idea embodies these interests; it becomes a (proposed) practice which has (potential) effects which can then be assessed. What befalls the analysis is that once interests are shown to become embedded in an idea, such as Keynesianism or protectionism, this institutionalization is cited to confirm that agents are besotted by the "power of ideas." No doubt, institutions can dictate policy "even in the face of declining elite consensus and divergent social interests"—though rarely for very long, at least not without bayonets. (Goldstein, p. 243) The danger in casting this "lag" phenomenon in terms of an ideas argument is that one quickly can lose sight of the material motives and forces driving the success of an economic idea, and so ends by fetishizing the idea alone as the cause. This flaw seems to be endemic in ideas approaches.

Goldstein and Keohane certainly "recognize that ideas and interests are not phenomenologically separate"; but their guiding question "is the extent to which variations in beliefs, or the manner in which ideas are institutionalized in societies, affect political action" and it is in pursuit of this purpose where slips tend to occur into unwarranted claims for the force of ideas. (p. 26) Institutionalized ideas can carry on regardless of circumstance but this phenomenon is also explicable as bureaucratic inertia, institutional sclerosis, political ploy ("stonewalling") or may be justified up to a point as sober conservativism. Institutionalized ideas also can become invested with different meanings as political actors fill old concepts with new content in order to adjust to environmental exigencies.[47]

Policymakers "rely on causal models in making policy choices," and policy entrepreneurs "depend on ideas about how to translate these forces into a political and economic program." However, the maps must meet stringent interest-bound criteria so that even "efficiency is valued only to the extent that the means to a goal adhere to existing ideas, values, and institutions." (Goldstein and Keohane, p. 255) An example is Charles Maier's study of industrialists contriving to "redefine [a national commitment to democracy] to square with the criteria of optimality and efficiency" in the highly undemocratic realm of the factory system.[48] However, these maps neither always originate with elites nor are elites always united behind one version.

International forces, Goldstein argues, are interpreted through institutional lenses. "If insufficient attention is paid to the agent who interprets changes in domestic group demands and in the national interest—often through institutionally biased lenses—the essence of the politics of making economic policy may be over-looked."—(pp. 240–241) Here Goldstein surely identifies a vital element in policy conflicts, but her restricted focus on formal actors underplays the ability of informal actors and of "mass publics" to perceive, and even make use of, economic ideas and environment changes as pieces in a power game. All these actors are well aware that rules established in the victory of an economic idea constrain future choices, as exemplified by the ferocity of the recent NAFTA debate. An understanding by the citizenry of the material interests at stake in a technical issue can even neutralize the mystique of specialist expertise.[49] Organized interests and even diffuse actors (motivated by the salience of the issue to organize) then can try to gain the interpretive "upper hand," propagate their views and seek the most sympathetic decision-making sites (congressional committees, the executive branch, the courts, regulatory agencies, etc.) in which their fates are to be determined.[50]

Economic ideas are most aptly treated as "clusters of ideas/interests" which, however, can be a slippery concept. (Sikkink in Goldstein and Keohane, p. 162) "It is not markets but ideas that establish the rules of the game, that demarcate for policy makers the proper forms of new policies and that privilege particular constituencies," Goldstein states; four pages later, we find that markets "define a viable policy space." (pp. 238, 242) So the market apparently is an objective force that defines a policy space even though it is also subject to ideas and can under certain circumstances become a site for a struggle about the rules. This makes a good deal of sense, but one is not quite sure Goldstein intends it. "To have causal weight," she demands, "ideas must have an independent effect on policy, apart from the interests of the actors who defend them." (p. 252) This is not convincingly demonstrated; rather, the impression conveyed is that all that is solid melts into ideational air, and vice versa, as it suits the analysis. Garret and Weingast, by contrast, plausibly argue that certain "ideas have properties that may lead to their selection by political actors and to their institutionalization and perpetuation. It is not something intrinsic to them that gives them their power." (Goldstein and Keohane, p. 178) In their study of the Single European Act there is an unusually acute and sustained sense of the material underpinnings of ideas.

IDEAS AS WEAPONS

Are economic ideas held despite material distress for the sake of other goods or long-term ends? The most promising cases are the former socialist economies where Stalinist central planning became the political economy paradigm, created a set of favorable social interests and afterward, Nina Halpern argues, "exerted an independent influence." (Goldstein and Keohane, pp. 92–93) The Chinese Communist Party adopted Stalinist political economy as a legitimate guide for economic development.[51] Yugoslavia's shift from Stalinist centralism toward worker management illustrates that not just any viable idea will do, but only those ideas that fit the balance of economic and legitimation needs required by a political regime at a particular juncture. By no means is it obvious that the adoption of either economic idea ever contradicted the national interests of China or Yugoslavia. Halpern overstates the "imperviousness" of Soviet ideology. Scholars have long noted how sincere Soviet scientists wielded "dialectical materialist" principles to legitimate their needs for flexible research programs, and to make credible scientific contributions.[52] The adaptation of ideologies, especially "official" marxist thought, to changing circumstance or to new political goals is almost as familiar a phenomenon as ideological lag or Gulag dogmatism. The point requires emphasis and illustration.

A recent article attributes the Soviet foreign policy shift in the 1980s to a "changing external environment and the advent of a reformist general secretary [who] created a series of policy windows through which aspiring policy entrepreneurs jumped."[53] The consequent benign interpretation of U.S. motives, however, was not the invention of policy entrepreneurs; it was a revival of one among several Soviet policy currents invoked whenever external events (Nazi invasion) or internal pressures (industrial modernization/more consumer goods) rendered it useful for justifying desired policy changes to domestic and foreign audiences.[54] If a relevant audience is adamantly unreceptive—e.g., the United States will not truck with the "evil empire"—the strategem will of course flop. Ideologies are politically pliable to a degree limited by circumstances, interests, and social beliefs.[55] Just as the Chinese in the 1950s could claim that "New Democracy was pre-socialist," leaders in newly industrializing countries cheerfully may explain to disgruntled Yanks that their managed market systems are in effect "pre-free market arrangements."

Garret and Weingast persuasively suggest that "the influence of focal points and shared belief systems is likely to vary significantly

> with the structure of given strategic interactions. The lesser the distributional asymmetries between contending cooperative equilibria and the smaller the disparities in the power resources of actors, the more important will be ideational factors. Similarly the effects of focal points will increase with the actors' uncertainty about the consequences of agreements can be expected significantly to influence the resolution of multiple equilibria problems, but the relative explanatory power of each is likely to vary significantly with the context. (p. 185)

However, we must not overlook moments when an idea ignites a struggle over control of this context, when politics becomes "a contest for the authoritative values that orient society. Here the control of mass media, the status and message of organized religion, the shaping of markets and consumption, the *correct* interpretation of poverty at home and revolution abroad become crucial political concerns."[56] The content of an idea alters over time or in the course of conflicts and compromises. As Goldstein reminds, the meaning of so apparently unambiguous a term as "free trade" is not the same today as in the last century.

THE IMPORTANCE OF BEING EPISTEMIC

In the *International Organization* number on "Epistemic Communities" (ECs) Peter Haas and Emanuel Adler contend that just as "structures are constituted by the practice and self-understandings of agents, so the influence and interests of agents are construed and explained by political and cultural structures." (p. 371) This "structurationist approach" echoes an earlier analyst who complained that the "materialist doctrine concerning the changing of circumstances . . . forgets that circumstances are changed by men and that it is essential to educate the educator himself."[57] However phrased, the dialectical point is worth making.

Haas and Adler argue expectations "come from interpretive processes involving political and cultural structures, as well as from institutions." (p. 371) This is a necessary addition to, and caveat for, institutionalist models. Certainly "the institutional framework provides the context in which groups and individuals interpret their self-interest and thereby define their self-interest."[58] However, this formulation confers all power on the institutional framework with no space allowed for creativity by actors within and around it. If we "ground these variables in the [institutional] context in which they are defined and interpreted" we get into conceptual quicksand when external change and/or internal challenges throw this institutional context into flux.[59] Haas and Adler, like the other ideas approaches, extend inquiry beyond the borders of institutions, and supply very sound reasons for doing so.

Haas and Adler argue that "the manner in which people and institutions interpret and represent phenomena and structures makes a difference for the outcomes we can expect in international relations." The drawback is that they want to lodge this interpretive power almost exclusively within epistemic communities, which are networks of knowledge-based experts who have "(1) a shared set of normative and principled beliefs . . . (2) shared causal beliefs . . . [that] serve as the basis for elucidating the multiple linkages between possible policy actions and the desired outcomes, (3) shared notions of validity—that is intersubjective, internally defined criteria for weighing and validating knowledge in the domain of their expertise, (4) a common policy enterprise—that is, a set of common practices associated with a set of problems to which their professional competence is directed, presumably out of the conviction that human welfare will be enhanced as a consequence."[60]

John Gerard Ruggie, who originated the term, says that epistemic communities "consist of interrelated roles which grow up around an episteme; they delimit, for their members, *the* proper construction of social reality."[61] Adler and Haas go on approvingly to note the need for the "political infiltration of an epistemic community into governing institutions" to promote their cause. (pp. 27, 374) Indeed, this definition snugly fits the Central Intelligence Agency (CIA), which is a "transnational knowledge-based network" if there ever was one, although Haas and Adler seem to believe what they are offering is a spruced-up version of Mannheim's free-floating intellectuals.

To take the comparison further, congressional hearings on CIA director-nominee Robert Gates disclosed that the Agency not only has made major errors—a fallibility which ought to give both clients and the public pause—but that it tailored information to suit the views of clients, which, in light of the *Pentagon Papers*, seems less an aberration than an organizational tradition.[62] Regarding Vietnam, policymakers were unwilling to believe pessimistic CIA appraisals, and the intelligence community itself soon split into factions. Why should experts located outside these policy circles fare any better when bearing bad tidings or views that conflict with policymakers prejudices?

Haas and Adler assume that if "confronted with anomalies that undermine their causal beliefs, [epistemic communities] would withdraw from the policy debate, unlike interest groups," which ignores a rather well-known intellectual inclination to resort to ad hoc statements or denial to defend cherished models. (p. 18) (Milton Friedman and Karl Marx, after all, can both claim with some justice that their ideas were never properly carried out.) There is also difficulty distinguishing who is influencing whom in these epistemic analyses. If "economic actors begin with an economic situation to which they link a policy preference, and then seek out a political strategy to make that preference prevail," and "politicians begin with a political situation for which they need support, and then seek economic policies which provide that support," then epistemic communities begin with a diagnostic model and seek out political and economic actors who need help to construct support for their own preferences.[63]

The definition of a community is disturbingly elastic. One contributor starts by stating that central bankers are not an epistemic community, and by the conclusion is flirting with the proposition that bankers may emerge from their crass chysalis someday to "become a full-fledged epistemic community." (Kapstein in Haas, pp. 266, 285)[64] Granted, a lot of political learning is going on, but if the decision makers whom EC members advise turn out to be themselves, then "epistemic community" simply collapses as a concept. Haas also is encouraged by increases in scientific staff in government and the "increasing deference paid to technical expertise and in particular to that of scientists." (p. 11) But this alleged deference hardly explains so extraordinary an event as Reagan's Strategic Defense Initiative (unless we declare Edward Teller to be an epistemic community of one).[65] Public attitudes toward experts are far more ambivalent than Haas suggests, and wisely so because the historical record on experts does not compare all that well with other citizens with regard to moral courage, prudence, foresight, or any other civic virtue.[66]

In any case, the data is usually ambiguous and scientists usually divided—often many ways—concerning environment, energy, and other public issues.[67]

The epistemic approach is a model of elites, by elites and for elites; an added difficulty is that the descriptive tasks undertaken tend to become prescriptive ventures.[68] This *is* a problem because the epistemic approach is driven by a dubious faith in the critical capacities of like-minded experts assembled in a community. Yet there is evidence that those experts who are closest professionally to controversial technological issues tend on the whole to be less critical than events soon prove was ever warranted. More physicists than biologists consider recombinant DNA research risky and more physicists than biomedical scientists consider nuclear plants safe; a researcher ascribes this phenomenon "to the influence of social networks within disciplines rather than to expertise" itself—and the obvious implication is that a community of any kind is unlikely to put a premium on dissent within its ranks.[69] This suggestion may annoy some scientists, but lay citizens certainly should ponder the proposition that it is not an epistemic community *per se* but rather the clashes among "communities" from different disciplines of science, and conducted in the public sphere, that produces the most valuable and self-critical input into policy decisions.[70]

Epistemic analysis ultimately is also a sponsorship argument regarding pedigreed groups who "create reality, but not as they wish." One may readily concede Haas and Adler's claim that where policymakers have no strong preconceived views, and the issue is a first foray, then these bands of experts will exercise a lot of influence. (pp. 380–381) Stating the proposition another way: if the issue does not matter very much, then experts do. This does not make for an alluring analytical agenda.

Finally, an epistemic community's influence on decisions "depends on the level of uncertainty" in a policy realm where, if uncertainty is high, an epistemic community presumably exerts an influence akin to a physician prescribing a remedy the patient is unable to evaluate. But political actors customarily summon epistemic communities "whose ideas implicitly align with their own preexisting political agenda and will help them further it," so that those "communities expressing ideas close to the mainstream have a greater propensity to acquire influence," or as Mayor Daley Sr.'s cronies succinctly put it: "We don't want nobody nobody sent."[71]

John Ikenberry is an interesting exception who veers away from epistemic claims in his analysis of Bretton Woods. In 1944, change was necessary and American and British elites, who shared underlying interests, were "interested in building institutions that have a measure of legitimacy." Neither state could politically tolerate old deflationary dogma, and free trade in conjunction with expanded control of domestic economies were actually quite compatible moves." (p. 294)[72] Policymakers were positioned to innovate a compromise because, as other analysts note, they used ideas to highlight "the potential gains that may accrue from exchange, especially [this situation] in which some change in behavior must occur before the gains can be captured." (Goldstein and Keohane, p. 204) Geoffrey Garret and Barry Weingast argue that the principle of mutual recognition in the European Community was, and indeed had to be, "consistent with the desire of the major political and economic actors in Europe to liberalized trade." But Ikenberry usefully points beyond this necessary but insufficient condition: "What ultimately mattered to the ratification of Bretton Woods agreement was not that it was based on policy ideas advanced by an expert community but, rather that the political ideas resonated with the larger political environment." (p. 291)

Kathryn Sikkink cites the cautionary example of an Argentine policy functionary whose technocratic frame of reference made him utterly insensitive to how his actions and words were eroding political support. (pp. 236–237) His economic reasoning, Sikkink explains, "made sense within the intricate reasoning of *desarrollista* thought but appeared contradictory to those not immersed in this thought"— which, when you are sufficiently outnumbered, describes the condition of autism. (p. 120) These particular politicians, and the developmental experts they consulted, were "dismally unaware" of the symbolic dimension of politics; they didn't know, so to speak, "how it would play in Peoria"—a grave oversight.

NATIONS AND NOTIONS

Sikkink, a Latin Americanist, comfortably applies that field's view of economic ideas as "projects" and so she manages nearly always to keep in mind that she is examining "clusters of ideas/interests," not ideas alone. (p. 223) She examines forms of "developmentalism" in Brazil and Argentina where state actors try to strike "a compromise between the demand of the international economy and the demands of domestic groups," and attempts to explain why economic performance was better, and policy more successful, in Brazil. Sikkink especially heeds Hirschman who urges attention to the crucial need for preparation of the population for acceptance of a new economic idea, a task which requires incorporating these "diffuse publics" into analyses.[73] So her focus isn't restricted to relations among policymakers, bureaucrats, or epistemic communities but also on relations between them and with the wider society as elites try to strike a "balance between the demands for reform and accumulation."

Sikkink plumbs a vital Gramscian level: "For common sense, defined the terms of public political discourse; it is embodied in social practices and therefore must be considered a material force"; and "civil society" is the sphere in which the "struggle to define the categories of common sense takes place."[74] The advantage of Gramsci's approach over others is that it emphasizes "an awareness of the material nature of ideology and of the fact that it constitutes a practice inscribed in apparatuses" (institutions).[75] Sikkink notes that "shared ideas are the products of agreements that originate in past material distributions of goods," and this assumes an experienced public has a reasonable memory and rational grounds by which to judge political proposals. Hence, the public isn't entirely at the mercy of experts and self-interested parties.

Argentine and Brazilian citizens "were wooed with images of industrialization, technification, and the future greatness of their country" by their respective leaders who needed "capable institutions and broad political support" to carry through their developmentalist projects. (pp. 70, 81) An "important means for mobilizing support is an appeal to commonly held ideas, "a project that captivates and inspires people"—though this would not be very easy inasmuch as developmentalism was "indifferent" to matters of distribution and equity.[76]

Argentine President Frondizi entered office with frail legitimacy because *Peronistas* were electorally excluded and because he proceeded to reverse himself on foreign investment and petroleum development, repress the trade unions, and failed to integrate industrialists into pro-business schemes. Citizens of all classes soon did not need a semiologist to tell them that Frondizi was volatile and unreliable. In Sikkink's symbolic action-oriented account Frondizi simply loses an "interpretive struggle." She treats concrete (and correctly interpreted) actions as "signals," as mere "perceived" events which fan a "chronic distrust" of government. (p. 222) Thus the analysis inexorably takes on the cast of a misperception argument, as though citizens can possibly "misperceive" whether or not they are employed or sheltered or are free to speak and organize.

In "a multilayered game of symbolic action," an International Monetary Fund (IMF) stabilization scheme may be a "symbol" to international investors but also inflicts real deprivation upon domestic wage earners. The analysis proceeds as if only the "intersubjectivity of language" mattered, and not the link of economic ideas to credible projects with material effects. In treating Frondizi's lies and contradictory acts primarily as "discursive incongruences," one slips easily into trivializing political activity, and what then matters is the relation between ideas and discourse, not of ideas to lived experience.

Brazilian developmentalists made "a social compact" with subordinate labor but their success was also based on "a convergence of interest between Kubitschek, state *technicos*, and industrial interests." (pp. 146, 154) Sikkink notes that the economic ideas of the Latin American Commission for Economic Development (CEPAL), an epistemic community or reasonable surrogate, dovetailed nicely "with existing ideas of the entrepreneurs, while providing theoretical justifications for policies that industrialists already had been advocating." (p. 157) Brazil's greater access to loans and credits is acknowledged, but Sikkink oddly credits policy success to "a stronger institutional framework" and identifies an "insulated portion" of the Brazilian bureaucracy as the vital ingredient.[77] Her verdict is contradicted by the essential role also ascribed to "bureaucratic rings," which integrated the preferences of private industrialists in a skewed way into public sector schemes.[78] Indeed, Sikkink points out there were "more clientelistic politics and more successful mobilization of technical resources" in Brazil. (p. 172) Hence, insulation is not obviously the answer and, anyway, genuine insulation would militate against the responsiveness to popular pressures which she cogently argues also is vital. Her study is afflicted by an unresolved tension between the attractions of an insulated technocratic mode of governance and her concern for inclusion of popular voice in policy.

Environmental changes are "stimuli for institutional development," Sikkink correctly writes. "The forms these institutional innovations take are contingent on the specific responses of government officials." (p. 173, fn. 7) But actors and coalitions also devise their own "interpretations" of changing economic circumstances, and promote corresponding programmatic messages to the wider citizenry (or potential allies) in order to reinforce their dominance or to displace that of others. Sometimes the message works, sometimes not. (The claim, for example, that there "is no health crisis in America" works only if it is not laughed away by voters.)[79] If the circumstances change dramatically, the notion of what is pragmatic widens and may even go up for grabs.[80]

A good strategy will "presuppose a knowledge of how the public, or how specific political and economic groups will respond to policies"—but these responses are not fixed. People "can under circumstances reconfigure what is happening to attain their own advantage or meet their needs."[81] It is less important in Sikkink's study that "different rationalities" were at war between proponents of different economic ideas than whether and how proponents communicated with and promoted popular needs. Neglecting this dimension is hazardous. In Argentina the reprisal came in a roundabout way, with worker unrest creating the pretext for a military coup in 1962; in Brazil, which was only *relatively* more successful, it came a little later.

Ideas certainly are "interpreted within the context into which they are inserted," and "by the way they are inserted," but the context is not an inert background although dominant groups portray a favorable context as immutable. (Sikkink, p. 252) "None of the supposedly nonpolitical sources of authority—not religious dispensation, not the social order, not the market or technology—can be established as legitimate without a prior political operation." Maier observes. "Its advocates must control the resources of politics, including influence over the media and the capacity to shape political discourse. Once stability had been achieved, the political pressures may disappear from discussion. Indeed, the objective for any strategy for stability must be to make people forget politics."[82] Nonetheless, contextual arrangements are not immune to challenge. The point is that elites and nonelites constantly "work" their environments: that is, they play upon the material and ideational elements available in their organizational and cultural contexts to protect or further their concerns, and they are usually well aware that opponents do too.[83]

Gramsci's writings on hegemonic ideology suggest a means for investigating the relations between cognitive and socioeconomic processes which judiciously retains elements of both while avoiding the excesses of either.[84] The concept of "cluster of ideas/interests" is a promising though, as we have seen, wobbly equivalent. What is needed is at least an application of Gramsci's work in non-marxian realms—where there is not yet a satisfactory equivalent—in order to advance research; particularly worthy of attention is the Gramscian concept of "articulation" which provides tools for a theory of contexts.[85] Such an approach would be better equipped to plumb problems regarding the variability of interest-formation, and the degree of public influence over the parameters of economic policy.

CONCLUSIONS

The revival of "ideas" approaches stems from a concern with the lack of specificity in rational choice explanations, and in the framing of choices according to ostensible material interests. This article conditionally endorses the claim that "beliefs about the casual connections between interests and policies are at least as important as the nature of the interests themselves." But the pervasive flaw in "power of ideas" arguments is their failing to abide by the recognition that ideas and interests are "not separate entities, only analytically separable ones."[86] Economic ideas matter because they are "clusters of ideas/interests" which define productive arrangements. Gramscian analysis handles this conceptualization deftly and is a valuable source for social scientists to elaborate and adapt to other paradigms. Sikkink attends to this task and so do Garret and Weingast in their argument that belief systems "do not always emerge without conscious efforts on the part of interested actors," that they "must be constructed." (Goldstein and Keohane, p. 176)

This chapter criticizes the notion of a passive public that is posited because many ideas enter the public fray already processed by elites, ranging from epistemic communities to policy entrepreneurs. But, with respect to economic ideas, nonelites are not so haplessly manipulated; they can engage in shaping the preferences of other actors regarding the framing of a situation and, consequently, the "correct" policy. Economic ideas are programs for action that must appeal not only to crucial interest groups but to deeply felt, if incompletely articulated, social needs.

These ideas/approaches, despite their problems, are an important avenue between elites, institutions, and the public realm, and alert us to the subtle political dynamics at play when elites must devise solutions to reach common ends they cannot attain through fiat. All these writers want to know how cognitive factors influence elite behavior. However, we should advance beyond the conceit that a tree in the forest really hasn't fallen unless a Council on Foreign Relations member hears it or it falls on her. Sikkink and Ikenberry, among others, lead a belated acknowledgment in international relations of the importance of legitimacy, that is, of the need to attend to the diffuse but definite bedrock interests of mass publics when elites meet to thrash out policy.

Finally, these studies imply a need for an enlarged notion of rationality—more "substantive" than instrumental—regarding models of actors' behavior. A recent inventory of the IR suggests "for progress to be achieved under conditions of complex interdependence, state elites must recognize that, at a minimum, national interests cannot be achieved at the expense of others, and at a maximum, their own interest depends on the realization of others' interests"—which may be more a revelation for IR analysts than for many state actors. The versions reviewed promote ideas approaches as supplements to interest-based paradigms so as to illuminate how structural and cognitive factors interact.[87] Yet, this is too modest an ambition. Whether cumulative additions culminate in a paradigm shift, or at least a reshuffling of the stature of paradigms within IR, remains to be seen—but seems highly desirable.

Notes

1. Jack Snyder, *Myths of Empire: Domestic Politics and International Ambition* (Ithaca: Cornell University Press, 1991) pp. 30–32, 95–96; Jeff Frieden, *Debt, Development and Democracy* (Princeton: Princeton University Press, 1992).
2. See Philip Green and Sanford Levinson, eds., *Power and Community: Dissenting Essays in Political Science* (New York: Random House, 1968); David Easton's 1969 American Political Science Association (APSA) presidential address "The New Revolution in Political Science," *American Political Science Review* 68 (1969). The key critique of behavioral methods in foreign policy came from outside; see Noam Chomsky, *American Power and the New Mandarins* (New York: Vintage Press, 1967), pp. 23–159. The era spurred interest in the Frankfurt School, Witttgenstein, Foucault, and other philosophers. It's common to raid across disciplines for ideas, see Stephen Toulmin, *Human Understanding*, Vol. 1 (Princeton: Princeton University Press, 1972).

3. Albert Hirschman, *The Rhetoric of Reaction: Perversity, Futility, Jeopardy* (Cambridge, MA: Belknap Harvard, 1991), p. 29.

4. Alexander Wendt objects to the term "reflectivist" because it smacks of radical relativism. He prefers the label "constructivist" because it denotes that the social construction of reality occurs with at least a tenuous link posited between word and object. See "Anarchy is What States Make of It: The Social Construction of Power Politics," *International Organization*, 46, 2 (Spring 1992), p. 393, and "The Agent-Structure Problem in International Relations Theory," *International Organization* 3, 41 (Summer 1987).

5. "Not ideas, but material and ideal interests directly govern men's conduct. Yet, very frequently "world images" that have been created by ideas have, like switchmen, determined the tracks along which action has been pushed by the dynamic of interest," Max Weber. "Social Psychology of the World's Religions," in *From Max Weber: Essays in Sociology*, eds., H. H. Gerth and C. Wright Mills (New York: Oxford University Press, 1958), p. 280. Keynes mocked "practical men, who believe themselves to be quite exempt from any intellectual influence usually are the slaves of some defunct economist. Madmen in authority who hear voices in the air are distilling their frenzy from some academic scribbler of years back": in, *The General Theory of Employment, Interest and Money* (New York: Harcourt Brace & World, 1936), p. 383.

6. John Hall acknowledges that Marx "did recognize the reality of belief," in his essay "Ideas and the Social Sciences," in Goldstein and Keohane *Ideas and Foreign Policy* (Ithaca: Cornell University Press, 1992), p. 37. Engels called the notion that marxism denies ideology any effectiveness in history "idiotic." For where "is there a superstructure, however airy and delicate its construction, which is not just as real as the foundation? . . . a foundation is not constructed as an end in itself but only so that a superstructure can subsequently be erected upon it . . . The superstructure is therefore that part of the building in which its meaning and purpose are accomplished . . . the social superstructure is that part of society in which historical actions take shape; but in order to be effective they have to operate on the basis and within the limits and capacities of the foundation . . . Ideas and views cannot arise out of themselves and exist out of themselves but require a foundation in men's relation of work and exchange, upon which they constitute themselves, and in relation to which they change, partly in correspondence, partly in contrast." Cited in Max Adler's 1930 essay "Ideology and Culture" in Tom Bottomore and Patrick Goode, eds., *Austro-Marxism* (Oxford: Oxford University Press, 1978), p. 254. Also, see Raymond Williams, "Base and Superstructure in Marxist Cultural Theory," *New Left Review* 82 (November–December 1973).

7. Stephen Krasner strongly takes the "hooks" view. "Ideas have not made possible alternatives that did not previously exist; they legitimated political practices that were already facts on the ground. Ideas have been one among several instruments that actors have invoked to promote their own mundane interests . . . Only after ideas became embedded in institutional structures were they consequential for political behavior." "Westphalia and All That" in Goldstein and Keohane, pp. 238, 257.

8. Other works in this vein are Peter Hall, ed. *The Political Power of Economic Ideas: Keynesianism Across Nations* (Princeton: Princeton University Press, 1989); Anthony King, "Ideas, Interests and the Policies of Governments: A Comparative Analysis," *British Journal of Political Science* 7, 3 (October 1979); Paul Egon Rohrlich,

"Economic Culture and Foreign Policy: The Cognitive Analysis of Economic Policy Making," *International Organization* 41, 1 (Winter 1987), Emanuel Adler, *The Power of Ideology: The Quest for Technological Autonomy in Argentina and Brazil* (Berkeley: University of California, 1987) and "Cognitive Evolution: A Dynamic Approach for the Study of International Relations and Their Progress," in Adler and Beverly Crawford, eds., *Progress in Post-War International Relations* (New York: Columbia University Press, 1991); John S. Odell, *U.S. Monetary Policy: Money, Power and Ideas as Sources of Change* (Princeton: Princeton University Press, 1982); Ernst Haas, *When Knowledge is Power* (Berkeley: University of California, 1990); R. J. Bullen, H. Pogge von Strandmann, A. B Polonsky, eds., *Ideas into Politics: Aspects of European History 1880–1950* (London: Croom Helm, 1984); Mary Furner and Barry Supple, eds., *The State and Economic Knowledge* (Cambridge: Cambridge University Press, 1990). Robert R. Reich, ed., *The Power of Public Ideas* (Cambridge, MA: Ballinger, 1988) and John Gerard Ruggie, "International Regimes, Transactions and Change: Embedded Liberalism in The Postwar Economic Order," *International Organization* 36, 2 (Spring 1982).

9. Countering this, see Peter R. Gourevitch, "The Second Image Reversed" *International Organization* 32, 3 (Autumn 1978); Robert Putnam, "Diplomacy and Domestic Politics: The Logic of Two Level Games," *International Organization* 42, 3 (Summer 1988), and Stephen Haggard, "Structuralism and Its Critics: Recent Progress in International Relations Theory," in Adler and Crawford (fn. 9), pp. 403–468.

10. See Paul Pierson, "When Effects Become Causes: Policy Feedback and Political Change," *World Politics* 45, 3 (July 1993).

11. On values see Ronald J. Inglehart, *Culture Shift in Advanced Industrial Society* (Princeton: Princeton University Press, 1992); on political culture see David Laitin, "Political Culture Political Preferences," *American Political Science Review*, 82, 5 (June 1988) and John Street, "Political Culture: From Civic Culture to Mass Culture," *British Journal of Political Science* 24, 1 (January 1994); on political psychology, Fred Greenstein, *Personality and Politics* (Chicago: Markham, 1969); on psychoanalysis, Harold Lasswell *Psychopathology and Politics* (Chicago: University of Chicago, 1977, 2nd ed.); on symbolism, Murray Edelman *The Symbolic Uses of Politics* (Urbana: University of Illinois, 1967). Also, see Robert Jervis, *Perception and Misperception in International Relations* (Princeton: Princeton University Press, 1977) and Deborah Welch Larson, *Origins of Containment: A Psychological Explanation* (Princeton: Princeton University Press, 1985).

12. On leader-specific studies see Ole Holsti, "Cognitive Dynamics and Images of The Enemy: Dulles and Russia," in Douglas Finlay, Ole Holsti, and Richard Fagen, *Enemies in Politics* (Chicago: Rand McNally, 1967); Holsti, "Foreign Policy Viewed Cognitively," in Robert Axelrod, ed., *Structure of Decision: The Cognitive Maps of Political Elites* (Princeton: Princeton University Press, 1976); and Alexander L. George, "The Causal Nexus between Cognitive Beliefs and Decision-Making Behavior: The 'Operational Code Belief System'," in Lawrence Falkowski, ed., Psychological Models in International Relations (Boulder: Westview Press, 1979).

13. See Nina Halpern, "Creating Socialist Economies: Stalinist Political Economy and the Impact of Ideas" in Goldstein and Keohane.

14. These beliefs form an "economic culture," that is, a "definitive set of agreed-upon assumptions about how social economics functions and which social outcomes are desirable," Rohrlich (fn. 8), pp. 68–69. Furner and Supple define "economic knowledge" as "those things that people 'know' in the essence of

believing them" including "theories or assumptions about the ways in which different types of economic structures promote or hamper civic progress, equality, and welfare; the relations between economic expansion and individual liberty (and indeed the very nature of liberty) and the links that unite particular forms of government and prosperity," (fn. 8), p. 24.

15. See Ruggie, "International Regimes, Transactions and Embedded Liberalism in the Postwar Economic Order," *International Organization* 36, 2 (Spring 1982). Also, see Adam Przeworski and Michael Wallerstein, "Democratic Capitalism at the Crossroads," *Democracy* 2, 3 (July 1982).

16. Furner and Supple (fn. 8), p. 34. Likewise, Sikkink notes that the Reagan Administration, despite a deep aversion, could not entirely abandon a concern with human rights. "The Power of Principled Ideas: Human Rights Policies in the United States and Western Europe" in Goldstein and Keohane, p. 166.

17. Daniel Ellsberg writes of witnessing as a special assistant in Washington, D.C. "a whole dimension of policy consideration that is often discussed but almost never written down for fear of leaks both within government and to the public." *Papers on the War* (New York: Simon & Schuster, 1972), pp. 77–78.

18. William Drake and Kalypso Nicolaidis claim "the issue is not where community members sit but what they say," in "Ideas, Interests, and Institutionalization: Trade in Services and The Uruguay Round," in Haas, *IO*, p. 39. And note that there are usually "many Pareto-optimal alternatives open to a society" and that it is a "value judgment" that a Pareto-optimal situation is superior to any number of suboptimal ones. Brian Barry and Russell Hardin, eds., *Rational Man and Irrational Society?* (New York: Sage, 1982), p. 141.

19. H. Bruce Franklin, *MIA or Mythmaking in America* (New York: Lawrence Hill, 1992).

20. See the pertinent essays in, *The American Prospect* 16 (Winter 1994).

21. See Wendt (fn. 4), p. 393.

22. Geoffrey Garret and Barry R. Weingast differ in arguing that "the central concern of reflectivists—the social and institutional bases of shared beliefs—hold the key to overcoming the deficiences of functional logic" in "Ideas, Institutions and Interests: Constructing the European Community's Internal Market," in Goldstein and Keohane, p. 176.

23. Also, see Jon Elster, ed., *Rational Choice* (New York: New York University Press, 1986), pp. 1–27. Elster "Further Thoughts on Marxism, Functionalism and Game Theory," in John Roemer, ed. *Analytical Marxism* (Cambridge: Cambridge University Press, 1986).

24. Peter Haas and Emanuel Adler, "Conclusion: Epistemic Communities, World Order, and the Creation of a Reflective Program," *IO*.

25. John Dryzek, "How Far is it from Virginia and Rochester to Frankfurt?: Public Choice as Critical Theory," *British Journal of Political Science* 22, 4 (October 1992), pp. 407–408. He discusses the work of Viktor Vanberg and James Buchanan.

26. See E. E. Schattschneider, *The Semi-Sovereign People* (New York: Holt, Rinehart & Winston, 1960); and Jurgen Habermas, *Knowledge and Human Interests* (Boston: Beacon Press, 1973).

27. On Britain, see Ian Gilmour, *Dancing With Dogma* (London: Simon & Schuster, 1992); on the United States, David A. Stockman, *The Triumph of Politics* (New York: Harper & Row, 1986).

28. James A. Kurth, "The Political Consequences of the Product Cycle," *International Organization* 33, 1 (Winter 1979); Peter Gourevitch *Politics in Hard Times* (Ithaca: Cornell University Press, 1986); Thomas Ferguson, "From Normalcy to

New Deal: Industrial Structure, Party Competition, and American Public Policy in the Great Depression," *International Organization* 38, 1 (Winter 1984).

29. Policy entrepreneurs do not parachute in from Mount Olympus; they usually are interested actors who benefit when their ideas are adopted. Indeed, Sikkink refers to premiers Frondizi in Argentina and Kubitscek in Brazil as policy entrepreneurs in *Ideas and Institutions* (Ithaca: Cornell University Press, 1991) p. 245.
30. Note Albert Hirschman on the dangers of *currozione* "by which [Machiavelli] meant . . . the loss of public spirit," in "How the Keynesian Revolution was Exported from the United States and Other Comments," in Hall (fn. 8), pp. 354, 357.
31. "He who determines what politics is about runs the country, because the definition of the alternatives is the choice of conflicts, and the choice of conflicts allocates power." Schattschneider (fn. 33), p. 66.
32. "Epistemologically, the world and our representations of it are not isomorphic; our concept of reality is mediated by prior assumptions, expectations, and experiences. There is no such thing as the direct and true apprehension of reality itself . . ." writes Haas, *IO*, p. 21. This is the litany across the hermaneutic fields. "The realities with which psychoanalysis concerns itself . . . are created, evolved, and constructed realities . . . The psychological impact of reality on the individual varies according to what a human being makes of it, consciously or unconsciously. There is no objective reality per se that carries psychological weight of its own." Robert S. Wallerstein, "Psychoanalytic Perspectives on The Problem of Reality," *Journal of American Psychiatric Association* 21 (1973), p. 7.
33. Fred Block and Margaret Somers, "Beyond the Economistic Fallacy: The Holistic Science of Karl Polanyi," in Theda Skocpol, ed., *Vision and Method in Historical Sociology* (Cambridge: Cambridge University Press, 1984), p. 62.
34. An exception is Charles S. Maier, *In Search of Stability: Explorations in Historical Political Economy* (Cambridge: Cambridge University Press, 1987).
35. Thomas Kuhn, *The Structure of Scientific Revolutions* (Chicago: University of Chicago Press, 1962). See Peter Euban's essay on Kuhn's impact on political science in Green and Levinson (fn. 2).
36. Feyerabend makes this case in *Against Method* (London: Verso, 1975). On political implications, see Chapter 1.
37. See Bronislaw Oyrzanowski and Magda Palecny-Zapp, "From One Economic Ideology to Another: Poland's Transition from Socialism to Capitalism," *International Journal of Politics, Culture and Society* 7, 1 (1993).
38. On ideologies as "maps of problematic social realities" which "so construe them as to make it possible to act purposefully within them." See Clifford Geertz, "Ideology as a Cultural System," in *The Interpretation of Cultures* (New York: Basic Books, 1973), p. 220.
39. Robert H. Jackson, "The Weight of Ideas in Decolonization: Normative Change in International Relations"; also Sikkink, 9; Ernst Haas (fn. 8), p. 2; Goldstein, p. 3.
40. Peter Hall, "The Politics of Keynesian Ideas," in Hall (fn. 8), p. 369.
41. Ibid., p. 370.
42. Peter Gourevitch, "Keynesian Politics: The Political Sources of Economic Policy Choices" Ibid., 73. Also, see Margaret Weir, "Ideas and the Politics of Bounded Innovation," in Sven Steinmo, Kathleen Thelan, and Frank Longstreet, eds., *Structuring Politics: Historical Institutionalism in Comparative Analysis* (Cambridge: Cambridge University Press, 1992). Bounded innovation characterizes "institutions whose existence channeled the flow of ideas, created incentives for political

actors, and helped to determine the political meaning of policy choices," p. 189. Claus Offe gives an earlier formulation in "The Theory of the Capitalist State and the Problem of Policy Formation" in Leon Lindberg, et al., eds., *Stress and Contradiction in Modern Capitalism* (Lexington MA: D.C. Heath, 1975). Weir suggests "economic coalition arguments overlook the more independent role that new ideas can play in causing existing groups to rethink their interests and form alliances," (p. 190) which is a point worth exploring although we lack any examples of this occurring in the absence of the uptake of similar (potentially threatening) ideas by competitors.

43. "[P]olicy ideas matter because they provide opportunities for elites to pursue their interests in more effective ways. This may be the most profound way in which ideas matter." Ikenberry, "Creating Yesterday's New World Order: Keynesian 'New Thinking' and the Anglo-American Postwar Settlement," in Goldstein and Keohane, p. 84.

44. A good recent example is Daniel Verdier, "The Politics of Preference Formation: The United States from the Civil War to the New Deal," *Politics and Society* 21, 4 (December 1993).

45. Ellis S. Krause and Simon Reich argue that the nature and competitiveness of a particular sector influences both the extent and the exact form of aid that the executive will extend—a pattern deriving from an ideology of American State. In their terms the U.S. "free but fair" trade fluctuations in policy make perfect sense. "Ideology, Interests and the American Existence: Toward a Theory of Foreign Competition and Manufacturing Trade Policy," *International Organization* 46, 3 (Summer 1992).

46. Karl Polanyi, *The Great Transformation* (Boston: Beacon Press, 1957) and E. J. Hobsbawm, *Industry and Empire* (London: Penguin, 1971).

47. See the case studies in Daniel T. Rodgers, *Contested Truths: Keywords in American Politics Since Independence* (New York: Basic Books, 1987).

48. Maier (fn. 40), 45. Also David F. Noble *Forces of Production* (New York: Knopf, 1984).

49. Paul Goodman's comment remains apposite: the average citizen may not be equipped to "judge the substantive issues relevant to the vast sums for research and development; medicine, space exploration, and technical training; *but it would be helpful if he understood the interests and politics involved* (emphasis mine). *People or Personnel and Like A Conquered Province* (New York: Vintage, 1969), p. 315.

50. For an example regarding nonproliferation, see Chapter 3.

51. On rationales used to justify central direction as a means to achieve the official goal of worker rule, see Kendall Bailes, *Technology and Society Under Lenin and Stalin, 1917–1941* (Princeton: Princeton University Press, 1978).

52. See Loren Graham, *Science and Philosophy in The Soviet Union* (New York: Vintage, 1974); George Fisher, ed., *Science and Society in Soviet Society* (New York: Atherton Press, 1967); David Joravsky, *Soviet Marxism and Natural Science* (London: Routledge & Kegan, 1961); and Thomas Baylis, *The Technical Intelligentsia and the East German Elite: Legitimacy and Social Change Under Mature Communism* (Berkeley: University of California, 1974).

53. Jeff Checkel, "Ideas, Institutions and the Gorbachev Foreign Policy Revolution," *World Politics* 45, 2 (January 1993), p. 273.

54. Ibid., p. 275. See Fred Halliday, *The Making of the Second Cold War* (London: Verso, 1985) p. 11. Gorbachev interestingly invokes Lenin as a supple interpreter of and adjuster to trends in *Perestroika* (New York, Harper & Row, 1987).

For an internal view of Soviet flip-flops on foreign policy, see Arkady N. Shevchenko, *Breaking with Moscow* (New York: Ballantine, 1985), pp. 77–79, 108–109, 120.

55. Halpern observes such flexibility in China where there were "distinct limits to the ideological reformulations that have been permitted, for example, the debate must still revolve around the proper combination of plan and market, the proper role of the law of value, and new forms of management rather than ownership," p. 104.

56. Maier (fn. 40), p. 16.

57. Karl Marx and Frederick Engels, *The German Ideology* (New York: International Publishers, 1957), p. 120.

58. Sven Steinmo, "Political Institutions and Tax Policy in the U.S., Sweden and Britain," *World Politics* (July 1989), p. 501.

59. Ibid., p. 502.

60. Haas and Adler's "limited constructivist view" is although "no description can exist independently of the social circumstances under which that description is made," some consensus is possible; hence, "correct beliefs may evolve over time, as progressively more accurate characterizations of the world are consensually formulated." This stance parallels that of Charles Sanders Peirce. See Habermas's pertinent critique in (fn. 12), pp. 91–141.

61. Ruggie, "International Responses to Technology," *International Organization* 29, 3 (Summer 1975).

62. Melvin Ott, "Shaking Up the CIA," *Foreign Policy* 93 (Winter 1993–94), 42. See Hans Morganthau's very prescient article on the dangerous adaptation of intelligence to preconceptions, "Vietnam and the National Interest." In Marvin E. Gettleman, ed. *Vietnam: History, Documents and Opinions* (Greenwich, CT: Fawcett, 1965), p. 374.

63. Peter Gourevitch in Hall (fn. 8), p. 89.

64. Ethan Barnaby Kapstein, "Between Power and Purpose: Central Bankers and the Politics of Regulatory Convergence." In Haas, *IO*.

65. See William J. Broad, *Teller's War* (New York: Simon & Schuster, 1992).

66. See Leonard A. Cole, *Politics and the Restraint of Science* (Totowa, NJ: Rowman & Allanheld, 1983) and Ellen W. Schrecker, *No Ivory Tower: McCarthyism and the Universities* (New York: Oxford University Press, 1986).

67. Haas recognizes that "choices remain highly political in their allocative consequences," especially "where scientific evidence is ambiguous and the experts themselves are split into contending factions . . ." *IO*, p. 11. What is rare in policy debates is scientific unanimity, not divided opinions.

68. Peter Haas rejects Ernst Haas's reliance on these communities' "beliefs in extracommunity reality tests." p. 17 (n. 39), in *IO*.

69. Allan Mazur, *The Dynamics of Technical Controversy* (Washington, DC: Communications Press, 1981), pp. 81–82.

70. This accords with the spirit of Geertz's comment that "competing ideologies are at least as important a check on ideological claims" as is scientific analysis, p. 230.

71. The Chinese went to the extreme of dispatching their unwanted "epistemic community" of market economists, who did not provide for Party power-retention needs, to a most severe reeducation.

72. Ikenberry, "A World Restored: Expert Consensus and the Anglo-American Postwar Settlement," in Haas, *IO*, p. 294.

73. See Hirschman's essay in Hall (fn. 8).

74. Antonio Gramsci, *The Modern Prince*, p. 112.

75. Chantal Mouffe, "Hegemony and Ideology in Gramsci," in Tony Bennett, Graham Martin, Colin Mercer, Janet Woolacott, eds. *Culture, Ideology and Social Process* (London: Open University, 1987), p. 223.
76. Cosmopolitan and nationalist developmentalists "agree about vertical industrialization programs promoted by vigorous state action but disagree over the role of foreign investment and the degree of state involvement in the economy." Ibid., p. 39.
77. On the implications of debt for Brazilian democracy see John R. Freeman, *The Politics of Indebted Growth* (Denver: Graduate School of International Studies, 1983), pp. 20, 65.
78. Ibid., 157. Sikkink notes that these "rings" aided the 1964 coup, p. 151.
79. See Geertz's discussion of why the claim that the Taft-Hartley Act was "a slave labor law" misfired. (fn. 47), pp. 208–210.
80. See Chapters 3 and 5.
81. See Alaine Touraine, *The Return of the Actor* (Minneapolis: University of Minnesota, 1988), pp. 1–14.
82. Maier (fn. 40), p. 268.
83. Margaret Archer reminds us of "the quintessential reflective ability of human beings to fight back against their conditioning [which] gives them the capacity to respond with originality to the present context—either by taking advantage of inconsistencies within it and generating new forms of syncretism, or by exploring novel combinations of compatible elements." *Culture and Agency: The Place of Culture in Social Theory* (Cambridge: Cambridge University Press, 1988), p. xxiv.
84. Stuart Hall, "Cultural Studies: Two Paradigms," in (fn. 108), p. 12.
85. "Articulation is a continuous struggle to reposition practices within a shifting field of forces, to redefine possibilities by redefining the field of relations—the context—within which the practice is located. . . . the practice of articulation reworks the context into which practices are inserted." Lawrence Grossberg, *Popular Conservativism and Modern Culture* (London: Routledge, 1992), p. 54.
86. Archer (fn. 121), p. xiii. Also, see Touraine (fn. 119).
87. Emanuel Adler, Beverly Crawford and Jack Donnelly, "Defining and Conceptualizing Progress in International Relations," in Adler and Crawford (fn. 8), p. 27.

PART II
INVESTIGATIONS

3

Safeguards and Profits:
Civilian Nuclear Exports,
Neo-marxism
and the Statist Approach

Stephen Krasner formulates a "statist approach" in *Defending The National Interest* which he argues is superior to both pluralism and instrumental marxism as a framework for explaining decisions by U.S. policymakers about promotion of raw materials investments abroad by U.S. firms. The statist model claims to better account for the role of ideology in decision making processes. A fundamental flaw in other models is that they "view formal government institutions as relatively passive recipients of societal pressure."[1] Krasner's case studies disclose a state that is more autonomous and dynamic than pluralist images imply while "instrumental marxism" is rejected because of instances where the state behaved more entrepreneurially than did private firms (e.g., Iran between 1951 and 1955), or else declined to support U.S. foreign investors. Krasner construed the destabilization campaign waged against Chile as a case of the state taking advantage of corporate predispositions—especially International Telephone and Telegraph (ITT)—to achieve its own aims in the Southern Cone.[2]

Hence, the state is comprised of a set of institutions that pursue aims "separate and distinct from any interest of any particular societal group."[3] The most autonomous institutions are the White House and the State Department which in foreign affairs form the "pivot of the state . . . Krasner believes that, unlike Congress, they "usually have been able to resist private pressures to take actions that were not perceived as furthering the national interest."[4] The "national interest" is defined as the preferences of central decision makers that persist over time, are rank-ordered, and relate to general societal goals. Private corporate actors presumably suffer when their preferences diverge from those of the state.[5]

Krasner claims a slimmer edge over the neo-marxist model because, though it is more difficult to distinguish structural marxist arguments from a statist paradigm, the importance that "central decision makers have at times attributed to ideological as opposed to economic or strategic aims is more compatible with the theoretical image that guides this study than with any materialist interpretation."[6] This verdict should evoke surprise (or sighs) among scholars familiar with the contributions of Gramsci and the Frankfurt School on the "material power of ideas."[7] Still, Krasner deems structural marxism his sturdiest rival since it too ascribes relative autonomy to the state which acts (or appears to act) as a 'neutral arbiter' maintaining the cohesion of the capitalist social formation even at the occasional tactical expense of particular powerful economic agents. In foreign investment Krasner finds a "happy convergence of interest between state and private corporations" so that "no firm judgment of the statist and structural marxist model" can be rendered.[8]

Our enterprise here is to apply both the statist approach and neo-marxist theory to the issue of the regulation of civilian nuclear industry exports so as to compare their explanatory merits. Unlike Krasner's investment cases, the "happy convergence" had shattered in the issue area of nuclear commerce during a fierce legislative struggle over the passage on the Nuclear Non-Proliferation Act of 1978 (NNPA), which thereby poses an interesting test for the models.

Nuclear vendors argued that the NNPA threatened their future as producers—a future they identified with the strength of the United States by emphasizing a series of pronuclear themes which shifted over time. First there was a short-lived promise of energy "too cheap to meter," then nuclear energy was portrayed as the *sine qua non* cutting edge of technical progress, and, eventually, these justifications ebbed into the Hobson's choice argument that no alternative exists. They pointed to mammoth "sunk costs" that in turn demand fresh capital infusions and more patience before dividends accrue; otherwise, markets are lost to foreign suppliers. Until the 1970s the nuclear industry enjoyed a robust "ideological hegemony" in the way its own interests fitted with cultural predispositions toward laissez-faire, belief in technological imperatives and desire for economic growth. An ideological notion aiding the industry's cause was the purely conceptual barrier that separated civilian nuclear applications from military use.[9]

In the relationship between ideology and decision making in the statist model, what is anomalous is the reversal of roles by "central decision makers" and the Congress during the NNPA debate, with respect to determining policy. Structural marxism provides clues why this anomaly occurs and for predicting its recurrence. We find that during moments of crisis in relations between state actors and private agents that structural marxism displays more explanatory utility. By "crisis" we mean sudden and protracted departures from Krasner's "happy convergences," departures that private elites view as disadvantageous. We do not deal with *systemic crises* that threaten to rupture and/or transform the socioeconomic structure of society. At a level of much "lower stakes" we refer to *policy crises* when the interests of the state and those of leading firms not only diverge but where no social crisis accompanies this divergence.

Our concern is the degree to which neo-marxism can explain not only the "outer parameters" of policymaking (which limit the range of policy options), but is able to contribute to the analysis of political behavior in policy areas where even sympathetic scholars believe that pluralist methods of investigation are superior.[10] In public policy "the parameters are economically determined but what takes place within them need not be."[11] Neo-marxists view the accumulation process as the most powerful constraint but not as the sole determinant of the content of policy. Our aim is to demonstrate the applicability of structural marxism in this significant range of short-term," incremental policy struggles.

In the contest over control of the content of the Non-proliferation Policy we review the relationship between the state and nuclear firms from 1945 through the the Carter administration during which period of policy compatibility there was little to choose between the statist and structural marxist models. We then examine the legislative struggle over the NNPA and draw conclusions as to the illuminative aspects of the models. Finally, we look at trends in nuclear export promotion and non-proliferation policy and discuss the importance of our conclusions for future research. The first task is clarifying distinctive features of the statist approach vis-à-vis neo-marxist theory.[12]

COMPETING AUTONOMIES OF THE STATE

"America has a strong society but a weak state" because of its notorious fragmentation of power and its multiple points of access to the decision making process which are so celebrated by pluralist writers as endemic features of the Lockean liberal legacy.[13] In this fragmented environment vetoes are easily imposed while positive policy initiatives are hampered by a purgatorial process of review, revision, and frequently, rejection because the state "confronts dissident bureaus, a recalcitrant Congress, and powerful private actors in its quest to manifest whatever central decision makers determine to be in the national interest.[14]

These interests are generally "national" in scope and are not supposed to discriminate for or against societal groups. The notion that U.S. decision makers formulate policy goals free from intrusive societal interests is at odds with Krasner's observation elsewhere that a weak state may seem to act "effectively in the strategic arena because its preferences are not likely to diverge from those of individual societal groups."[15] Policy goals are rank-ordered to facilitate choices when conflicts occur and they include not only specific material interests but also "ambitious ideological goals related to beliefs about how societies should be ordered."[16]

The successful implementation of policies depends on the arena in which decisions occur and upon adroit leadership. If policy implementation is confined to the executive branch or is dependent upon executive resources, the state usually succeeds even when it must gore powerful oxen in the private sector.[17] On the other hand, if policy implementation requires "authorization from Congress, or required the cooperation of private companies" central decision makers are frustrated or are "forced to compromise some of their aims."[18]

However, state institutions carry prestige and deploy real resources that imaginative leaders can convert into decisive instruments in the face of strong opposition. Because "international politics presents options that are not available for purely domestic issues and because political leaders can themselves define a dispute and change both its scope and the arena in which it is decided," Krasner deems the United States to be a "moderate state" with respect to the latitude its decision makers wield in foreign policy. When the policy instruments at their disposal are deftly employed, state authorities not only resist societal interests but can change the behavior of societal groups to accord with, or acquiesce to, state ends.

Splits inside Congress and among interest groups can be exploited: the scope of an issue may be expanded to include favorable constituencies to tip the balance; and the way the policy is defined can be modified by soothing presidential rhetoric. Franklin D. Roosevelt often is cited as a master of these maneuvers.[19] When zero-sum disputes arise in regulatory or redistributive issue areas a president may shift the matter out of vulnerable realms into the higher plane of "power politics" where reasons of state hold sway.[20] During policy crises the president and private interests both can play at identifying their preferences with the national interest because no immediate peril looms and a swing vote is yet to be won. Credibility (or credulity) is the key to success.

MARXIST PERSPECTIVES

"The executive of the modern state, Marx and Engels asserted, "is but a committee for managing the common affairs of the whole bourgeoisie.[21] Anyone who ever served on a committee will be disabused of the idea that consensual policies are fashioned easily and then effortlessly implemented. Although Marx displayed a rich analytical appreciation of the complex multivariate relations between state and society in his empirical studies *The Civil War in France* and *The Eighteenth Brumaire*, a cartoonish caricature of ruling class domination arose. Yet, Marx bequeathed no such image—nor any theory of state and bureaucracy at all.

Structural marxists view the state as a mediator and arbitrator of conflicts among an internally divided capitalist class and between the latter and other classes and organizations.[22] The state is itself divided into relatively autonomous branches and must both preserve conditions for economic growth through profit (accumulation) and maintain its own ideological credibility and of the entire economic system (legitimation) to serve the long term interests of a capitalist society. Hence, "class reductionism" and economic determinism are repudiated while an intertwining of ideology and material interests in the course of policymaking is stressed. Accumulation and legitimation are rank-ordered functions because the latter (e.g., welfare provisions) cannot be secured unless the former is in good working order. The state manages recurrent contradictions between these functions although it cannot solve them for once and for all.

One can stumble into a "hyper-structuralist trap" that deprives "agents" of freedom of choice and views them as "bearers of objective forces which they are unable to affect."[23] Krasner, like Poulantzas in his early work, characterizes the state as a unitary actor guided by omniscient managers. The result is that structural marxism resembles nothing so much as a mechanistic realist model positing the closest possible congruence of means to ends. Like realists, marxists are thought to disdain "the independent role of ideology"[24] and so cannot explain, for example, the "nonlogical manner in which U.S. leaders pursued their anticommunism in Vietnam.[25] Structural marxism is discarded for failing to achieve the very objective that it explicitly resists— that of forging an economic deterministic theory for predicting outcomes.

Structural marxism is not quite in the dire dogmatic straits to which Krasner consigned it. Neo-marxist scholars emphasize that to "endow the state with an essential class unity or an inevitable bourgeois character is to engage in crude reductionism," and that "there is no reason to expect a purely marxist approach to exhaust the analysis of the state."[26] Riven by struggles inside and between its component institutions the state is a highly problematic entity since, within broad limits that vary with the situational context, relative autonomy increases the likelihood of unpredictable outcomes, i.e., policy decisions unfavorable to actors wielding the most resources.

Moreover, during policy crises—moments of jeopardy for particular sets of firms rather than for the capitalist system—the relative autonomy of the state increases. By this we do not mean that a Bonapartist situation is in the offing or that the executive is thereby strengthened. Rather, all policy contestants are compelled by their deadlock to conduct a "war of position" and to concentrate their resources inside the indeterminate terrain of the state apparatuses. These apparatuses—that is, agencies and institutions—are "indeterminate" because economical and social power does not translate proportionately into political power there, and most certainly not so in each component institution of the state. Other things being equal, uncertainty of outcomes will increase when powerful actors are unable to muster a quick, decisive victory in periods of expanding autonomy—or "elasticity"—within state institutions.

We emphasize that increasing "elasticity" of the relative autonomy of state apparatuses (or component institutions) does not necessarily cumulate into an increase in the autonomy of the state itself. Pressed too far and for too long, increasing elasticity impairs the functioning of the state. Second, the degree of elasticity of the apparatuses of the state is limited by the need for functional compatibility between the economic system and the state structure. A state that is infinitely elastic is not capitalist or will not remain so for long. Third, increased elasticity is not only a dependent variable; it can be cause and consequence of policy crises.

STRUCTURAL REFINEMENTS

Fred Block and Paul Joseph aimed to refine marxist theory for policy analysts and move beyond structuralist formalism.[27] Block observes, like Weber, that the power of state managers is based on a monopoly of legal violence. State managers are interested in "maximizing their power, prestige and wealth," and their power is constrained by the institutional rules of the game and the particular class context in which they operate.[28] The competitive international state system compels state managers to

> protect their nation's positions within the international state system since those who preside over a decline in their nation's political, economic, or military strength are likely to find their own power reduced as their nation's freedom to maneuver internationally declines.[29]

Therefore he adds a security function. In practice security, accumulation and legitimation come into conflict, and this can breed policy crises. Different state institutions champion different goals. Because no harmonious ruling class directs the economy and because state isn't a unitary actor shepherding myopic capitalists toward their best interests, neither contestant has "a monopoly on rationality." Block analyzes the goals state managers pursue and how their choices are constricted while Joseph delineates different ways in which given goals may be attained. Policy currents, a term borrowed from Franz Schurmann, are:

> basic prescriptions governing the role of the U.S. in the world arena: a response to the forces of opposition on the part of defenders of capital foreign and domestic; ideological bridges between the capitalist class and state mangers; and they embrace special interests which influence but do not determine policy.[30]

Joseph's account of presidential decisions is highly revealing. A president may be attached to a particular current, but "the actual decisions of the president . . . shift between different currents, especially during periods of crisis" and these conversions stem from a "shifting calculus of costs."[31] That is, the balance of forces changes and the president, acts accordingly.[32] A president will try to shift the arena in which policy is decided and other central officials may try to change the definition of an issue or the scope of interests. In response, private interests can likewise attempt to shift the site of real power over the issue area

> In other words, the organization of the bourgeois state allows it to function by successive dislocation and displacement through which the bourgeoisie's power may be removed from one apparatus to another: the state is not a monolithic bloc but a strategic field.[33]

Poulantzas described strategies—short of disinvestment—that capitalists pursue to guard their interest when leftist governments take power. These strategies apply in "low stakes" situations such as regulatory conflicts where the interests of only a few firms are involved and which other firms do not believe affect their own survival (and toward whose interests they may be indifferent or antagonistic). In policy crises the "conjunctural primacy of politics" is underscored. David Abraham in his study of the Weimer democracy argues that at the systemic level

> The less obvious the dominance of any particular capitalist fraction, the greater the impact of the bureaucracy and of the executive on the one hand, and of the private interest groups on the other . . . The years of stabilization rendered the bureaucracy a stronger force in mediating interclass conflicts.[34]

In policy crises executive power is not enhanced nor can the bureaucracy maintain the cohesion necessary to mediate conflicts because the "elasticity" of the autonomy of component state institutions is increasing. The state is a strategic field where decision makers fight to realize their definitions of "national interest". The affected private agents will respond by, among other things, trying to shift the power over policy to a favorable site. At the same time the influence of groups with fewer resources *improves*.[35]

So we expect that in a policy crisis the greater the increase of the elasticity of the component institutions of the state, the more that asymmetries in access to power will be neutralized—and so the policy outcome grows more uncertain. Groups with intense interests but few resources also mobilize to exert influence through sympathetic sites within the state. A president who aims to draw support for his policy preference by expanding the participative scope of the issue may wind up diluting the power of the state (and of private elites) by opening the policy process to new groups which must be reckoned with. One may regard this as a democratizing side effect. While

Krasner's central decision makers determine the national interest, they cannot decide or implement it just as they please.

Incidentally, in contrast to the distinction between policy crisis and legitimation crisis, John Campbell's study of the nuclear industry distinguishes between *internal* legitimation crisis and *external* legitimation crisis because he stresses the importance of opposition occurring *inside* formal organizations such as the Nuclear Regulatory Commission. This dissent, however, is unlikely to become visible until "members of the technical staff [begin] to struggle against current safety policy by posing alternative policy-making criteria"—and successfully reach out and ally with public groups.[36] In our view this intraorganizational grumbling is irrelevant until it links up with forces in the public sphere so as to stoke a policy crisis.[37]

The foregoing refinements comprise a modified neo-marxist model that we compare with the statist approach. Before proceeding to the NNPA policy crisis, however, we review the foundations of the "happy convergence" in interest between the state and private industry. To cast the argument into sharper relief we also include the economic determinist hypothesis that the stringency of the regime for nuclear fuels and facilities varies inversely with the civilian sector's commercial success. This "vulgar hypothesis" represents the crude determinism attributed to marxism, which is not to be confused with a similarly crude determinism found in a liberalism that attributes allocative virtue solely to the market.

ATOMS FOR PEACE

Robert Oppenheimer observed nine months after the Hiroshima and Nagasaki blasts, and amid predictions that the force that leveled cities today would illuminate them cheaply tomorrow, that "the science, the technology, the industrial development involved in so-called beneficial uses of atomic energy appear to be inextricably intertwined with those involved in nuclear weapons.[38] That this link was recognized by authorities was evidenced in a declaration by the United States, Canada, and Great Britain that they "were prepared to share, on a reciprocal basis with other of the United Nations, detailed information concerning the practical applications of atomic energy just as soon as effective enforceable safeguards against its use for destructive purposes can be devised."[39]

The Acheson-Lilenthal Report recommended establishment of an international authority with ownership of nuclear facilities and exercising stringent control over all activities susceptible to diversion to weapons manufacture. After a proposal for international ownership of uranium mines was discarded, the "Baruch plan" entered the UN where the Soviet Union summarily rejected it as a disguised approval of the United States' nuclear arms monopoly. The United States then passed the McMahon Act of 1946 establishing civilian control of atomic energy, broke its agreement with Canada and Great Britain to share research, and stipulated that

> until Congress declares by joint resolution that effective and enforceable international safeguards against the use of atomic energy for destructive purposes have been established there shall be no exchange of information with other nations with respect to the use of atomic energy for industrial purposes.[40]

The Atomic Energy Commission (AEC) was responsible for developing and regulating atomic energy programs while a Joint Committee on Atomic Energy (JCAE) decided policy "with the advice and consent of the Executive." From the start the JCAE behaved as a promoter of a fabulous new energy that promised to reap international prestige, foreign earnings, domestic growth, skill-intensive employment, and political influence over those nations that sought to import these technologies.[41]

The JCAE hastened to close the considerable gap between promises and payoffs by enticing reluctant private investors. The U.S. state formed partnerships with industry in order to absorb high costs and risks so that this cumulative investment tended to diminish the state's "autonomy in this policy area and limit its ability to respond to public concerns."[42] The state was the prime mover in France, Germany, and Canada too where firms were beneficiaries of military programs or other subsidies which fed research and development (R & D) throughout the 1950s on a scale unparalleled by any previous industrial effort.[43]

Such was the legal and financial dependence of private industry on the state that Hyman Rickover, supervisor of the U.S. Navy's atomic submarine program, virtually dictated corporate nuclear development through his discretionary award of contracts.[44] Westinghouse, especially, reaped the benefit of subsidized Navy projects while commercial prospects for nuclear energy improved to an extent not otherwise so quickly attained. On the eve of Eisenhower's "Atoms for Peace" speech in 1953, research had progressed as far as construction of the federally funded shipping port nuclear power plant. Meanwhile, policymakers were rudely apprised not only of their wishful miscalculations about Soviet nuclear capabilities, but also with respect to competing reactor programs in Great Britain and the USSR. Accordingly, pressure to accelerate the nuclear program intensified.

The "vulgar hypothesis" cannot explain Eisenhower's proposal which, coming months after the first Soviet blast, had been a half-hearted disarmament bid. But neither is the hypothesis a negligible one. After a proposal for an International "atomic pool" was rejected an amended Atomic Energy Act of 1954 permitted private ownership of fissile materials and nuclear facilities, and pledged to "make available to cooperating nations the benefits of peaceful applications of atomic energy as widely as expanding technology and consideration of the common defense will permit."[45] In hope that technological fixes could solve contradictory goals, the United States ranked the promotion of civilian nuclear power above the goal of non-proliferation. A consistent ranking of objectives is discernible.

Industry had to be encouraged with cost-plus contracts into lines of research that policymakers deemed critical. These state initiatives confound determinist or pluralist beliefs that weak states merely respond to private sector desires. (Despite the vesting of authority in a civilian Atomic Energy Commission, a Military Liaison Committee, run by armed services personnel, actually exercised authority over the military "which, was, after all, the prime user of the atom.")[46] This typical conduct by states concerned with their relative military and economic position in the international order is consistent with both the statist model and with neo-marxism.

The U.S. state and the nuclear industry cultivated a mutually advantageous relationship. The AEC, in fact, "sought to create the very constituency that would 'pressure' it."[47] In 1955 the AEC initiated a Power Reactor Demonstration Program that would evolve through three phases of aid (including subsidized R & D and fuel for seven years), and declassification until investors showed interest. The Price-Anderson Act indemnified private industry while the AEC and Export-Import Bank would engineer overseas sales. The AEC chairman announced that his regulatory objective to "minimize governmental control of competitive enterprise" was a self-liquidating one.[48] In response to the 1956 Gore-Hollifield Bill, which wanted to compel the AEC to construct six reactors and thus raised the specter of an "atomic TVA," the AEC chairman stated that his agency would "give industry the first opportunity to undertake the construction of the nuclear reactors."[49]

U.S. light-water-reactor technology was preferred by West European buyers in the 1960s.[50] These reactors were fueled with enriched uranium and so America's monopoly on enrichment facilities guaranteed its dominance. To dissuade rivals from entering this sensitive trade, the United States had to foster an image as a reliable supplier of low-cost, abundant fuel. Enrichment facilities became a state monopoly where costs were kept down in service of a nonpecuniary "national interest." The State Department conducted secret negotiations with uranium suppliers to enforce adoption of safeguards at a time when membership in the International Atomic Energy Agency (formed in 1956) imposed "no affirmative obligation either to refrain from military nuclear activities or to submit to agency safeguards."[51] These factors enabled the United States to police frontiers where nuclear trade was otherwise free to flourish.

So the policy priorities of the White House and State Department never conflicted with those of the JCAE, AEC, or private industry except insofar as a frugal Republican administration was unenthusiastic about long term financial commitments.[52] Beginning with "loss leader" sales to wary investors, the nuclear industry rapidly grew in the 1960s—supported by federal spending, legislation, and sales campaigns. At the end of the 1960s only R & D and enrichment remained predominantly in state hands; the Atomic Industrial Forum tried to secure these for the private sector too.[53] Private industry opposed the formation of the European Atomic Energy Committee (Euratom) which the U.S. state had encouraged both for geopolitical reasons and because it was a useful channel for sales.[54] U.S. firms entered joint ventures (with France's Framatome) and licensing agreements (Germany and Japan). Predictably, foreign firms soon grew with the aid of their states to become rivals.

Technology transfers to noncommunist countries were unrestricted until 1972. Industrial nuclear energy was viewed benignly until the Chinese bomb test in 1964, the abetting of the Israeli bomb project by a French plutonium-producing reactor, and cumulative fears of proliferation prompted the Non-Proliferation of Nuclear Weapons Treaty (NPT) in 1970.[55] As far as exporters were concerned the NPT was a harmless document that guaranteed to signators the right to share in peaceful nuclear benefits. It fell short of being "geographically comprehensive" and hardly inhibited the spread of sensitive nuclear facilities.[56] The United States diluted its "continuous inspection" proposal to appease Japan and West Germany which feared that they would suffer a discriminatory rise in inspection costs on their breeder reactor projects.

Indeed, the NPT reaffirmed the primacy of marketing over vigilant non-proliferation.[57] So porous were the safeguards, particularly with respect to export of reprocessing technologies to nations with thinly disguised ambitions for military use, that a European observer credited the Ford and Carter administrations with "triggering of an awareness in Europe of the fact that exporting of nuclear materials and equipment is a special business" for which unique standards might have to play.[58] Might mercantilist motives account largely for this remarkable nuclear naiveté?

One cannot "allege that sheer economic need conditions the choices available and alone determines state policy outcomes"[59] Economic logic alone did not ordain state support for nuclear energy. Instead, the synergizing effect of optimistic forecasts of boundless energy plus substantial state investment resulted in the formation of a symbiotic bloc of public and private institutions. This development could not have been predicted on the basis of simple economic analyses or by an accounting of their social utility. Instead this outcome stemmed from a mutual integration of the interests of state elites and private elites.

"Fragmentation of power" and "insulation" are double-edged terms whose meanings change with the situation in which they are examined. A fragmentation of public authority fosters the creation of "many, partially overlapping and often competing vertical policy networks seeking to control the flow of public policy in their particular sphere of interest."[60] These policy networks contribute to the formation of interorganizational coalitions of elites. Fragmentation may "free political elites to act with fewer constraints" and "place them more under the influence of the most strongly organized interest groups and social classes."[60] By virtue of "expertise, hierarchical control, and ability to mobilize resources," coalitions of elites dominate policy outcomes because of the prohibitive organizational and information costs which discourage challengers.[61]

"Insulation" denotes insulation from popular demands only, not from corporate pressures. The influence of powerful groups upon political elites is undiluted where these elites are "insulated" from popular demands. This relationship between fragmented political elites and organized private interest groups is Krasner's "happy convergence," which I will term "a policy concordance." A *policy concordance* presupposes that (1) an interorganizational coalition of elites shares basic policy premises and (2) that they are insulated from nonelites or counter-elites. A faltering in either prerequisite creates conditions for a policy crisis.

An intimate interlock of state and private agents in the nuclear realm was dictated both by security concerns and the costly nature—long lead time, high capital requirements, intensive R & D—of this ambitious enterprise. What was good for Westinghouse, Framatome, or KraftWerk Union was good for their respective states and so it was no surprise to find policy concordances abound. Neo-marxism is consistent with these findings; even the "vulgar hypothesis"—that the stringency of the non-proliferation regime varies inversely with profitability—survives scrutiny if one views the latter as a retardant on the former as global competition intensifies. The policy concordance breaks down when the centrifugal effects of dissension expand the autonomy of the institutions of the state.

This policy crisis was precipitated by the intensifying competition signaled by formation of the Uranium Enrichment Corporation (URENCO), a Belgian-French-Spanish-Italian consortium in uranium enrichment, shortfalls in the nuclear promise domestically, a waning of the conceptual barrier between military and peaceful use, and, not least, the inept promotion of the industry by a neo-mercantilist Nixon administration. The Nixon administration hardly conformed to Krasner's image of an executive branch coordinating policies that maximize U.S. goals. In nuclear matters as in other issue areas (soybean embargo, closing the gold window) the political horizons of the White House were myopically domestic and the repercussions were counterproductive. Irreparable damage was self-inflicted on the United States' reputation as a reliable supplier.

The AEC projected a $3.5 billion yearly market for U.S. reactors and ancillary items. Nixon wanted to transfer enrichment centers to private hands even though private control augured hikes in prices that must undermine one of the few buttresses of the non-proliferation regime. When Congress blocked the sell-off of three enrichment plants, Nixon impounded funds for enrichment expansion in order to create a supply squeeze to "force favorable action on privatization."[62] The White House played morale booster to the sluggish private sector, revised rate schedules upward, imposed onerous new contracts on foreign customers, and the subsequent squeeze resulted in a 1974 freeze on exports. The AEC resisted privatization but was quickly subdued by Nixon appointees.[63] State Department personnel who had misgivings were marginalized. Only after the enrichment snafu and the Indian nuclear blast was the alarmed and querulous "voice" of the State Department "restored."[64] Ironically, a zealous pro-business White House had destroyed the policy concordance.

A private consortium offered qualified support for a transfer of enrichment centers to their control; the catch was a demand for guarantees of what an American Enterprise Institute analyst gingerly termed "subsidy-like provisions."[65] The Ford administration's Nuclear Fuel Assurance Act was vigorously opposed by the General Accounting Office and Congress. This privatization campaign continued into the autumn of 1976 when the India test, the enrichment freeze, and prospective sales of sensitive equipment to "pariah states" finally perturbed the White House. By this time a de facto moratorium on domestic reactor orders constrained United States and European industries—France excepted—because of construction costs, declines in electricity growth rates, conservation measures, a global recession, and public outcry over safety violations. Nuclear advocates no longer were able to persuade significant sectors of the public that nuclear energy was safe or economical or that "those with interests in the expansion of nuclear power, in government or in the public sector, can be trusted to act in the public interest."[66]

The policy concordance dissolved and the measures taken to restore public confidence only served to increase the "elasticity" of the autonomy of state institutions and thus widen participation, diffuse power among sites, and stoke public controversy. The 1975 Energy Reorganization Act apportioned the duties of an abolished AEC between the Nuclear Regulatory Commission (NRC) and the Energy Research and Development Administration (ERDA). The JCAE's jurisdiction over nuclear matters was weakened in 1974 and ultimately dispersed in 1977 among seven congressional committees.

The essential anomaly for a statist explanation is that it was Congress, not central decision makers, that "took the first step" after the Indian bomb hearings to stiffen regulation of nuclear exports.[67] Until the end of the Ford administration (when breeder reactor and plutonium recovery programs were deferred) commercial objectives consistently took precedence over non-proliferation. As the Nixon episode testifies, the goal of non-proliferation, even when not in direct conflict with marketing, was quite dispensable for ideological reasons. The election of Jimmy Carter signaled an outbreak of full-blown policy crisis—but we should note that the "vulgar hypothesis" no longer holds up because competition among domestic industries for expanding export markets was accelerating.

LEGISLATING THE NUCLEAR NON-PROLIFERATION ACT OF 1978

On 27 April 1977, President Carter said in his message to Congress that "the need to halt nuclear proliferation is one of mankind's most pressing challenges." A year later Carter signed the NNPA in which it was declared to be the policy of the United States to

(a) actively pursue through international initiatives mechanisms for fuel supply assurances and the establishment of more effective international controls over the transfer and use of nuclear materials and equipment . . . for peaceful purposes in order to prevent proliferation . . ."
(b) . . . confirm the reliability of the United States in meeting its commitment to supply nuclear reactors and fuel to nations which adhere to effective non-proliferation policies by establishing procedures to facilitate the timely processing of requests from subsequent arrangements and export licenses;
(c) strongly encourage nations which have not ratified the treaty on the Non-Proliferation of Nuclear Weapons to do so . . .
(d) and cooperate with foreign nations in identifying and adapting suitable technologies for energy production and, in particular, to identify alternative options to nuclear power in aiding such nations to meet their energy needs, consistent with the economic and material resources of those nations and environmental protection.

Congress was concerned not only with preventing proliferation but also with restoring the United States as a reliable supplier. In amendments of the Foreign Assistance Act and Export-Import Bank Act, Congress had created sanctions—which the president could waive—on nonnuclear states engaging in weapons-related nuclear activities.[68] The General Accounting Office (GAO) noted that U.S. firms over 1970–1973 "supplied 86% of the nuclear capacity exported to the free world, but this share declined to 45% for 1974 to 1977. From 1978, when the NNPA was enacted, through 1980, the U.S. share of this market was 39%."[69]

The Office of Technology Assessment predicted the value of U.S. reactor exports to developing nations would be 5 to 7 billion dollars by 1990, assuming a U.S. share of 35–40 percent over the early 1980s and 25–30 percent in the latter half of the decade.[70] An ERDA report estimated that the

United States would get 120–140 billion dollars in export revenue from nuclear sales through the year 2000.[71] As market shares declined and competitors' "sweetener deals" abounded, the U.S. nuclear industry feared that unilateral legislation might jeopardize its waning competitiveness. Accordingly the industry fought to weaken the non-proliferation bills pending in Congress in 1977 and 1978.

The NNPA also was perceived negatively by foreign competitors. Europeans suspected that the United States was changing the rules of nuclear trade to protect its portion of the market just when the Europeans "developed an impressive technological edge" in reprocessing and fast breeder technology.[72] In West Germany a 50 percent excess capacity was built into the industry for export purposes, and so the response was livid. A KraftWerk German executive assailed the United States' self-declared role of "policeman on the world-wide beat of non-proliferation" and charged that the NNPA was designed to maintain dependence of importing countries on the United States.[73] European officials and executives fretted that the new U.S. policy served the sinister purpose of aiding and abetting domestic opponents of a "nuclear society." A pronuclear international alliance formed to oppose the NNPA and to complement the domestic U.S. industry activities. Next we examine whether advocates of tough controls succeeded.

In the 95th Congress nonproliferation bills were attacked on the grounds that a unilateral tightening of export controls would injure U.S. industry and undermine chances to devise realistic strategies. The nuclear industry and its congressional allies sought to limit the regulatory power of the NRC over licensing and to transfer authority to the State Department which the industry believed would exercise more lenient licensing procedures.[74] This strong corporate preference appears peculiar inasmuch as the NRC was such a strong supporter of private industry. But, in contrast to the AEC's routine approval of licenses through 1975, the new NRC had taken its task seriously—at least in the realm of exports—so that its procedures slowed the export licensing process.[75] In 1977 the NRC, after a report acknowledging the inadequacy of agency safeguards against diversion of nuclear material, decided it could no longer go along with International Atomic Energy Agency (IAEA) criteria.[76]

Senator McClure of Ohio, a state dependent on nuclear-related jobs, was a vehement opponent of the non-proliferation bill and expressed particular concern over Section 304 of the NNPA requiring the NRC to "make independent judgments" on the implementation of safeguards in foreign nations for exported materials.[77] McClure cited State Department views that such a policing function would be resisted abroad and that "any such result would completely undermine the international safeguard system and certainly throw existing international commercial procedure into greater turmoil."[78]

The NRC was divided.[79] As the NNPA prescribed, export licenses were to be issued by the NRC only after notification by the State Department that the administration concluded that the proposed export will not be "inimical to common defense and security." If the NRC withholds a license the president, subject to review by Congress, could overrule the decision. The NRC's importance was exemplified in decisions in 1978 and 1980 to refuse fuel shipments to India despite the administration's urging.[80] In debates over the bill one NRC commissioner had favored executive branch rule while another took the opposite stand, replying:

> While it is true that the executive branch can and should influence whether nuclear export goes forward, it must provide the NRC . . . with convincing justification. This extra element of protection is of course, an inconvenience to the laissez-faire exporters, to say nothing of those officials, who regard U.S. nuclear fuels and equipment as modern day equivalents of glass beads and Indian blankets—prime items of international barter . . .
> In giving export licensing authority to an independent regulatory commission in 1974, Congress was saying in effect that it wanted this country's nuclear trade to be handled consistently and not be subject to explicit protective standards rather than the political exigencies of the moment. This still makes sense.[81]

Senator McClure and like-minded legislators failed to shift "last word" authority on license to the State Department but some favored amendments were passed. One amendment reaffirmed the U.S. commitment to a more liberal trade. Nuclear lobbyists were disturbed by a section of the bill proposed by Senators Cranston, Glenn, Javits, Percy, and Ribicoff who urged it be U.S. policy "to cooperate with other nations in protecting the international environment from radioactive, chemical, or thermal contamination from nuclear activities." For example, regulations drafted by the Council on Environmental Quality would require environmental assessments for nuclear exports.

Senator McClure opposed both actions because their restrictive guidelines "would have a devastating effect on nuclear exports, not unlike the impact such statements have had on our domestic nuclear power and other activities."[82] To accelerate licensing, McClure fastened an amendment that enabled the NRC to make a single finding for more than one application and also to use an alternative procedure for licensing, based on a finding of "no material changed circumstance." The State Department opposed congressional initiatives involving the NRC in review procedures, or imposing U.S. standards on other nations because it would "impair our ability to remain a major international nuclear supplier, a role that is closely connected with our ability to achieve our non-proliferation and other foreign policy goals . . ."[83]

Regarding the Glenn-Percy Bill provision to procure research funds for nonnuclear sources for developing countries, the Senate Committee on Energy and Natural Resources was informed by the executive branch that they prefer deletion because the section conveyed an "implicit bias" against nuclear development.[84] Although not deleted, the provision "has not been implemented. The Congress has neither pressed the executive branch to implement Title V nor appropriated any funds for it," the GAO reported.

In Congress Senator McClure stressed the significance of the nuclear industry on jobs at home and for offsetting the balance of payment deficits. The Carter administration was by no means heedless of the economic significance of nuclear exports. An ERDA spokesperson told the Senate Committee on Energy and Natural Resources:

> these nonproliferation bills . . . have a significant impact on our power reactor vendors. This impact could be favorable if the result, as we hope, is to reassure other countries of our reliability as a nuclear supplier. It obviously could be unfavorable if Congress allows those features of the Glenn-Percy bill to remain which would give a basis for concern to other countries that we are unreliable . . . It is obvious that maintaining a position as a nuclear supplier has tangible benefits to the United States from a commercial point of view . . . although in the judgment of the administration and regardless of commercial benefits, nonproliferation considerations must prevail over commercial factors.[85]

The nuclear industry highlighted the question of reliability and the ways in which a complex licensing process involving several branches of government could go awry. Lobbyists warned that new legislation appeared "unfair, arbitrary, and inconsistent" and thus would divert customer countries to non-U.S. suppliers. A General Electric vice president pleaded for "flexibility" on criteria for export licenses and went on to define the proper role of Congress as establishing "goals and criteria" toward which the executive branch should move, with periodic reports to Congress and the establishment of a straightforward licensing procedure.[86]

The White House and State Department were concerned that zealous congressional action might restrict their latitude in foreign policy and thereby unnecessarily antagonize other nations. A restrictive approach might adversely affect delicate negotiations in the International Nuclear Fuel Cycle Evaluation (though it was really little more than a study group). The Carter administration won its fight against a one-house veto regarding presidential waivers of the NNPA. Certainly non-proliferation was not the administration's foremost foreign policy concern; non-proliferation goals conflicted, for example, with the tilt toward Pakistan after the Soviets invaded Afghanistan.

What was the bottom line on non-proliferation? Note that the Glenn-Percy Bill that stood for floor debate in February 1978, was itself a compromise between the Percy and Glenn bill (S. 897) and the administration bill (S. 1432). Glenn and Percy were hardly antinuke radicals, but rather were politicians concerned to restore the United States as a reliable supplier while carrying out "the delicate surgery that is needed to separate these Siamese twins so that . . . we can have benefits without bombs." Nonetheless the Committee on Energy and Natural Resources argued that even the compromise bill established procedures that were "cumbersome," "time-consuming," and so "highly unpredictable" that the bill might lead "to an effective moratorium on new nuclear exports."[87]

Did Carter's non-proliferation policies represent a radical departure? Referring to Carter's 1976 UN statement, two analysts argue that the president's policies moved "away from restrictions on U.S. participation in the world nuclear market, away from penalties and pressures on other suppliers and purchasers, and towards inducements and incentives for countries which supported U.S. market policies." The NNPA in the long run might enhance the export potential of the U.S. nuclear industry "by encouraging it to develop and market 'proliferation-resistant' fuel cycles." Yet this outcome depended on reactions of customer and other supplier nations and how effectively the United States could sell its "dual denial" approach—dissuading others from building indigenous enrichment and reprocessing facilities.[88]

However, a 1981 GAO report concluded that foreign reactions were overwhelmingly negative—with the exception of Canada and Australia—and that the NNPA was the decisive factor. Recipients of U.S. nuclear products were upset by NNPA provisions that unilaterally altered the terms by which the United States engaged in nuclear cooperation, and by the restrictions imposed on what customers were permitted to do with U.S.-supplied products. This posed a quandary to the U.S. industry insofar as the NNPA is only one of the many factors affecting nuclear purchases. In 1978–79 the U.S. industry sold four reactors to foreign customers. "As a practical matter" Yager notes, "since all nations with which the U.S. has had agreements for cooperation met the criteria of the NNPA when the act entered into force, no immediate export embargoes were effectively imposed."[89]

STATISM, NEO-MARXISM AND POLICY CRISES

Congress, not the executive branch, proposed and fought for strict export controls. The NNPA passed 411–0 in the House and 88–3 in the Senate. Certainly the nuclear lobby's preference that central decision makers retain ample leeway vis-à-vis Congress is incongruent with Krasner's portrait of the U.S. political system. Does this case prove that the White House and State Department were easy targets for corporate influence, and that Congress remained aloof, if not immune?

Congress opted neither for non-proliferation nor profitability. It rejected the most domestic element in Carter's "dual denial" policy—the halt of the Clinch River Breeder reactor. Many congressmen believed that this halt would obstruct technological progress and meeting the goal of energy independence. Brenner suggests that congressional debate could more easily be controlled by staunch non-proliferationists than by the nuclear industry because the NNPA was not a salient issue to most members. Congressional actions concerning different issues depend upon the kind of issue in question and its local pertinence. Krasner correctly stressed that the way in which an issue is defined and the arena in which it is decided are critical dimensions of policy formulation. But his characterization of the arenas is misleadingly static.

Another flaw of the statist model is that it portrays decision makers as autonomous shapers of policy in service of a nebulous national interest. Krasner justifiably rejects a bureaucratic approach to politics that implies "government action does presuppose government intention."[90] His case against the "anti-intentionality" of early formulations of structural marxist theory was surely warranted because, as policy shifts under Nixon attest, the intentions and strategies of actors in the Oval Office do make a distinct difference. Eisenhower and Carter were no less pro-business than Nixon or Reagan, but the *intensity* of their adherence to liberal economic ideology sharply distinguishes the approaches these presidents took to non-proliferation.

A strong ideological orientation will make the White House more permeable to the preferences of some societal interests. Perhaps this ideological convergence was coincidental. But it must be rigorously examined in an investigation of the imputed autonomy of decision makers. The Carter administration sought to "sanitize," not ban, nuclear exports and to adhere to the "reliable supplier" creed. It pursued goals that differed from the interests of the nuclear industry, rival suppliers, and potential customers. The State Department sacrificed stringency in non-proliferation in order to mollify vital allies, particularly Western Europe and Japan. Against this background, the administration placed a premium on flexibility. That international pressures worked to the advantage of domestic nuclear industry was a fact that did not escape the attention of private executives. This conciliatory *realpolitik* also was a response to a display of the force of international capitalism. When subjected to these political dynamics the "national interest" became a more pliable commodity than Krasner would lead one to believe.

NEO-MARXISM

Central decision makers, contrary to Krasner's expectations, did not comprise a united front based on pursuit of predetermined ends. Conflicts occurred between the White House and State Department, and between these sites and a divided NRC. When the formulating and implementing of policy departs markedly from intentions of central policymakers, Krasner attributes the deviation to external opponents, who certainly were multitudinous. But

an explanation of outcomes requires conceptual tools that enable us to identify the structural constraints under which policies are formulated and of
how those constraints are expressed in competing sites within the state.

Michael Brenner divides the main administration actors into categories
that dovetail with Joseph's "policy currents." The "mainstream" current held
that non-proliferation took precedence over commerce but were willing to
make pragmatic adjustments. A "purist" current totally opposed plutonium
recycling and advocated exacting controls. Although purists were a small
group, they soon allied with "like-minded staffers on key congressional committees and in the NRC."[91] At the other end of the spectrum was the
nuclear establishment (Right current) whose influence was concentrated within
the ERDA. Bureaucratic infighting led to transmission of confused signals
by the administration to Congress and so exacerbated the effects of the increasing "elasticity" in the relative autonomy of the agencies and institutions
of the state. A struggle occurred in the "strategic field" of the state wherein
the contenders maneuvered so as to shift ultimate authority over policy to
their most favorable sites. That the participative scope of the issue increased,
too, is reflected in an NRC commisioner's worried remark that "nothing is
going to shut this trade-off faster than for the public to decide it really is a
trade in bombs."[92] Even Brenner's labyrinthine account does not suffice to
trace the struggle among different factions within the administration and over
the component parts of the state. To judge by subsequent events, the Right
current was the loser and Congress clearly a winner.

The Carter administration did not support the nuclear industry nor did it
champion a "national interest," as the statist model assumes. The NNPA
neither appeased the nuclear industry nor lived up to Carter's crusading
expectations. The administration housed in its branches many oppositional
forces; eventually the pressures these forces brought to bear were compounded
by foreign events (such as the Soviet invasion of Afghanistan and the "discovery" of Soviet Brigades in Cuba). These events pushed Carter from a
"purist" position toward the Right current. But Congress did not follow.

The Reagan administration immediately set out to "streamline" the licensing process, lift the embargo on domestic reprocessing, ease the rules on
foreign reprocessing of U.S.-origin uranium, exploit loopholes in the NNPA
on "dual use technologies," minimize congressional review of executive
expeditiousness, cheer on the private sector, and even suggested that spent
fuel be reprocessed for military purposes. Despite Reagan's effort to "remove
impediments" to nuclear trade, the beneficiaries were highly dissatisfied with
the extent of the aid offered. "I think it is a religion of this administration,"
complained the president of Power Systems, Inc. (Westinghouse), "that there
will be no subsidies, that we've got a free market economy—which would
be fine if markets were truly free."[93] Facing a skeptical and antagonistic

Congress, the administration abandoned efforts to alter or repeal the NNPA.[94]

Domestic dissatisfaction with the cumulative adverse aspects of nuclear energy grew. The 1982 Nuclear Waste Management Act directed the Department of Energy to build permanent *and* safe (which may be impossible) storage sites for nuclear waste. (By 1994 the Energy Department was confessing that twenty-six metric tons of plutonium had been stored unsafely since the production of fissile weapons materials halted in the late 1980s— and foresaw 20 years elapsing before truly effective measures are agreed upon and implemented.)[95] Observing Reagan's decisions to peddle nuclear fuel to non-treaty signators Argentina, South Africa, and India, Senator Percy was "concerned that we as a nation—and in particular, we in Congress—may be losing our grip on non-proliferation." In House hearings on loophole-closing amendments, an exasperated member noted that one "cannot escape the conclusion that the administration sees the NNPA not as a means of halting the spread of nuclear weapons but as a hurdle to overcome in order to conduct nuclear commerce overseas."[96]

The specter of a "nuclear Sarajevo" spurred passage in the House of two amendments designed to stanch this cowboy capitalist trend. The Reagan administration proved unable to recreate the old "policy concordance." Fragmentation had cut the other way, adversely affecting all aspects of civilian nuclear power policy. From 1979–82 utilities registered no new orders for nuclear plants while thirty-three nuclear units were cancelled; over 1982–88 thirteen more units were cancelled and four more deferred indefinitely.[97] U.S. nuclear development, in the absence of centralized planning, "tended to reflect the commercial interest of individual private enterprise to a greater extent than in other countries" yet nuclear power is "particularly vulnerable in countries where authority is fragmented, as in countries with federal structures and/or judicial systems with broad mandates."[98]

The concerns of a wider public audience were reflected by congressmen who, during the amendment hearings, cited troubling matters such as the Israeli air strike on the Osiraq reactor in Iraq, reports that Libya tried to buy a bomb from Pakistan, "what-if" speculations over possession of a bomb by Argentina during the Falklands war (and, of course, the prevention of Iraq from acquiring a nuclear device was prominent among the justifications for U.S. intervention in the Gulf in 1991). In the aftermath of the break up of the Soviet Union non-proliferation became an acute issue again—what with more than forty countries believed capable of making bombs.[99] Witness the military threats made by the United States against North Korea in 1994.

Accidents at Three Mile Island and Chernobyl, near-meltdowns at Browns Ferry and Dresden, and revelations of numerous close calls offer little reason to cheer the pronuclear cause.[100] In 1990 the U.S. energy secretary admitted that nuclear weapons complexes had contaminated many workers with excessive radiation.[101] The risk of ignoring such developments for the sake of adding to profits, even if billions of dollars, no longer seemed worthwhile. Discretion became the better part of mercantilist valor. As structural marxists aver, the "economic" did not translate proportionately into power in the "political realm"—and even less so in times of policy crisis.

Obviously, this realization did not set in everywhere. In France a new right-wing government in March 1993 fired up the Superphoenix, the world's "fastest" breeder reactor. "We want to try to transform long-life radioactive materials into short-life ones . . . and lower their radioactivity," claimed an environment ministry adviser. Opponents retort that safety problems persist since the plant was shut in 1986 after six months of continuous technical mishaps. Nuclear energy is "a religion of the state," lamented Jean-Luc Thierry of Greenpeace. "In France there is no public debate because everything is rigged . . . the opposition was crushed in the 1970s."[102] (A German high-speed breeder reactor was built near Kalkar but was not brought into operation and the Japanese have been reticent about their breeder reactor program.) The French government in 1995 proceeded to demonstrate an impressive degree of impervious idiocy in conducting a series of nuclear tests in the Pacific.

CONCLUSION

One may regard this new institutional equilibrium as a positive democratic gain—though not necessarily a lasting one. The decision to promote nuclear power was not immanent in the "motion of capital" nor "inscribed" in the apparatuses of the state. Like Krasner, who examines relations between the state and specific firms, this chapter did not address *classes as such* because neither the survival of the world capitalist system nor of any single state is contingent on the prosperity of the nuclear industry. We have assessed the explanatory capacities of the statist model and of structural marxist theory in understanding discordant developments in what was for decades a "happy convergence" of interest between the state apparatus and domestic nuclear industry.

Our analysis of the policy crisis disclosed defects in the statist model which was unable to account for the anomalous behavior of central decision makers and Congress in this arena. The degree of insulation of central decision makers from societal interests is more *variable* than Krasner indicates, and is mediated by shared ideological affinities that reach across public-private boundaries. Congress can thrust (or be thrust) forward as initiator and guardian of the "national interest" as a consequence of this extended "elasticity."

Unlike cabinet systems, the U.S. Congress (and, to a lesser extent, the courts) is the crucial site because it determines the allocation of power and missions among all the other sites in the system. Structural marxism predicts concentration of lobbying effort in Congress because it is (1) most permeable to efforts by nonelites and counter-elites; (2) the most equitable—or least inequitable—site where groups with highly varying resources contend; and (3) a repository of power over the institutional structure of the "policy concordance." In short, Congress does engage in adversarial struggles with the executive branch over the definition of the "national interest." Here is where the statist model is found particularly wanting and where structural marxism provides the better analytical basis for explaining the dynamics of a policy crisis.

The U.S. state was unwilling to promote nuclear exports *at any price* or, on the other hand, to unilaterally alter the non-proliferation regime. Hence it is "vital to reject any attempt to establish the functionality of the state on behalf of capital on *a priori* essentialist grounds."[103] In a policy crisis the state is not just an arbiter of the conflicting interests of factions of the bourgeoisie but rather a strategic field in which the increasing elasticity of the component institutions generates opportunities for influence by nonelites and counter-elites who join the struggle to shift policy authority to a favorable site.

This is not the stuff of bureaucratic politics models; this is a wider "war of position" in which the agencies and branches of the state become the focal points and vehicles for access to policy influence by new entrants (or by old contestants making up for earlier imbalances in the distribution of political resources), mediated by a level of popular mobilization, the range of permissible and viable options will expand while the relative weight of the options changes. Since the "policy concordance" is by definition an elitist equilibrium, these tendencies exercise a democratizing effect in specific policy areas. This is a *trend* that is neither irresistible nor irrevocable. At minimum, these trends enhance the indeterminacy of policy outcomes. This argument differs from Campbell in that it demonstrates that we can conduct analyses that are sensitive to both institutional and ideological variations *within* the neo-marxist tradition, rather than apply marxism at one moment and an institutionalist model at another moment, in syncretic style.[104]

The impact of a policy crisis is intensified by shifts of actors and agencies across "policy currents." A sympathetic critic of marxism cogently cites the need for "a theory of the *interiorté* or the limited freedom of the subject, which goes together with the autonomy of the cultural and political factors" because actors have a built-in "internal distance" that enables "a limited but real range of choices about the roles they are going to play, not to speak of the ways in which they are going to play them."[105]

Motivated by fresh evaluations, new evidence, coalitional possibilities or even moral misgivings actors may redefine their institutional missions and, at very least, switch allegiances among policy currents. We do not undertake construction of a theory of "internal distance" here, but we advance the thesis that "the internal distance" of actors will increase with the increasing elasticity in the component institutions of the state during a policy crisis.[106] The behavior of NRC members and of Congress provides suggestive evidence for this elasticity effect.

Structural marxism is modestly elaborated here to account for a significant range of short-run, relatively low stakes policy outcomes. We argue that structural marxism yields useful insights into the dynamics of policy formulation in distributive, regulatory and "power politics" areas as well as the redistributive one.[107] This applicability, however, is likely to correspond to the potential the issue has for conversion into a redistributive one. In the case of nuclear exports, opponents of "nuclear laissez faire" worry not only whether the regime-destabilizing transfers may occur but also about the repressive shape of a "nuclear society" to come.[108]

The usefulness of a middle-range operationalization of "policy crisis" and "elasticity" can only be tested in further studies. Candidates include trade legislation, regulatory battles over pollution or occupational safety and health standards, and industrial policy. In comparative analysis we should expect political systems to display different "elasticities" during a policy crisis. The French state is likely to be less elastic than the West German or U.S. states, and individual agencies in one state will exhibit significant variance in their elasticity as compared with those of other states. One can anticipate different policy outcomes.

This chapter illuminated a pattern of political events and institutional conditions that enhance the *indeterminacy* of outcomes in formerly closed policy processes termed "policy concordances," and thereby provide opportunities that nonelites and counter-elites can exploit in order to press their own preferences effectively. But a success in one policy area (e.g., stringent safeguards on nuclear exports) does not have to spill over into other areas of public concern (e.g., Reagan's economic policy agenda). An increase in the elasticity of the autonomy of the component institutions of the state does not necessarily cumulate into increased autonomy of *the state* from societal interests.

Given this analysis, the notion that an entity called "the state" can exist apart from the relationship of social forces constituting (and penetrating) its many institutional components is a dubious one. Structural marxism's abstract view of the state as "a condensation of a relationship of forces among classes and fractions of classes" but one not "reducible to the relationship of [these] forces" seems for once to be a vivid and appropriate view. Finally, we note just as there are limits to the autonomy of the state, so too are there limits to the applicability of structural marxism. While this chapter encourages marxist policy studies, need we say that the tantalizing dream of constructing a "universal solvent" of a theory is the height of philosophical innocence?

Notes

1. Stephen D. Krasner, *Defending the National Interest: Raw Materials Investment and U.S. Foreign Policy* (Princeton: Princeton University Press, 1978), p. 26.
2. Ibid, p. 311. Krasner certainly has a point. See, for example, the account of U.S. aims regarding Allende's Chile in Seymour Hersh, *The Price of Power: Kissinger in the Nixon White House* (New York: Summit Books, 1983), pp. 258–294.
3. Ibid., p. 10.
4. Ibid., p. 18.
5. See Charles H. Lipson, "Corporate Preferences and Public Policies: Foreign Aid Sanctions and Investment Protection" *World Politics* 28 (1976).
6. Krasner, *Defending the National Interest*, p. 34.
7. See Antonio Gramsci, *The Modern Prince* (New York: International Publishers, 1971); Herbert Marcuse, *One Dimensional Man* (Boston: Beacon Press, 1968); Jurgen Habermas, *Legitimation Crisis* (Boston: Beacon Press, 1973) and Martin Jay, *The Dialectical Imagination* (Boston: Little, Brown, 1973).
8. Ibid., p. 133.
9. Mans Lonroth and William Walker, *Nuclear Power Struggle: Industrial Competition and Proliferation Control* (London: George Allen & Unwin, 1983), p. 176.
10. Robert Alford, "Paradigms of Relations Between State and Society"; in Leon Lindberg, *Stress and Contradiction in Modern Capitalism* (Lexington: DC Heath, 1975); Patrick McGowan and Stephen G. Walker, "Radical and Conventional Models of Foreign Economic Policy," *World Politics* 33 (1981).
11. Alan Wolfe, "New Directions in the Marxist Theory of the State" *Politics and Society* 4 (1974), p. 137; Claus Offe, "The Theory of the Capitalist State and the Problem of Policy Formation"; Lindberg, *Stress and Contradiction*, 1975; and Adam Przeworski, "Proletariat Into a Class: The Process of Class Formation from Karl Kautsky" *"The Class Struggle* to Recent Controversies" *Politics and Society* 4 (1977).
12. Nicos Poulantzas, *Political Power and Social Classes* (London: New Left Books, 1969); Louis Althusser and Etienne Balibar, *Reading Capital* (London: New Left Books, 1970).
13. Louis Hartz, *The Liberal Tradition in America* (New York: Harcourt, Brace, 1955); Krasner, *Defending the National Interest*, p. 61.
14. Krasner, ibid., p. 63.
15. Ibid., p. 70.
16. Ibid., p. 10.
17. Ibid., p. 18.
18. Ibid., p. 19.
19. Franz Schurmann, *The Logic of World Power* (New York: Random House, 1974); Theda Skocpol, "Legacies of New Deal Liberalism" *Dissent* 30 (1983). See my comments on Roosevelt's wartime role in Chapter 8.
20. Theodore Lowi, "American Business, Public Policy, Case Studies and Political Theory," *World Politics* 16 (1964).
21. Robert Tucker, *The Marx-Engels Reader* (New York: Norton, 1978), p. 475.
22. Ralph Miliband, *Marxism and Politics* (Oxford: Oxford University Press, 1977), p. 68.
23. Ibid., p. 73.

24. Krasner, *Defending the National Interest*, pp. 333, 345.
25. See John G. Ruggie's review of Krasner in *American Political Science Review* 74. There he notes that Lockean liberal ideology and an attendant "irrational anticommunism" are highly implicated in the expansion of U.S. capitalism in the postwar era.
26. Bob Jessop *The Capitalist State* (New York: New York University Press, 1982), pp. 220, 223.
27. Paul Joseph, *Cracks in the Empire* (Boston: South End Press, 1981).
28. Fred Block, "Beyond Relative Autonomy: State Managers as Historical Subjects," in Ralph Miliband and John Saville, eds. *Socialist Register* (London: Merlin Press, 1980), p. 229.
29. Block, "Cooperation and Conflict in the Capitalist World Economy" *Marxist Perspectives* 2 (1979), p. 84.
30. Joseph, *Cracks in the Empire*, p. 72.
31. Ibid., pp. 73, 272.
32. Joseph also notes that "specific state agencies do not 'belong' to one current or another. During the Vietnam war policy disagreements occurred both within and between agencies."
33. Poulantzas, *Political Power and Social Classes*, p. 138.
34. David Abraham, *The Collapse of the Weimar Republic* (Princeton: Princeton University Press, 1981), p. 45.
35. John L. Campbell likewise observed "that activists tended to channel their dissent through whatever institutional opportunities they felt would lead to success." These accessible institutions include, above all, Congress. *Collapse of an Industry: Nuclear Power and the Contradictions of US Policy* (Ithaca: Cornell University Press, 1988), p. 83.
36. Ibid., p. 51. Detailed case studies of this process are presented in Brian Balogh, *Chain Reaction: Expert Debate and Public Participation in American Commercial Nuclear Power, 1945–75* (Cambridge: Cambridge University Press, 1991), p. 77. See especially his discussion of the Bodega Bay reactor.
37. Campbell cites Habermas's *Legitimation Crisis* as well. Here I employ "policy crisis" as a subset of what Habermas calls a 'rationality crisis' which is a term intended to set apart short-term, limited conflicts from system-threatening ones. A rationality crisis occurs when a state appears unable to manage the economy. Only if prolonged and unalleviated can this fester into a legitimation crisis. Campbell applies the latter term to all degrees of crises.
38. Mary Ames, *Outcome Uncertain* (Washington: Communications Press, 1978), p. 13.
39. Quoted in William Epstein, *The Last Chance* (New York: Free Press, 1976), p. 5.
40. Ibid., p. 8. "By 1950, MacMahon, who had built a career championing the peaceful uses of atomic energy, spearheaded the quest for the hydrogen bomb." in Balogh, *Chain Reaction*, pp. 149, 244.
41. Lonroth and Walker, *The Viability of Civilian Nuclear Industry* (New York: International Consultative Group on Nuclear Energy, 1979) pp. 1–3; J. Yager, *International Cooperation*, p. 51; and Michael Brenner, *Nuclear Power and Nonproliferation* (Cambridge: Cambridge University Press, 1981), pp. 24–30.
42. Dorothy Nelkin and Michael Pollak, *The Atom Besieged* (Cambridge, MA: MIT Press, 1981), p. 188.
43. Lonroth and Walker, *The Viability of the Civilian Nuclear Industry*, p. 10.
44. Peter Pringle and J. Spigelman, *The Nuclear Barons* (New York: Avon Books, 1981), pp. 147–164; Balogh, *Chain Reaction*, pp. 88–90. Rickover in the 1950s

did not believe that nuclear power would become commercially viable.

45. Atomic Energy Act, 1954, Section 3(e).
46. Harvey Wasserman and Normon Solomon, *Killing Our Own: The American Experience with Nuclear Radiation* (New York: Delta Books, 1984), pp. 47–48.
47. Balogh, *Chain Reaction*, p. 93.
48. Daniel Ford, *The Cult of the Atom* (New York: Simon & Schuster, 1982) p. 52.
49. William H. Lambright, *Governing Science and Technology* (Oxford: Oxford University Press, 1976), pp. 78–79.
50. Irving Bupp and J-C Derian, *Light Water* (New York: Basic Books, 1978).
51. Pringle and Spigelman, *Nuclear Barons* pp. 203–204; Yager, p. 155.
52. Lambright, *Governing Science and Technology*, p. 77.
53. T. G. Moore, *Uranium Enrichment and Public Policy* (Washington: American Enterprise Institute, 1978), p. 33.
54. Bupp and Derian, *Light Water*; Lonroth and Walker, *Nuclear Power Struggles*, p. 12.
55. On the French-Israeli connection see Seymour Hersh, *The Samson Option: Israel's Nuclear Arsenal and American Foreign Policy* (New York: Random House, 1991).
56. J. Yager, *International Cooperation in Nuclear Energy* (Washington: Brookings Institution, 1981), p. 30.
57. On problems that the contradictory goals of promotion-versus-regulation generated within the NRC, see Campbell, *Collapse of an Industry*, pp. 79–81.
58. Lellouche, "Breaking the Rules . . . ," p. 43.
59. William Potter, *Nuclear Power and Non-Proliferation: An Interdisciplinary Perspective* (Cambridge: Oelgesschlager, Gunn & Hain, 1982).
60. Alford, "Paradigms of Relations," p. 158.
61. Lindberg, *The Energy Syndrome* (Lexington: DC Heath, 1977), p. 332.
62. Brenner, *Nuclear Power and Nonproliferation*, p. 34.
63. On the Nixon administration see Chapter 4 of Alba Alexander, "Playing Fair: Social Citizenship and Tax Reform, 1942–1986," Ph.D. dissertation, University of Chicago, 1994.
64. Ibid., p. 64.
65. Moore, *Uranium Enrichment and Public Policy*, p. 36.
66. Lonroth and Walker, *The Viability of Civilian Nuclear Industry*, p. 42.
67. Pringle and Spigelman, *Nuclear Barons*, pp. 376–377.
68. John Dunne, *Controlling the Bomb* (New Haven: Yale University Press, 1982), pp. 104–105.
69. GAO, *The Nuclear Nonproliferation Act of 1978 Should be Selectively Modified* (Washington: GPO, 1981), p. 125.
70. OTA, *Nuclear Proliferation and Safeguards* (New York: Praeger, 1977), pp. 255–256.
71. ERDA, 1976, pp. 4–15.
72. Pierre Lellouche, "Breaking the Rules Without Quite Stopping the Bomb," in George Questor, ed. *Nuclear Proliferation* (Madison: University of Wisconsin, 1978) pp. 41, 46.
73. G. Hildenbrand, "A German Reaction to U.S. Nonproliferation Policy," *International Security* 3 (1978), p. 56.
74. Smith, "Nuclear Industry Seeks to Weaken . . . ," p. 5.
75. Brenner, *Nuclear Power and Nonproliferation*, pp. 80–88.
76. Smith, "NRC Safety Experts Split on Safeguards" *Washington Post*, 17 January 1978, p. 12.

77. U.S. Congress, *Legislative History of the Nuclear Nonproliferation Act of 1978*, 1979; p. 788.
78. Ibid., p. 789.
79. There were some distinctly domestic reasons for the intra-NRC expressions of nervousness about nuclear energy. By 1979, the NRC had recorded nearly 2,300 operational errors in U.S. nuclear plants. In Wasserman and Solomon, *Killing Our Own*, p. 229. Also, see Peter Stoller, *Decline and Fall: The Ailing Nuclear Power Industry* (New York: Dodd, Mead & Co., 1985), pp. 2–4.
80. Brenner, *Nuclear Power and Nonproliferation* pp. 199–204.
81. Victor Gilinsky, "The NRC's Valid Role in Nuclear Exports," *Washington Post* 26 January 1978, p. 23.
82. U.S. Congress, *Legislative History*, p. 784.
83. U.S. Congress, *Nuclear Exports: International Safety and Environmental Issues*, 1980, p. 30.
84. U.S. Congress, *Legislative History*, p. 555.
85. Ibid.
86. Ibid., pp. 581–582.
87. Ibid., p. 496.
88. G. Duffy and Gordon Adams, *Power Politics: The Nuclear Industry and Nuclear Exports* (New York: Council on Economic Priorities, 1978), pp. 67–68.
89. Yager, *International Cooperation in Nuclear Energy*, p. 177.
90. Graham Allison, *Essence of Decision* (Boston: Little, Brown, 1971), p. 175.
91. Brenner, *Nuclear Power and Proliferation*, p. 127.
92. Victor Gilinsky quoted in J.P. Smith, "Nuclear Industry Seeks to Weaken Nonproliferation Bill," *Washington Post* 3 February 1978, p. 5.
93. *Nuclear Industry Monthly*, Atomic Industry Forum 8 (1981), p. 10.
94. J. M. Hamilton and Leonard S. Spector, "Congress Fights Back" *Transaction/Society* 20 (1983).
95. "Tons of Plutonium Stored Unsafely, U.S. Concedes," *Chicago Tribune*, 7 December 1994.
96. U.S. Congress, *Legislation to Amend the Nuclear Nonproliferation Act of 1978*, 1983, p. 9.
97. David P. McCaffrey, *The Politics of Nuclear Power: A History of the Shoreham Nuclear Power Plant* (Dordrecht: Kluwer Academic Publishers, 1991), p. 2.
98. Lonroth and Walker, *Nuclear Struggles*, p. 42; and Nelkin and Pollak, *The Atom Besieged*.
99. Mitchell Reiss, *Without the Bomb: The Politics of Nonproliferation* (New York: Columbia University Press, 1988). Also, see the analysis of diplomatic costs and controls on proliferation in Jordan Seng, "Prospects for Stable Nuclear Proliferation in the Developing World" (University of Chicago, mimeo May 1994).
100. See the discussion of safety in Charles Perrow, *Normal Accidents: Living with High Risk Technologies* (New York: Basic Books, 1984), Chapter 2; and Scott Sagan, "Organizations, Accidents and Nuclear Weapons" mimeo, presented at the University of Chicago PIPES (April 1992).
101. Michael D'Antonio, *Atomic Harvest: Hanford and the Lethal Toll of America's Nuclear Arsenal* (New York: Crown, 1993), p. 271.
102. Sharon Waxman, "France Fires up Nuclear Breeder," *Chicago Tribune* 8 December 1994.
103. Jessop, *The Capitalist State*, p. 235.

104. Campbell, *Collapse of an Industry*, pp. 192–193. Campbell is in accord with our analysis when he notes that it "is misleading to talk about the institutional autonomy of 'the state' at all. Sensitivity to these sort of institutional variations forces us to realize that states are composed of many different apparatuses and that each one's institutional autonomy may vary dramatically from each other, in different policy areas and over time." n. 8, p. 194.
105. Victor Perez-Diaz, *State, Bureaucracy and Civil Society* (Atlantic Highlands, NJ: Humanities Press, 1978), p. 91.
106. Theories of "internal distance" have long been a concern of the Frankfurt School.
107. See Lowi, "American Business, Public Policy . . ."; and McGowan and Walker, "Radical and Conventional Theories."
108. Lindberg, *The Energy Syndrome*; and Nelkin and Pollak, *The Atom Besieged*.

4

Peripheral Postindustrialism: Ideology, High Technology, and Development

Although their luster has dimmed lately the new industrializing countries (NICs) achieved impressive growth rates, hefty hikes in manufactured exports, diversifications of industrial structures, and a multiplication of trade outlets.[1] The developing countries' share of global value-added edged up 3 percent between 1965 and 1980, but ten NICs recorded almost 75 percent of the gain. Seven NICs—Hong Kong, Taiwan, Singapore, South Korea, Argentina, Mexico, and Brazil—were sources of over 60 percent of the South's manufactured exports.[2] The product-cycle virtuosity and the industrial "deepening" of the NICs were evident not only in the steel, textile, shipbuilding and other "mature" industries but also in high-technology sectors such as electronics in which the Asian "gang of four" (Hong Kong, Taiwan, South Korea, and Singapore) boosted their share of the South's exports in the 1980s.

Although beset by Northern protectionist tendencies, foreign debt, authoritarian regimes or precarious transitions from them, the NICs demonstrated that "late-comers" need not be condemned by an "iron law" to perform as hewers of wood and drawers of water, or as assemblers of final-stage products in peripheral enclaves. Contrary to bleak "dependentista" prognoses, a few Third World nations moved briskly from import-substitution and consumer goods phases to the production of intermediate producer goods and of consumer durables. Brazil, Mexico, and India—endowed with requisite natural, human, and organizational resources—developed capital goods industries, and are shifting (as were smaller NICs) into "more skill- and technology-intensive areas of production." However, over the decade of the 1980s Latin America's gross domestic product (GDP) growth plummeted from 6.1 percent to 1.6 percent even as East Asia sustained a 7.9 percent, South Asia (mainly India) was 5.1 percent and mainland China shot up to nearly 10 percent.[3]

Surveying outward-oriented development policies, Ruggie contends that liberal economists and *dependistas* alike overstated "the determining impact of the international division of labor on national welfare." Liberals "ignore the critical importance of, and dependistas to discount the generative potential in, domestic political structures."[4] Worse are neo-marxists who ignore "the opportunities in developing countries created by new institutional arrangements for indigenous entrepreneurs, states, and the process of local accumulation."[5]

These charges appear extremely odd in light of the neo-marxists' virtual obsession with the role of the state. They also are puzzling if one bothers to scan the fierce critiques exchanged among the dependistas and between them and neo-marxists.[6] Fernando Cardoso long ago (before his political career began) spurned "overly static, mechanistic views of the relationship between the polity and the economy," urging scholars to focus upon the political forces and political possibilities unfolding within dependent developers in terms of a "double determination"—a task requiring the "formulation of concepts linked to the effort to explain how internal and external processes of domination relate to one another."[7] Cardoso and Enzo Faletto cite the dynamic developmental role, class composition, institutional structure, and consequent internal and external sensitivity of states that certainly have gained wider "margins of maneuver" within a changing international division of labor.

Dismissive appraisals of dependency literature too often and too conveniently confined themselves to ritualistic scorn for the stagnationist theses of Paul Baran and of Andre Gunder Frank.[8] Nonetheless, critics of dependency and world-systems analyses have made welcome efforts "to contextualize the economism of the debate in larger institutional terms and frameworks."[9] Attention was usefully directed upon local factors and social forces promoting or hindering adjustment to changing patterns of global production and trade.

The prescriptive implication is that peripheral polities, instead of prattling about imperialism, repressed alternatives and quixotic aspirations for autarchy, ought to put their own houses in order so as to maximize the substantial benefits that the capitalist world-economy offers to the adept. So research agendas now strive to explain the differential impact of exogenous events upon local producer groups, economic sectors, institutional structures, policy networks, and state strategies—and to assess their implications for coalition formation and for policy choices.

However, political and social elites try to guide the manner and to limit the extent to which any changes required to upgrade the economy occur so that policy measures designed to aid accumulation will not upset the internal distribution of power. Specifying conditions under which these vital trade-offs occur between economic adjustment and power-retention, and their consequences, has been the special province of the bureaucratic-authoritarian literature.[10]

An implicit (or insufficiently explicit) premise of studies of the political dynamics of adjustment is that global economic changes rarely are presented to policymakers as an unambiguous "stimulus" demanding an invariant "response." Rather, these impinging forces are, in effect, appropriated through the interpretive (ideological) capacities of domestic coalitions and actors to reinforce their dominance or else to weaken or displace the dominance of rivals. Global shifts *signal* the need for internal adjustment, but these signals, and the very real pressures accompanying them, are converted by ideological mediation into programmatic *messages* to the citizenry as to the form the policy response should take. Cardoso and Faletto adumbrate this thesis in their depiction of the state not only as a vigorous agent (in the Gerschenkronian sense) but also as a crucial field of contest for groups and classes with competing "projects" whose success will be determined by "how international conditions are used in the internal power game, rather than by the particular conditions themselves."[11]

In this chapter I elaborate conceptual means by which the role of ideological activity can be incorporated into explanations of choice in the politics of adjustment. Another concern is the consequences of these ideological conflicts (in which developmental projects are cast in the most persuasive terms to gain the consent of groups crucial to the outcome of policy debate) for the limits of state "autonomy." Finally, I argue that the Irish case exemplifies a syndrome of wider significance, "peripheral postindustrialism."

Peripheral postindustrialization connotes: (1) the policy-induced diffusion of "postindustrial industries" within peripheral nations; (2) a truncated form of development (minus linkages and a local technology-generating capacity), where developing states latch onto the more labor-intensive paths of industry with a "post-industrial" vocation (electronics, chemicals, pharmaceuticals, etc.); and (3) an *ideological* strategy for extending hegemonic developmental schemes against challenges presented by global economic trends and by local counter-elites.[12]

The Irish Republic is an intriguing case because it is an excolonial nation with durable democratic institutions which embarked upon export-led industrialization in the late 1950s. In 1975 the Republic selected electronics as the basis for a new local structure of "complex-factor cost industries" (which I call "postindustrial") that ideally would maximize the competitive advantage of skilled labor against lower-wage export platforms vying for markets and foreign investment.[13] The Irish experience, like other European "intermediaries" should "shed light on the predicaments facing both the large advanced industrial states and the less-developed countries."[14]

STATE-SOCIETY RELATIONS AND POLICY CHOICE

Dependistas and nondependistas agree that the state is a pivotal actor with interests and resources of its own, but they differ in their depictions of state-society relations.[15] Nondependistas favor a "statist approach" which asserts that strong states like South Korea, Taiwan, Mexico, and Brazil can shape policy performance and "the behavior of societal groups so as to serve state-defined ends."[16] The stronger a state is, the more autonomous it is and the more likely are the preferences of societal groups to be overruled when they conflict with the course plotted by policymakers. Such states may appear to act as autonomously as Frankenstein's creature, but studies usually yield ambiguous findings.

In their statist analysis of South Korea, Stephen Haggard and Chung-In Moon note that the "state relied heavily on domestic entrepreneurs to perform the miracles" and that the business-state alliance proscribed through going liberalization politically and economically.[17] Raymond Duvall and John Freeman find that "state entrepreneurship" is triggered when the private sector is unable or unwilling to undertake developmental tasks or else may "generate some substantially undesirable patterns of development." In the view of some dependistas, the state is intent on creating or "reinventing" a bourgeoisie that gradually will acquire control over the state itself.[18]

I refer to states as "catalytic" if they rely on market mechanisms and incentives to guide economic activity; as "complementary" when engaged in substantial commercial activity and planning in tandem with private capital (indeed abetting the latter); and as "entrepreneurial" only if the state undertakes directive planning, public-private coordination, and commercial activity in a manner superordinate to the private sector. A genuinely "entrepreneurial state" would be a risk-taker in a dual sense, with respect to international market challenges, and with regard to challenges from internal economic elites.

Dependistas tend to explain the evident "bias of statism" (toward private capital) in terms of structural marxist models.[19] The reproduction of capitalist relations requires relatively autonomous states whose managers attend to the ofttimes divergent tasks of promoting conditions enhancing *accumulation, legitimation,* and *security.* The weight policymakers allocate to each function depends on the balance of class forces and the intensity of their conflict (which penetrates all branches and institutions of the state in different degrees and ways) as well as on state "strength" (measured by the resources and instruments at its disposal). An important implication is that state managers may act not only against the short-term interests of certain capitalists but also, under certain sets of conditions of "conjuncture," adopt programs that infringe on and even endanger capitalist dominance.

The state is a curious entity (a "material condensation" of class conflicts but "is not reducible to them") that is capable of playing off class-based organizations, class fractions, and societal groups in order to realize goals designated according to the policymakers' calculus. But when situational factors seem to augment their autonomy, state managers cannot do just as they please because at very least tacit alliances are needed to assure civil compliance with policy. (Analysts must tend to the class origins, positional interests, and ideological stances of policymakers or "technobureaucrats"). Obviously the state's resource base constricts its range of responses to market changes. However, the level of resources policymakers can summon is contingent on the kind of cooperation they are able to elicit. The *quality* of cooperation—from consent to coercion—is itself a resource. In other words, politics really matters.

Let us posit that *accumulation* goals are realizable by any one of several strategies that will pose different consequences for the distribution of the benefits of development and the burden of adjustment. The form of the policy response will be guided according to the implicit *legitimation* scheme of state managers (who may be impelled by social resistance to reappraise whose oxen they can least afford to gore). Pragmatism is at its zenith when state managers, motivated by economic exigencies, support policy packages, based on new coalitional formations, which challenge the interests of dominant groups. ("Pragmatism" is a term more evocative of the crucial blending of political entrepreneurship with brokerage that portends policy change; capitalist states, with certain vile exceptions, are never purely autonomous.)[20] What remains to do here is to identify conditions that precipitate "pragmatic" state action.

Among these conditions are foreign debt crises, the exhaustion of industrialization phase (e.g., horizontal import-substitution), mismatches between internal production structure and international markets, and other forms of severe pressure to adjust in costly essays. International influences will be investigated here, as Cardoso and Faletto urge, as an endogenous variable, whose local expression enables us to understand and perhaps predict the content of responses by nations on the weak side of asymmetries.

One useful means for reinvigorating the dialogue between dependistas and nondependistas is for the latter to apply the "sensitivity-vulnerability" distinction in *intrastate* relations (between and among components of the state apparatus which intersect with societal groups) as well as to interstate affairs, and proceed to inquire how changes in "sensitivities" affect national policy formulation, economic performance, and the distribution of power and wealth. But even this enterprise is likely to neglect crucial determinants that do not readily lend themselves to easy transcription into tables and graphs. The most resistant is ideology.

INTERESTS, IDEOLOGY AND POLICY STRUGGLES

John Odell's study of U.S. international monetary policy argues that a cognitive perspective, which claims that reigning ideas exert an "independent
effect on policy content, ought to be considered in a multiple explanatory
framework, including four other perspectives: security, market, domestic structure, and bureaucratic politics." He traces the ways in which their relative
importance changes. A cognitive perspective is least significant for explaining policy in states under extreme market or "situational" pressures. It is
most useful when studying states twice-blessed with structural power and
domestic tranquillity that allow a "breathing space" where ideas play a major
role in decisions. The scope of choice is "conditioned not only by global
impacts and domestic forces but by the pool of policy ideas" that are available and politically permissible. I say *conditioned* rather than *constrained* because critical conjunctures can draw authoritative attention to ideas that enlarge
the pool of choices.

Given the esoteric nature of monetary issues, Odell restricts his analysis of
cognitive factors to the "circulation of policy ideas in Washington." His
approach is less useful when dealing with issues where a wider public recognizes the stakes they have in policy outcomes. Helpful clues for investigating
these explanatory foci are found in the work of Antonio Gramsci, whose
writings on hegemony have gained currency among non-marxian students of
political economy.[21]

Hegemony occurs in a "socio-organizational phase in which ideologies,
which were germinated earlier, become 'Party' and enter into struggle" until
one (or a combination) of them

> tend to predominate, to impose itself throughout the whole social sphere,
> causing, in addition to singleness of economic and political purpose, an
> intellectual and moral unity as well, placing all questions around which
> the struggle rages not on a corporative, but a 'universal' plane and creating
> in this way the hegemony of a fundamental social group.... the ruling
> group is coordinated concretely with the general interests of the subordi-
> nate groups and State life is conceived as a continual formation of unstable
> equilibrium (unstable within the ambit of the law ... equilibriums in which
> the interests of the ruling group predominates but only up to a point, i.e.,
> not as far as their mean economic-corporative interest would like.[22]

The state ideologically is an "educator" and in the economic field it is an
"instrument of rationalization."[23] Gramsci argues that counterhegemonic parties
must engage in a wide-ranging "war of position" to garner support and, in
effect, surround as well as penetrate the state because economic crises do
not, and formal assumption of state power cannot, guarantee "transformative"
or socially progressive results. He notes that "the fact that international relations

are interlaced with the internal relations of nation-states, creating new, original and historically concrete combinations" which present important political opportunities for opponents. Gramsci emphasizes both the systemic sources and conflictual undercurrents because "it is at the level of ideologies that men become conscious of conflicts in the world of the economy."[24]

But for analysis of short-term nontransformative situations (second-stage struggle occurring within the "fundamental existing frameworks"), Albert Hirschman contributes the notion of "propensity to defer" to "economic exigencies."[25] To take his concept a step further, societal actors exhibit differing "propensities to defer" to market conditions and, for that matter, to state policy. Whenever the term "deference" appears from here on, I refer to the propensity of groups to defer to prevailing policy.

Why do actors defer? The reasons are interrelated: rewards or coercion, organizational impotence, lack of persuasive alternatives, costs and risks of opposition, apathy, "poor" information, and outright approval. The lattermost depends on ideological dispositions that invade the calculus of self-interest: hence, one recently witnessed the resonance of the phase "Stay the Course" even among those most mauled by the "magic of the marketplace." While state managers and dominant coalition members obviously differ in their attachment to the product of their negotiations, I will focus here on subordinate groups.

This "propensity to defer" must be imbued with Gramsci's acute sense of the material underpinnings of prevailing ideology. This definition is not exclusively marxist. Schumpeter's remarks on the manipulation of ideas and of public opinion should be familiar. Charles Lindblom examines the institutional sources of "constrained volition" in polyarchal systems that result in a "lopsided competition of ideas" and Walter Dean Burnham discusses the "politics of excluded alternatives in the United States. We should be astonished, Barrington Moore Jr. observed, if social systems did not propagate core beliefs favorable to elites insofar as such beliefs preserve "absence of a demand for change."[26]

A high "deference" is defined by this "absence" because all a dominant coalition needs is acquiescence, not approval. A low deference is indicated by the usual measures of protest and dissent: strikes, demonstrations, rapid rises in support for opposition and fringe parties, and a knitting together of the various elements of resistance. Dispersed and inchoate protest is no challenge: organization is the key.

Policymakers are spared a test of their skills if there is high public confidence in the state's ability to cope efficiently and equitably with economic problems. If public confidence (deference) is low at the outset or diminishes rapidly after the onset of economic adversities, the state can undergo a "policy crisis" whose outcome is determined by the severity and duration of the adjustment, the capacity of dominant groups to repress or appease opposition and the capability of counter-elites to mobilize support for alternative programs.[27]

If policy crises are acute and protracted, and conflict sharpens within the dominant coalition, state managers have an opportunity to exercise political entrepreneurship to the extent that new alliances are formed with formerly subordinate groups championing alternative schemes. This pragmatic scenario is less likely to unfold where a "triple alliance" reigns: it is more likely to occur in societal corporatist frameworks where the alliance is a quadrupled one (i.e., included an assertive labor representation).

The Irish case fits Peter Evans's definition of dependent development as a "special case of dependency," characterized by "capital accumulation at the local level accompanied by increasing differentiation" of industrial structure.[28] But Evans and the bureaucratic authoritarian literature focus on repressive renditions where "ambivalent alliances" of (a fraction of) the local bourgeoisie, multinationals and states rule. The Irish Republic resembles the small European corporatist polities where consent must be managed through democratic institutions. When the hard choices appear on the horizon, elites will resort to material concessions and ideological appeals long before bayonets are unsheathed.

If the elite's policy choice is portrayed as a Hobson's choice, or else the wisest one, then "the openness of the economy provides the means to combat the demands of the working class for higher wages and for economic and social reforms."[29] But even where "the logic of economic vulnerability prevails over the logic of worker militancy" democratic structures provide incentives for bargaining on other grounds—such as obtaining investment controls in exchange for "wages foregone."[30] Of course, a policy crisis, if untended or mismanaged, can flare into systemic crises that no prudent elite desires.

To reiterate: international market forces signal the need to adjust, but the precise forms of adjustment will depend on how signals are converted by social contestants into programmatic messages to the citizenry. One should not suppose *a priori* that these diagnostic and prescriptive messages reflect only the narrow self-interest and redound exclusively to the benefit of elites. Nor should one suppose that the state always obeys elite preferences (even when these are unambiguous), especially when hotly contested and, in system-maintenance terms, differ marginally from other programs.

Further, we should not assume that counterprograms are less congruent with international economic shifts or are inferior to the adjustment schemes proposed by dominant groups. The reverse may well be the case. If so, and the opposition can become strongly organized, a policy crisis ensues that will pose an interesting trial for the pragmatic capabilities of state managers.

DEPENDENT STATES AND HIGH-TECH STRATEGIES

The Organization for Economic Cooperation and Development (OECD) Interfutures Report portrays microelectronic as "a decisive qualitative leap forward" such that "the electronics complex . . . will be the main pole around which the productive structures of the advanced industrial societies will be reorganized."[31] Among these post-industrial industries are computers and software, semiconductors and lasers, fiber optics, electronic consumer goods, biotechnology, and ancillary activities. Although research and development and other sophisticated functions are metropole-oriented, the strategic fragmenting of standardizable aspects of production has brought a heady taste of the "micro-millennium" to poorer climes.[32]

Envisioning many silicon valleys, glens, and highways, several NICs and peripheral European states (the Irish Republic, Scotland [or its Developmental Office], Spain, Portugal, and Greece) selected the electronics sector as the cornerstone of their development schemes or else situated it prominently among their aims. The success of the "East Asia Edge" in the 1970s with standardized electronic goods production was widely noted, and with expansion of the market proceeding at a rapid rate, newcomers rushed in to share the bounty.[33]

South Korea and Taiwan actively direct their economies to attain an R & D-based competitive structure. Ireland and Scotland are "catalytic" in approach, attracting foreign industries whose cumulative implantation in native soil will form not only an integrated network, but prod local entrepreneurs to supplement, complement, and perhaps surpass them. A "catalytic" mode of intervention, however, will be ineffective if local entrepreneurial elements are weak (because of high risk, uncertainty, higher rates of return elsewhere, etc.), but states tend anyway to strike different balances among intermingling modes of intervention over time.

These societies are not content to await the expiration of product-cycles. Job creation and investment are immediate goals; but the ultimate aim is to create a base of gleaming "postindustrial" industries and to endow themselves with R & D resources that give their products a "cutting edge" in the global market. This ambition is consonant with the assumption that as a state's "capacity for action" (administrative skills improve, industry diversifies, entrepreneurship improves, savings and investment rates rise, etc.), strengthens the state will be motivated to pursue the goal of "alleviating dependence on foreign capital and technology."[34]

Liberal economists surely score points when questioning the welfare-enhancing wisdom of too zealous a pursuit of this aim. States trade off a degree of autonomy to reap the benefits of interdependence. But there are domestic reasons why autonomy cannot be consistently pursued. These reasons can be characterized in the form of two satisfying bargains, (1) *elite* and (2) *consensual*. What is sacrificed is the goal of autonomy. A consensual bargain is endorsed across social cleavages because autonomy is really a means to other ends (full employment, rising living standards, economic opportunities) that may be achieved only by embracing interdependence.

In an elite bargain (triple alliances, comprador coalitions, state corporatism, and some forms of societal corporatism) dominant groups resist policy proposals that portend a loss in their shares of power or wealth. Thus, ideologically-linked societal interests (or "pact of domination") seek to impose policies that not only consign autonomy goals to oblivion but also harm nonelites by sacrificing their most important concerns (jobs, living standards, social services) which, when improving, otherwise win consent. Nonelites may be better served by policies promoting autonomy (e.g., enhanced R & D, active state coordination in commercial and financial arenas, shading the developmental emphasis toward local resource base). Freeman and Duvall argue that "there is no reason to believe that the state's activities are an effective means of achieving control over industrialization and of alleviating dependence on foreign capital and technology."[35]

This empirically sound verdict founders analytically on the premise of invariantly high "deference" by subordinate strata no matter what their organizational capabilities, the feasibility of alternatives, the form of social conflict, or the "pragmatic" capability of state managers. Of course *situational factors can press so powerfully that no alternative to orthodox adjustment prescriptions is possible.* Even so, the analytical tack taken here requires the consideration of counterfactual alternatives that serve to sharpen any interpretation. These theoretical concerns will be fleshed out in the ensuing case of Ireland's peripheral postindustrialization strategy.

IRISH DEVELOPMENT AND COLONIAL HERITAGE

As England's "first colony" Ireland was integrated into the core economy in the seventeenth century as a "vast cattle ranch." Rebellious natives were stripped of their land until only 14 percent remained in their (Catholic) hands by 1603. English legislation stifled Irish industrial competitors (and, briefly, cattle exports) through the eighteenth century. Ireland was forcibly united to Britain after the 1798 rebellion and the result was "a colony—not of the classical English form, but rather of the style of Algeria, nominally part of the United Kingdom, but in practice governed on different principles."[36]

While industrialization did occur in the northeast corner, exposure to free trade snuffed incipient industries elsewhere, so that Ireland became, as Marx remarked, "only an agricultural district of England, marked off by a wide channel from a country to which it yielded corn, wool, cattle, industrial,

and military recruits."[37] Capital was yielded in the form of rents and investment to the more lucrative money market across the Irish Sea. A singularly
adverse effect on Irish development was a fourfold rise in cattle prices relative to grain prices in George III's reign:

> The expanding Irish cattle-exporting industry, by supplanting other agri-
> cultural enterprises with a high output/acre, caused a decline in demand
> from the land intensive export sector. Simultaneously competing exports
> were depressing nonexport industries. The combined effect was greatly to
> reduce total demand, scale of operations, and hence overall efficiency in
> labor and capital-intensive industry in Ireland.[38]

As unit costs rose due to declining scale, the 'remedy' of wage reduction
only aggravated the fall in local demand. Meanwhile, the expanding cattle
trade ("on the hoof" for mainland value-adding) displaced small farmers and
tenants who were crowded onto ever smaller parcels of land. The stage was
set for a gruesome display of "deference"—the great famine of 1845–49. A
Malthusian tragedy prompted by Manchester liberalism, the famine made
emigration the fatalistic substitute for social radicalism, an invaluable prop
for the social order.

The population fell from 8.5 million in 1845 to less than 5 million at the
turn of the century. Still, the struggle for land reform intertwined with the
Home Rule movement. Incremental concessions culminated with the 1903
Wyndham Act, which created a new class of peasant proprietors who, like
the large "ranchers," undertook an undercapitalized but socially conservative
existence. Home rule was thwarted by a league of English and Ulster Tories
(supported by Protestant underclasses) and a minor insurrection eventually
erupted into the Anglo-Irish War of 1919–1921.

In the 1922–23 civil war the new Free State, run by the "most conservative revolutionaries in history," defeated the rebels who opposed partition,
and also beat down wage levels below those during the infamous 1913 Dublin
lockout. Bereft of the industrial northeast (containing 40 percent of taxable
capacity, 30 percent of population and a third of port trading), the new
regime presided over a primary commodity-exporting economy. Technically
a dominion, the new state was a Gaelic hodge-podge of British institutions
and economic ideology. Party cleavages were based on civil war (i.e., nationalist) affiliations, and enduringly so. The Catholic Church, source of solace
and identity in colonial days, guarded the gates against Bolshevik demons
and bawdy authors while emigrants poured out.

Appointing agriculture as motor for the growth of secondary industries,
the first government "aimed at the reduction of all costs of production in
order to enable producers to compete successfully abroad; this entailed low
taxation and low expenditures."[39] "Abroad" meant Britain, and "exporters"

meant the cattle ranchers. "Low taxation" meant low direct taxes only, and "low expenditure" meant misery, migration, and self-prescribed "low stateness."

In 1926 57.1% of the male working population were employed in agriculture and the same year 33.7% of the national income was earned by this sector. In the same year 88.99% of exports by value were agricultural and 42.08% came from the main export to Britain, mainly cattle; 92.3% of exports went to the United Kingdom . . . 58% of imports by value were manufactured goods and 78% of imports came from the United Kingdom.[40]

Despite arterial emigration, unemployment never fell below 6 percent. By 1930 Irish investment in British industry was twice the reverse flow. An ardently *dirigiste* government was impelled to create "state-sponsored bodies" to fill the entrepreneurial gaps in the economy—utilities, credit, transport, and later, commercial public enterprises.[41] But the "great spurt" of industrial development under organized direction, noted elsewhere by Alexander Gerschenkron, occurred in sporadic dribbles in Ireland. Why?

The "advantages of backwardness" were superseded by, in part, "advantages of dependence" for particular strata. Dominant rural and petit bourgeois interests shunned Sinn Fein reveries of national self-sufficiency, and were better served by free trade. Liberal economic orthodoxy was embedded in the institutions inherited from Britain. The "island behind an island" felt no pressing military threat to motivate state-directed development and, as a marginally privileged member of the "Celtic periphery," Ireland was *insufficiently* backward because of earlier British infrastructural investments (albeit to facilitate particular patterns of trade and traffic) and political reforms.[42] How the inclusion of industrial Ulster might have changed the character of an all-Ireland state is a much pondered, imponderable.

As in Latin America the depression made a necessity of the Sinn Fein virtue of import-substituting industrialization (ISI), which the new populist government of Fianna Fail intended to pursue in 1932. Yet Irish exponents of Friedrich List's autarchic gospel never imagined that infant industries can be nurtured during contractions of trade—and these doldrums were soon aggravated by an "economic war" with the United Kingdom over retention of payments for tenant-purchases funded by British government stock.

The value and volume of cattle exports fell more than a third by 1935 while dependence on the United Kingdom market went unchanged. The dispute was resolved in 1938, but in the midst of it, the Fianna Fail government (comprised of most of the defeated rebels of the civil war) tapped an aggressive populist nationalism to increase state autonomy vis-à-vis "prometropolitan" interests who were motivated by economic losses to flirt with a clumsy and ineffective fascist movement.[43] As the global economy foundered

and emigration outlets clogged, a populist government rejected the preferences of elites for free trade in order to pursue autarchy.

Under ISI industrial employment rose from 100,589 in 1931 to 166,513
by 1938. Industrial output increased by 40 percent (and skidded quickly
with the exhaustion of "easy" opportunities). In the absence of exchange
controls or specific policies to induce use of indigenous raw materials and to
direct linkage paths, prices rose in a complacent industrial climate. Tariffs
and low taxation were approved by small-scale industries and agricultural
exporters. British investors were undaunted by a porous Control of Manufactures Act, which decreed that firms must be Irish-owned.[44]

By the mid-1940s Fianna Fail, its radical populist period spent, had become a classic "catch-all" party presiding over development.[45] Although creating public enterprises in peat, sugar, chemicals, steel, airlines, and food
processing, the party's deputy leader asserted "private enterprise should be
supported by the state until it matured and that private enterprise, if strong
and willing, should then be permitted to take over public enterprise."

The state never entertained "scale-down" tariff designs to improve efficiency nor was there any effort to rationalize firms or coordinate relations
between private and public sectors in order to enhance economies of scale
and factor utilization.[46] Capital-deepening was not on the agenda although
producer goods, imports, and the overall ratio of imports to national income
rose in the Sinn Fein haven from the 1930s to the 1950s.

From 1946 to 1951 industry created one job for every thirty job seekers.
Total employment had risen one percent since 1926 despite emigration of
one of every three citizens. In a saturated home market industrial production (and the volume of agricultural exports) was static from 1953 to 1958.
The population had declined and unemployment was rising. Balance of payments problems met with non-Keynesian responses that only exacerbated
the crisis of 1956–58. (Kieran Kennedy and Brendan Dowling argue that,
given signs of an export upturn, an expansionary policy might have fostered
an export drive off the protectionist base.)[47]

However, by 1958 with the Common Market forming, dollars converting, and transnational firms roaming, Irish policymakers abandoned autarchic
ambitions for industrialization by invitation. As the legitimacy of economic
nationalism bled away in the form of emigrants and capital, state managers
utilized the crisis and international market forces to subdue any resistance
from a weak bourgeoisie—although they sugared the pill with requipment
subsidies and formal discouragement of internal sales by grant-aided foreign
firms. Agricultural exporters certainly were eager for European Economic
Community (EEC) markets and higher prices.

Since the anemic deference by subordinate strata was literally expressed by
"exit," the "voice" in the policy switch belonged to a pragmatic state elite

during this instructively labeled "Whitaker-Lemass revolution." (Whitaker was Secretary of the Department of Finance; Lemass, formerly Minister of Industry and Commerce, was premier from 1959 to 1966, and their "revolution" was a mild updating of economic orthodoxy to fit the Rostovian age.) Coinciding with a world-trading boom, the policy shift paid off handsomely from 1958 to 1964 with a 4 percent annual gross national product (GNP) growth rate and a 7 percent industrial growth rate. In this period foreign firms accounted for 70 percent of start-ups and 77 percent of new industrial jobs— provoking some apprehensive, if ugly, rural sneers in high places. Quoth one discussant

> The cry that industry is "away" and all because a few Japs, a few Jews, and a few Negroes come in here for the taxpayers to build factories for them, contribute to the cost of machinery, give them slave labour—if it can be got—protect them from every side so that they can export their goods to other countries under the label "Irish," I warn the Minister that they will pack their bags tomorrow or the day after and clear off, and they can tell this government or any government where to get off.[48]

But jeremiads, racist or otherwise, were rare. That comparatively modest growth was declared an "economic miracle" speaks volumes about the gravity of the 1950s crisis. Over the 1932–1957 era quasi-autarchic policies proved incongruent with international market forces and so became insupportable in terms of providing the "material bases of consent."[49] State autonomy increased as state managers were forced to devise an effective response to the long-exhausted, "easy" ISI phase. In the absence of popular mobilization behind alternative programs (the Labour Party was notoriously weak and pliable), the policy shift occurred in timid accordance with modern capitalist precepts about indicative planning, active macroeconomic policy, and unhampered trade.

State authorities saw themselves in effect as "Leninists of the bourgeoisie" whose mission was to enlighten and aid myopic private entrepreneurs in realizing their long-term interests. As economic nationalism was slowly shed, the dominant coalition was reinvigorated by a new consensual policy course: export-led industrialization from which a legitimating stream of benefits quickly flowed. In this respect, the Irish policy shift accorded with the verdict that "while the apparent determinants of state action may involve the political defeat of the bourgeoisie," the effect is "to reproduce and to reinforce that class."[50]

Was there an alternative course? Yes, but only in the outermost reaches of counterfactual speculation. Emigration, which in the 1950s was equivalent to one-seventh of the population, was both an indicator and dampener of crisis. No substantial support could be drawn from any quarter for more dramatic state intervention, expansion of public commercial activities, and more forceful measures to upgrade native firms so as to mount a home-market-based export drive.

INDUSTRIAL RENAISSANCE AND SYSTEMIC
TECHNOLOGY GAPS

Like Chile and Argentina in the 1960s, the Irish aimed to improve small-scale industrial base, expand and diversify exports, and thereby diffuse dependence. Foreign firms were envisaged as "pump-primers" for an *Irish* dynamism. Some efforts were made to encourage primary export-substitution (exporting goods that previously had been substituted), but these shrank to an ineffectual defensive posture against strong competitors swarming across the lowering tariff walls because of mutual tariff reductions agreed with the United Kingdom in the mid-1960s.

But the response of indigenous firms to free trade was sluggish, almost resistant. In 1961 only 31 firms employed 500-plus workers and produced 28 percent of gross output while over half of the total firms employed fifteen or fewer workers and accounted for 6 percent of output.[51] Glittering growth rates in GNP (4.2 percent over 1960–1970) and industrial exports (17 percent over 1964–1974) were attributable to foreign firms that garnered three-fourths of state subsidies, but likewise contributed 75 percent of new industrial jobs. The proportion of exports in national industrial output rose from 13.8 percent to more than 30 percent by 1972.

Rising internal demand brought reprieves, not pardons to local firms using standardized technologies, minimal export orientation (10–20 percent), a relatively nonexistent research base, archaic management practices, and which were more import-intensive and less value-adding to local primary resources than incoming firms.[52] The level and range of state inducements—"adaptation grants," a Management Institute, an Industrial Research Institute, etc.—failed to counter the private prerogative to search for the highest or least exerting rate of return (real estate, service, foreign investment, and some defensive investment, rather than an aggressive adjustment to stern challenges). The state mollified local capital via requipment aid, export-encouraging subsidies, eventually a fifty-fifty split of grants, and in 1981 a flat 10 percent tax on *all* manufacturing activity.

However, basking in the early glow, state managers (1) dabbled with "economic programmes"; (2) depoliticized the developmental process by investing responsibility in a technobureaucratic entity, the Industrial Development Authority; and (3) attempted to contrive corporatist arrangements expressly including trade unions in order to influence wage restraint. As Kaufman observed:

> Manufacturing exports of any sort require policies which threaten a variety of domestic populist interests: devaluation and subsidy burdens on urban consumers; liberalization of import policies; and stable expectations about price and exchange level—in short, many of the requisites of predictability and stability that O'Donnell suggested were necessary for deepening.[53]

Corporatist experiments fizzled. The small scale of industry inhibited both managerial adjustments and the organization of the labor force. Neither labor nor capital was organized sufficiently to "deliver" on commitments. Although the Irish Congress of Trade Unions (ICTU) eagerly participated in the National Industrial Economic Council, this tripartite body collapsed at the decade's end when the ICTU, seeking *quid pro quo* investment guarantees, balked at income policy proposals. Under statutory threat the ICTU finally agreed in 1970 to annual "national pay agreements" bargaining.

Governed by Fianna Fail, or else by an even more conservative Fine Gael party in coalition with a hapless Labour Party, the state gave short shrift to Labour's pet idea of a national development corporation that was intended to coordinate private activity with the public commercial sector (which in 1970 accounted for 8 percent of GDP, 6 percent of employment, 15 percent of gross investment, and 46 percent of public gross investment). Ignoring the public sector role in underwriting local demand, generation and use of local resources, infrastructural and welfare value, and of "socializing" private sector risks, the economically illiterate cry that "four private jobs support each public job" sounded credible.

Foreign firms became the driving force. In 1966 grant-aided firms (78 percent foreign) accounted for 9 percent of industrial jobs, 42.5 percent of manufactured exports, and 11 percent of gross output. By 1973 the respective figures were 29 percent of jobs (10 percent in the United Kingdom, 22 percent in West Germany), 62 percent of exports (24 percent in the United Kingdom and 30 percent in Belgium) and 30 percent of output—though two-thirds of increased export revenues stemmed from other sources, invisibles and agriculture.[54] The bulk of foreign direct investment (FDI) was British, American, and German. American investment predominated by the mid-1970s.

The role of FDI in Ireland was expressed bluntly in a government-sponsored report which warned critics that if these sources were discouraged, "Irish people will still have to work with capital that is not owned by Irishmen—but they will be working with it outside Ireland rather than at home."[55] This celebration of the disciplinary virtues of emigration—together with exhortations to restrain wages so that capital could "remunerate, renew, and expand"—became the battle cry of the new developmental ideology.

The 1972 referendum over EEC entry was the next pivotal moment in which the Labour Party's struggle to present a viable alternative was overwhelmed by a combination of official and private pro-Common Market forces. Labour spokesmen argued that associated status served Irish needs equally well, while preserving state discretion over the timing of tariff scale-downs and industrial upgrading schemes. But the Finance Minister balked "for the simple reason that foreign investors would not regard the two situations as equivalent." A massive pro-market propaganda campaign carried the vote exactly in line with Party affiliation: a combined Fianna Fail and Fine Gael total of 83 percent for entry versus Labour's 17 percent against.

Contrary to stereotyped dependista claims the international market and foreign firms dictated nothing; rather it was indigenous interests, persuasively converting market "signals" into programmatic messages, that determined the precise form of policy response. The active state direction implied in Labour's program was rejected. Hence this analysis is consistent with the "recurring dependency syndrome" by which Duvall and Freeman describe an inverse relation between growth and state entrepreneurial activity. Rather than focus on technobureaucrats, however, I argue that this syndrome is the outcome of broader social struggles for the political power to define the developmental project.

The argument that state-aided industries provided the otherwise unemployed with the privilege of paying taxes seemed pragmatically sound, if not strikingly equitable. But this tactic became a substitute for the upsurge of private initiative that the policy was intended to trigger; official reports recognized that "repeated injections" were needed to sustain the developmental project. So the Industrial Development Authority (IDA) ingested funds and issued "job projections" which, while they were credible, conferred political capital on governments. However, the IDA was running too many races: against demography ("youngest and fastest growing population in the EEC"); job losses from import competition, rising expense of capital-intensive technology, and rivals for footloose capital.

Concerned over the final-assembly bias and weak linkages of foreign firms, the IDA responded in the mid-1970s by targeting high-tech electronics firms for location in Ireland to create a secure web that might transform the Emerald Isle into a silicon island. However, obscured by energy crises and global recession, the benign consensus-generating basis of "peripheral postindustrialism" project eroded as a result of systemic technology gaps—systemic in terms both of internal socioeconomic organization and of international economic relations. The sources and effects are identified below:

1. Foreign *control over technology transfer is the most familiar problem*. Duty-free technologies give rise to balance of payments strain. Imported with the technologies is their "interest-composition," i.e., their design embodies the criteria of potent social interests elsewhere. Among the potentially inappropriate criteria:
2. *Capital-intensity bias and "segmentation."* Though never achieving full employment, the Irish state is not situated badly compared to labor-surplus Third World economies. Trends toward automation are not necessarily a disadvantage in a relatively developed society that produces a surplus of science and engineering graduates. Nonetheless they have taken a toll.

Segmentation is the allocation by parent firms of partial, specialized production processes among a variety of sites. If "final assembly" they are
low-skilled. Segmentation retards host state capacity to make Vernon's
"obsolescing bargain" obsolesce, and militates against linkage. A related
concern is:

3. *The "volatility" of new technologies* hampers a turn of bargaining advantage to the host. That parents of foreign affiliates retain control over R & D
for rapidly changing sophisticated products is well documented. If local
firms and the state are unable or unwilling to match (presumably in product lines of specific competitive advantage), these R & D outlays, then
product cycle virtuosity suffers. If so, reliance on high-tech foreign affiliates will exacerbate these effects. Finally,

4. *1, 2, and 3 are interrelated* and their negative impact is intensified by
economic downturns and by global competition, especially when the state
is restricted to a catalytic role and the local bourgeoisie lacks what Evans
nicely terms a "vocation for hegemony." In downturns R & D is devoted
rationalization (producing a given amount of output with less labor) rather
than product innovations which provides a basis for capacity-extension
(and more jobs). But in upturns high-tech firms are more likely to locate
affiliates in Asian or East European low-wage areas. The competition for
mobile capital to feed the "peripheral postindustrial path" is keener than
ever. The greater the competition for these firms, the more remote the
possibility that this strategy can succeed.

The adverse effects of automation were evident long before the oil shocks
of the 1970s. Between 1964 and 1974 new grant-aided firms "accounted for
59 to 68 percent of the increase in gross output and 24 to 33 percent of the
increase of exports, which was *achieved with a lower labor force than in 1966*.[56]
Another Irish economist observed that a curious feature of the economy
during the 1960–73 "miracle" years

> was the very high level of investment (averaging 19% of GNP over the
> period) and the poor performance on total employment which rose from
> 1,052 in April 1960 to 1,066 in April 1974 . . . In the more recent period
> 1974–1977, investment has averaged almost 25% of GNP. Despite a rise
> of investment to 30% of GNP (compared to 14 percent in the United
> States, 17 percent in the United Kingdom, and 31 percent in Japan) *total
> employment fell to the lowest level in the history of the Irish state*.[57]

By 1984 the unemployment rate exceeded 16 percent (even in the 1960–73
heyday averaged 6.5 percent). State spending rose from 35.8 percent of GNP
in 1962 to 53.0 percent in 1974 through regressive tax policies that triggered massive street demonstrations in 1979 for reform. Capital taxes were
less than 1 percent of total revenue while the share contributed by taxed-at-
source wage earners rose from 62 percent in 1970 to 90 percent by 1980.
The consensus-generating aspects of the economic strategy were faltering.

A fiscal crisis loomed and an elite bargain ("satisfice") composed of foreign and local exporters, some small Irish "supplier" firms, elements of the bureaucracy, the two main parties and some branches of the trade unions) formed.

THE "PUSH BUTTON" REPUBLIC AND THE POLITICAL EXHAUSTION OF INDUSTRIAL PHASES

DIAGNOSIS

When the foregoing problems of development were cited, an IDA official confidently replied that the Republic was so compact, its population so skilled and educated, and its economic and political climate so obliging that there would be enough push buttons to go around for Irish fingertips.[58] A similar optimism informed the "new strategy" in Puerto Rico, which hoped to lure enough high-tech firms to emerge as the "technological axis" of the Caribbean.[59]

South Korea and Taiwan undertook "statist" direction of production of high-tech equipment, and other Third World states followed even though this route "is just about the most difficult and least effective way of entering industrial production." The dice are loaded against a newcomer that has a small home market, is short of capital and skilled manpower, and is rich in unskilled labor.[60] Even Scotland, an early "peripheral postindustrializer," duplicated, often in a more exacerbated way, Irish adversities. Viewing a Scottish scene of poor linkages, automated unemployment and foreign firm departures, a scholar asked if:

> indigenous firms have not *yet* escaped commercial dependence upon the local multinational sector. However, the fact that external investment in electronics manufacturing in Scotland has been taking place for nearly 30 years casts doubt upon this explanation, especially in light of the small size of this group (native firms provide 9% of total electronics employment).[61]

The most damaging appraisal of the Irish strategy was presented in 1982 by an independent consulting agency. Pertinent to the waning consensual nature of the Irish project, Telesis observed:

> Irish industrial policy aims to create jobs. As it is now designed, it expends too much energy creating job "approvals" . . . Only 30% of the jobs approved in foreign-owned firms between 1972 and 1978 were actually on the ground in 1981 . . . An even greater discrepancy exists for indigenous industry. Sustainable jobs as a percentage of job approvals is only 14%.[62]

Telesis reported the good news for indigenous firms that the "shake out" attending EEC entry was nearly over; the bad news was that few Irish firms had adjusted to new competitive conditions. (Puerto Rican figures, incidentally, were even worse.) The Telesis report criticized the state for encouraging a "businessman's dole mentality" among small firms and noted that "most of the largest and strongest Irish companies are investing abroad in businesses only minimally related to Irish employment and export."

As for ambitions for an integrated electronics industry (60 percent of job "approvals" were in electrical and mechanical engineering), Telesis found "manufacturing satellites performing partial steps in the manufacturing process" whose skill demands and linkages were "limited," as in Scotland, Puerto Rico, Singapore, and elsewhere. Telesis laid the blame upon "timid" government, which failed to press for creation of a "corporate base with sufficient resources and time horizon to undertake removal of obstacles" to indigenously based export growth. The report cited the "ultimate limiting factor" on Irish strategy as the rival strategies of parent multinationals, but another comment squarely hit the mark regarding structural constraints.

Telesis noted "private capital, both Irish and foreign, would find better opportunities in other countries if market forces alone were dictating their choices."[63] This constraint is a stimulant of a high "propensity to defer" during turbulent adjustments when elites call upon subordinate strata for sacrifices. But this high deference is agreement to an *interest-based depiction of economic exigencies* when alternative schemes of dividing the burdens of adjustment are possible. A need to adjust is distinct from the struggle to formulate acceptable allocations of "austerities." A class, organization, or group does not display deference when accepting the least worst of all possible policy choices, but rather when it accepts a narrowly defined set of options that serve the interests of another class or ruling bloc. In this case, the subordinate strata accedes to a "surplus" burden in the adjustment process.

The ironies of chasing progress in this "information age" became painfully evident in Ireland. Elites tell job holders that to "catch up" with EEC living standards they must deliberately lag behind the rates of wage (and by extension, social wage) growth in the trading partners. The external environment "demanded" it. The living standard gap between Ireland and the EEC average actually increased slightly since entry, and only the admission of Greece buoyed Irish living standards, wages, and social services from the bottom of the Common Market charts. A quarter to one-third of the citizenry subsists in poverty while a tenth holds two-thirds of all wealth.

In the absence of proof of "wage-led" losses of jobs or competitiveness, elites admonish workers to restrain wages even when productivity gains are robust. These admonishments testify to the *exculpatory* and *extenuating* functions of a hegemonic ideology, which depicts international economic conditions as omnipotent forces requiring invariant reactions from the private sector. If this characterization seems credible, then no decline in deference will occur.

Workers are instructed to invest—via wages foregone and rising taxation—

in job-destroying productivity measures. Irish-owned firms, reliant on internal demand, suffer more from ebbing demand than they gain from wage "relief." As Hartmut Elsenhans nicely illustrates in historical perspective, investment will decline because demand is much more vital to capitalist calculation than wage scales *per se*. Still the message is driven home that Irish workers are implicitly competing with *Asian* wage levels. (The Central Statistics Office reveals that the average wage level for "high-tech" employees in Ireland is slightly *less* than the overall manufacturing wage.[64] The state responds by raising aid and incentive levels through further revenue extraction from fewer wage earners—until fiscal crisis erupts. External "shocks" do not by themselves cause the crisis.

One may raise the objection that rising demand elsewhere will stimulate export-oriented investors but the trends analyzed here are arrested and the material basis for support of the state strategy is restored only if sustained trade growth occurs, and if the local economy is equipped to take full advantage—both dubious assumptions. Belgium recorded productivity increases of 90 percent from 1970–80, but with fewer workers producing a roughly constant output of goods it passed even Ireland to the EEC unemployment statistics.[65] Multiplier effects are weak in Ireland and the microchips impact on tertiary employment should not encourage these interested in attaining even politically tolerable levels of unemployment—and it is the *political* exhaustion of industrial strategies which is our analytic concern.

A second objection is that a "lump of labor" fallacy occurs here; that is, that our analysis ignores the demand creation attending a progressive cheapening of products. This is an open question. The least skeptical investigators foresee mismatches between the labor-shedding effect of process innovation and the timing of product innovations—which have not appeared in profusion.[66] An OECD study found that "consumption of information goods and services still plays a minor role in the budget of the average household."[67]

Export-oriented investment in the absence of strong external demand converts "peripheral postindustrialism" into a subset of dependent development, which is defined by Evans as excluding local consumers due to its basic export-based strategy. The process is regressive in a way akin to Frank's notion of underdevelopment. Unlike Frank, this analysis stresses the indigenous sources supporting this *choice* among possible responses to international forces; the consequent fragility of the ideological basis of the dominant coalition (which Cardoso regards as the "state"); and, the effects on the limits of the states autonomy in democratic polities where subordinate groups are less reliably—because more ideologically—contained than in authoritarian NICs.

Borrowing rose precipitously in the 1973–76 period to offset energy prices and otherwise depressed consumer spending (which, when high, is import-oriented). The Irish never considered an "indebted industrializing" tack in conjunction with expansion of public commercial firms. The premier in the 1973–77 coalition explained that although he had no prejudice one way or another, any "completely different deployment" of state-sponsored bodies "risked alienating the investment on which our future depends." The 1977–81 Fianna Fail government increased borrowing for short-term electoral reasons but also in the belief that private investment would be stimulated. Borrowing was the only option for a democratic state whose developmental strategy resulted in diminishing returns and a shrinking pool of revenue sources.[68]

By 1982 borrowing was 18 percent of GNP. Overall the debt equaled GNP and debt service consumed a quarter of government revenue.[69] Deference remained high through three elections fought over 1981–82 as parties competed for the right to impose deflationary programs that differed marginally. Austerity packages were portrayed as a secular pilgrimage, a collective repentance for "sins" that barefoot treaders of (as a Fine Gael minister colorfully phrased it) the "rough stony path" may not recall having committed. They were induced to feel guilty because the international marketplace, like God, moves in mysterious ways that demand perfect obedience.

Deflationary policies feed the vicious cycles and erode the sources of regime stability. By 1983 the "average earner" paid 43 percent of income to taxes, while indirect taxes further depressed purchasing power—and the fortunes of local businesses. The real level of personal consumption was 15 percent lower in 1984 than in 1979 (and investment fell by a third as the foreign debt rose fivefold). Irish economists found it "something of a paradox" that, despite a stricken home market, manufacturing output rose 5 percent in 1983 and 17 percent in 1984 so that economic recovery "was all output, no jobs."[70]

Unemployment rates passed the 16 percent mark. By 1984 "leakages" into debt service and profit repatriation amounted to 10 percent of gross domestic spending, reducing a 4 percent GNP growth to 2 percent. The beneficiaries of growth in world trade were high tech firms, primarily U.S. ones. United States investment in Ireland grew from 986 million Irish pounds to 3.8 billion between 1977 and 1983—an annual reinvestment rate of 24 percent. In their most profitable EEC outlet, U.S. manufacturers recorded a 24 percent real return compared to an average 5.6 percent elsewhere in 1984 (although this is substantially due to transfer price mechanisms in a favorable Irish tax climate).

The espoused solution is to do the same things, only somehow better. Thus a minister decried "unreal wage demands" and argued that future productivity gains be rewarded not by vulgar wages (as opposed to refined profits) but, incredibly, in the "satisfaction and security of a long-term job." This minister admitted that management efficiency, marketing expertise, and new product development were more crucial to Irish competitiveness than wage curbs, but gave no pause for thought on the implications of infringing on private prerogatives to correct deficiencies. The emphasis on wages diverts attention from serious questions about industrial strategy and state intervention.

This skewed view cannot be construed simply as an expression of self-interest by "capital" if only because so many Irish businesses are harmed. Ideological "lag" best characterizes the problem. However, this "lag" is conditioned by an institutional environment that keeps "nondecisions" at bay. The dissident voice of the small Labour Party was muffled during its periodic coalitions with Fine Gael. So by itself "lag" is an insufficient explanation; those who prosper through the current strategy know very well where their interests lie.

THE ROLE OF IDEOLOGY

An investigator of the Peruvian case argues that a "new bourgeoisie" may arise as a "hegemonic candidate" in dependent developers. Particularly where "bonanza resources appear, domestic industrialists'" fear of the state

> as restrictor of entrepreneurial initiative diminishes in direct proportion to their self-transformation from an individualist to an organization-based class; to the restructuring of the state apparatus along technical-managerial lines and the infusion within it of the managerial ideology, and to the growth of the 'bonanza,' which enables them to enjoy the advantages of a strong local state without paying for it.[71]

If unblessed by a "bonanza" a "mature" and "developmentalist" bourgeoisie can engineer the integration of the working class into the capitalist order by reliance on the spread of high-productivity enterprises which enable a rising wage basis for accommodation of trade unions.[72] However, our analysis of peripheral postindustrialism identifies disturbing features that vitiate this progressive scenario.

Wage "give backs," work rule erosion, and union-busting efforts so recently evident in advanced industrial nations testify to the contingent nature of "mature" private enterprises when opportunities to "roll back" labor arise. Whether rollback or sophisticated bargaining will occur in a specific case depends not on enlightened ideology of management but, foremost, upon the relative strength of the contestants and their capacity to enlist the support of the state.

High sensitivity to international market conditions induces corporatist-style bargaining (e.g., wage controls in exchange for job guarantees, public investment and project expansion, tax reforms, and monitoring of investment) only if (1) the requisite conditions of centralization and concentration among the bargaining groups obtains; (2) deference is diminishing rapidly; and (3) the level of organization enables a counter elite to promote credible alternatives that influence policy. The political exhaustion of an economic policy course then impels policymakers to search for new coalitional arrangements.

Peter Gourevitch too argues that crises "render politics more plastic," emphasizing how the "international situation shapes the internal group behavior according to varying sectoral locations in the global division of labor." The conditions of the cohesion of a coalition give way, opening up possibilities for new coalitional configurations (a process which "political entrepreneurs" may or may not guide, depending on the resources they can summon or to which they are forced to resort). My argument is that just how "plastic" politics becomes during crises will be retarded or accelerated according to an ideological interpretation of the response "demanded" by economic exigencies. This is a vital supplement to the more sociological approach of Gourevitch, who writes

> A given policy preference is not necessarily in the "interest" of the actor. On the contrary, it is possible to posit a calculus or frame of reference that could make a range of conflicting policies reasonable from the standpoint of different strategies . . . The way out of this interpretive trap is to be sociological, to ask what sorts of strategy various groups actually did prefer.

The "interpretive trap" had sprung on the actors before the crisis; the "way out" is confined by the frame of reference, and the latter may be swamped by international market forces so that the "calculi" of various groups becomes indeterminate. Although the opportunity can be missed, a critical moment occurs when the governing coalition loses cohesion, becomes porous vis-à-vis subordinate group demands, incorporates new components, and in which the preferences of coalition members change.

A high deference is an *ideologically-induced vulnerability* that serves the interests of an export coalition, but also is based on the diffusion of material benefits to other groups. Waning deference is by no means irreversible nor are counter-elites always poised to exploit it. The British miner's strike of 1984–85, an essentially defensive struggle, failed because they had no positive program by which to galvanize public support (and indeed lost union and Labour Party support) and because they faced a well-prepared Tory government (deploying superior resources) that proved adept at promoting its own "definition of the situation" and so the miners were easily outflanked in the media. In the Irish case adversities sparked demonstrations for tax reform, worker sit-ins in shutdown factories and a mild rebuke of the Labour Party for its "anti-working class measures." But these sporadic indications of declining deference amount to no more than impotent grumbling.

PRESCRIPTIONS AND COUNTERHEGEMONIC CONTENT

The Telesis report urged adoption of an alternative strategy to restore a consensual development bargain. Telesis advised the state to maximize skill barriers (versus low-wage rivals) by reallocating a third of public expenditure from foreign firms to indigenous exporters and subsuppliers. A "national enterprise agency" should serve as a "corporate shell" for Irish firms because "the industrial infrastructure does not exist in Ireland and *the network of subsuppliers has to be created in a more planned and organized way*."[73]

The state should encourage mergers, rationalization, joint ventures and private-public coordination while phasing out low-wage sectors a là the Swedish policy pattern. The state must emphasize competitive advantages in exploiting native raw materials—food processing, fisheries development, processing of mineral deposit finds (small oil strikes were made offshore) and research capacities expanded for "selected" industries, including small-batch production for capital goods. This strategy requires a "carrots and stick" approach to private industry and the creation of coordinating mechanisms and forums (presumably, a revival of societal corporatist efforts).

Telesis did not dwell on the role of public commercial enterprise; given its caustic diagnosis of local capital's shortcomings, one may chalk it up to tact. Telesis provided a programmatic basis for new coalitional possibilities, which could prove subversive because there is scant reason to believe that the *degree* and *kinds* of intervention suffice to meet social goals.

As the "peripheral postindustrializing" strategy falters on, one might anticipate splits inside the dominant coalition over policy, enabling a new coalitional configuration to arise (trade unions, left groups, hard-pressed small businesses, "technobureaucrats" who can swing either way and pragmatists in the major parties). Relevant here is the Stephens's observation on Jamaican politics that where popular loyalties are primarily "clientelistic" rather than ideological, the "party leadership is allowed a greater flexibility to change its ideological stance without alienating (or educating) its supporters." Envisioned here a "democratic-entrepreneurial state," which also goes by more emotive names. The ideological basis for the strategy can dissolve during the course of a long-term political struggle, so it really is important to inquire why it is "people in that situation [are] likely to think that way."[74]

However the potential resistance is powerful; the dominant coalition is justifiably apprehensive that the pragmatic course agreed by Telesis—seeing it as the "camel's nose beneath the capitalist's tent." A weak Irish bourgeoisie knows it needs the state, but fears that the state will "act for itself" or, less metaphysically, "act for others." Small business shares this view and is primed to join the antistatist chorus whenever key industrial, financial, and agricultural groups begin it.

A "recurring dependent development syndrome" comes into play if a satisficing level of employment—anything under 10 percent these days—and rising living standards occur. In the short term, social pressures on elites tend to be "populist," centered around no specific programs and so are highly manipulable. If elites are unwilling or unable to defuse popular protest through concessionary measure, the threat of a concerted movement grows as economic adversities continue.

CONCLUSION

I have argued that international economic forces alone do not determine the precise response engendered in a given state or the definitions of interest made by domestic actors as to the policies they prefer. *This obviously presupposes some degree of choice and the presence of resources that make choice possible.* Global economic shifts and shocks are "interpreted" through mediation by dominant coalitions in ways that are designed to uphold their power versus challengers who stand to benefit from altered patterns of policy and state activity.

Powerful groups may even exacerbate sensitivity when the means for diminishing it are present. External forces become (not totally tame) pieces to deploy on the political game board. When acute and protracted, economic adversities, however, can erode the deference of subordinate strata (and of separate components of the dominant coalition) to the prevailing development policy and adjustment schemes, triggering a situation of indeterminacy (regarding policy content and outcome) within policy networks, within the dominant coalition, and between the latter and the nonelites, and between these shifting influences and policymakers.

The "politics of debt" in Latin America offers further material for the study of state responses to declines in deference. The International Monetary Fund (IMF) can provide internal leverage for some groups against the resistance of others. The IMF is not the only agent that can be invoked for such purposes and this function is not invariably a malign one. In the case of that exceptional debtor Israel, Washington applied pressure on Israeli leaders to put their finances in some semblance of order. "The message Shimon Peres and Yitzhak Modai tacitly convey is that they welcome Washington's discipline," a commentator observes. "It helps them make the case for austerity in their bids for consensus at home."[75]

When mysterious market forces become embodied in specific agents, the market itself becomes, in many aggrieved eyes, coteries of affluent aliens who decide over their own tax-deductible lunches whether and how long the citizenry must starve. Market forces no longer appear intangible and inexorable. Restive publics in Argentina, Brazil, Venezuela, and the Dominican

Republic have forced governments to tread warily toward fiscal propriety. Mexico has counted on ruling party ties to trade unions to enforce severe austerity measures.

In the Bolivian case an ultimatum by the Bank of America, on behalf of creditors to the nation, to resume interest payments was not acted upon by either party. "It's not a case that we ignored the deadline," a bank negotiator explained afterward. "There was no one to talk to." Social distress does not worry bankers, but institutional instability does. Banks are forced to consider conciliatory actions when the perceived capacity of states to enforce rules is diminishing.

A declining deference among subordinate strata permits a breathing space for government (whether they want it or not) when dealing with international lenders; it *may* also stir a search for alternative adjustment packages that broaden the scope of "orthodoxy" in the international regime. The political implications of a widespread decline in deference are not lost on local elites, even where their own misfiring strategies are most to blame, dominant groups can co-opt populist pressure into a "nationalist" course that restores their authority. The international implications are cited by the Latin American Debt Commission:

> In virtually every Latin American and Caribbean country; there are major pressures to turn inward, to reject cooperation with the IMF, to turn their backs on existing obligations and to look to solutions which stress a higher degree of protectionism and state control.[76]

Popular attention can be diverted successfully from internal shortcomings by pointing fingers at external agents. But any act tantamount to repudiation of international market forces is a hazardous precedent to set. Although local capital and foreign bankers alike may want Pinochets to proliferate, both Chicago-style economics and the military option are at least temporarily discredited in the larger debtor states.[77] This enhances the question of how "situations of indeterminacy" regarding state strategy, coalition formation, and debt negotiation, are contained or exploited by domestic contestants for political power.

This chapter focuses on democratic states pursuing, and coping with the consequences of, "peripheral postindustrial" development. This term denotes (1) a policy-induced diffusion of high-tech affiliates on the periphery with the objective of installing them as the leading local sector; (2) a truncated form of development (low linkages, meager R & D, less sophisticated elements); and (3) an ideological extenuation of prevailing policy, designed to counteract the political exhaustion of a development pattern. The lattermost was a strong motive of Irish elites, given that the alternatives of a state-capitalist kind were ruled out by a hegemonic ideology. The negative effects of a "peripheral postindustrial strategy" are most extreme in states employing "catalytic" policy instruments, but the probes cited earlier are manifested across the spectrum of regime type, levels of development, modes of intervention, and state-society configuration—as we shall see in the next chapters.

South Korea and Taiwan take a strenuously statist approach to promoting electronics industry, but remain primarily reliant on Japan for technology generation (with the "cutting edge" technologies being withheld).[78] By incorporating microelectronics advances into older processes the advanced industrial states can even roll back the Third World's comparative advantage in cheap labor. The debt crisis worked to curb severely R & D spending in Brazil, Mexico, Chile, Peru, and Venezuela.[79] The "scope of offshore activities is decreasing" even for standardized segments of production.[80] The increasing concentration of control by transnational firms over such products is associated with decreases in offshore production, and the skill mix and the complex "systems nature" of innovation—which must underlie a successful pursuit of this strategy—pose formidable barriers to even the most capable of imitators.

By incorporating microelectronics into older processes the industrial states potentially can roll back the Third World's advantage in cheap labor although there is probably little incentive for multinational firms to do so. Martin Carnoy notes that multinationals' training programs allows them to take full advantage of low-cost labor without sacrificing much quality or productivity—and they already do this successfully in the Pacific rim and in parts of Mexico.[81]

Even the prospect of rolling back Third World advantages in cheap labor should not be a source of good cheer for First World work forces. In the United States the Federal Bureau of Labor Statistics expect between now and 1995 that high-tech industries will create from 3 to 17 percent of new jobs. The EEC Brussels office estimates that in 1978, 7.5 percent of the EEC work force was employed in the electronics industry, broadly defined, but that since 1969 these firms have shed an average of 20 percent of labor.[82] The impact of automation on tertiary activities is far from encouraging in the present global context. Ultimately, demand growth must outpace productivity gains to sustain or raise employment levels, and the fabled forces of the market are not so very evidently poised to accomplish this. "Trade," Nathan Rosenberg writes,

> means a willingness to accept new patterns of specialization as the industrializing countries establish new competencies and displace more advanced industrial economies from traditional niches based upon earlier, but now eroding, comparative advantages. These adjustments, however, are coming into increasing conflict with other domestic goals, such as high employment, strong expectations about the continued growth of real wages, and

increasing sensitivity to the distributional aspects of adjustment processes left to the market.[83]

The present interaction of high-tech development with international market patterns will exert pressures on states to adopt protectionist measures or to engage in policy innovations domestically and perhaps to explore new cooperative arrangement internationally over the allocation of niches in the changing international division of labor. Certainly market mechanisms and the remarkable advances in high technology offer indispensable benefits. But as the current scramble for advantageous niches continues, political pressures will mount for leaders to devise means to avoid negative aspects of this chase.

"Perhaps the profoundest problem that faces modern society," Paul Goodman noted several decades ago, "is to decide in what functions the automatic and computer style is not relevant—and therefore to curtail and forget it."[84] The same may be said for the role of the market, and when deference to what Galbraith called the "conventional wisdom" is declining, these social tasks effectively begin.

ADDENDUM

In December 1992, the Irish Labour Party doubled its parliamentary count from 16 to a historic high of 33 (of 166 "Deputies") and formed a coalition in January with Fianna Fail. Fianna Fail had governed the Republic since February 1987—initially as a minority government and after June 1989 in coalition with the Progressive Democrats. In the 1980s Irish governments imposed austerity programs with the most remarkable, even insouciant, ease. At the onset of the debt crisis in the early 1980s Irish citizens were exhorted in quasi-religious tones to "walk the rough stony path" to fiscal rectitude, as if everyone were equally to blame. This masochistic twaddle should have been difficult to peddle.[85]

But a media campaign propounded the dangers of the debt, diverted attention from profound inequalities, and carried the day. Labour too acknowledged that debt was a serious problem. The belief that social needs must give way to the debt crisis culminated in 1987 when the chief opposition party Fine Gael endorsed the economic aims of the Fianna Fail government. Putting the books "in order" meant savage cuts in health, education, and environment. Taxes were onerous yet no reform of a regressive tax structure was in the offing. The major parties weren't interested—beyond commissioning unheeded studies—nor were the Progressive Democrats, except to sound their refrain of the twin imperatives of cutting taxes and spending. These three parties, the banks, large firms, and an ascendant crew of neoliberal economists combined to mount a relentless public barrage of messages promoting harsh economic policies.

"People don't like what's going on," lamented Labour Party leader Dick Spring, "but they are convinced there is no alternative." By 1991 even The Guardian praised what the editors beheld as a "continuing Irish miracle."[86] Because of prudent economic management and a deal with the Trade Unions (which, unlike Thatcherites, the Irish state acknowledges), Ireland boasted the fastest growing economy in the European Community in 1990 led by a vigorous export performance from its sleek new foreign sector of industries. If rapid economic growth without prosperity is a miracle then that is indeed what the Irish were experiencing.

Irish unemployment was twice the European Community average. In a population of three and a half million, a million citizens—and 40 percent of all children—lived in poverty. Emigration was stemmed only by British doldrums and a recent study foresaw no prospect of a halt in rising joblessness.[87] A notable recent volume has as its theme a "state of aimlessness" stemming from a widespread and, for many citizens, realistic sense that Ireland "does not have a future."[88] The editor cites the unabating problems: unemployment, emigration, poverty, indebtedness, right-wing triumphalism, and the deceptively distant sounds of fury in the North. In a hauntingly symbolic act postal workers during a strike in 1991 excepted people mailing applications for "Morrison visas" to emigrate to (or remain in) the United States.

What happened? Or to put it another way, what is not happening? The key "irony," as conservative commentators delicately put it, is that the republic contrives to get high aggregate growth rates and export performance while suffering simultaneously from the highest unemployment in the EC, a hemorrhage of repatriated profits, and regressive taxes. Still, the country has voted over and over again for right-wing parties.

How is it that the Irish vote this way? Historians trace this predilection to the civil war (which emphasized nationalism over class), emigration (drains off dissent), the "distractions" of Northern Ireland, late industrialization (no sizable working class), and a fiercely conservative Catholic Church. Not to be overlooked is the mediocrity, with some exceptions, of Irish economists who set the narrow terms of public debate.[89] As a consequence the Labour Party, and all left-wing groups combined, never managed until recently to attract more than one voter in five.

In lopsided coalitions with Fine Gael, Labour barely impeded its partner's reactionary impulses. So Labour was punished at the polls in 1987, dipped to 12 seats and was overtaken in votes in Dublin by the Workers Party, an offshoot of the Official IRA whose leaders in 1972 had called a cease-fire in the North. In March 1992, six of the seven Workers Party (WP) deputies bolted to form the Democratic Left. Their aim was to break with a "closed disciplinary organizational style," promote a democratic internal structure and generate credible societal alternatives.

Labour formed a new coalition with Fianna Fail. In the suspenseful negotiations, after the election, Labour rejected Fine Gael as too "condescending
and patronizing"—a habit Fine Gael hardly could help. In turn Fine Gael
chided Labour for consorting with corrupt Fianna Fail and ritualistically chided
both parties for their "overoptimistic belief in state intervention." No fan-
tasy, however, could be more optimistic than to expect private enterprise to
save the economy. Even the Fine Gael leader, who had nothing but business
tax cuts to offer, pronounced the state-subsidized private enterprise policy of
the last thirty-five years as a failure.[90]

ECONOMIC QUANDARIES

The result of the Industrialization strategy? The Irish state now has fewer
jobs than at any time since achieving independence in 1922. In the 1980s
there was an explosion in cost of tax reliefs in Ireland—amounting to 700
billion pounds for the corporate sector alone.[91] The IDA in 1992 claimed to
create 12,056 jobs, which were more than offset by losses. Only 54 percent
of jobs "projected" in the 1980s actually were created.

Over 1981–1991 the Irish netted 7,000 net jobs at a cost of 1.6 billion,
or 228,000 pounds per job. (The IDA estimate of cost per job was 14,300.)
But an investigating review authority into industrial policy set up its own
data unit. Add tax relief plus European Social Fund and other aid and the
figure soars to 500,000 pounds (about $800,000) per job.[92] A Green Party
wag figured on a calculator that the sum could be divided into 18,000 pounds
per unemployed person, who, even at a fraction of the sum, would be
better off as a direct recipient.

SOURCES OF AUSTERITY

The Fine Gael-Labour coalitions of the 1980s stemmed inflation and borrowing levels. In 1987 Fianna Fail, promising "a better way," commenced a
heavier round of cuts in the health and social services. Fianna Fail resumed
bargaining with a battered Trade Union movement that accepted a consultative role in exchange for pay restraint. The government and unions forged
agreements. Fianna Fail also resorted to privatization and sold B & I shipping line at a bargain rate—part of a pattern of rescuing failed public firms
while denying funds to public enterprises that have expansive potential—a
"perverse investment policy."[93]

Fianna Fail took aboard the Progressive Democrats after the June 1989
election. (Fianna Fail fell from 81 to 77 seats while Fine Gael got 55, Labour 15, Workers Party 7, and Progressive Democrats 6.) The coalition
responded to trade unions' demand to close some tax loopholes and be-

tween 1990 and 1992 company tax revenue tripled (83 million to 280 million). There also was a move to increase taxes on bonds and dividends. In December 1991 the government reacted to rising costs and falling revenues by taxing welfare benefits and trying to retract a public sector pay increase. The Progressive Democrats managed to advocate ethical conduct while at the same time urging the state to renege on agreed pay guidelines of the union bargain (3 of 4 citizens opposed breaking this agreement).

The Finance Minister evaded the query whether the government was depressing demand and feeding a downward cycle.[94] The IDA chairman did attribute a drop in Irish firm start-ups (and net job losses in 1991 and 1992) to falls in domestic demand.[95] The deflationary bind was obvious. The government reported that net pay went up in 1990 and 1991, yet other reports note these gains got gobbled by value-added tax (VAT) taxes on phone bills, footwear, and clothing. A rash of company failures followed. As the state cut public capital spending from a half to a third of investment, gross investment rates dropped from 28.4 of GNP in 1982, to 18   percent in 1987 (21.1 percent in 1990).[96] Despite cutbacks the debt rose: in 1986 it was 6,103 for every person, by 1990 it was 7,170.[97] The core problem has been the ideological insistence on treating the debt problem in isolation from reform of industrial policy and of the tax system.

The solutions of the 1950s became, as critics warned, the problems of the 1990s.[98] Why not try more wage restraint? "Wage demands have been moderated since 1987," an Irish analyst dryly observes. "We now have the highest unemployment in the history of the State."[99] The government asserted that since 1989 about 35,000 jobs were created, but there also were 35,000 fewer people at work than a decade before. Economic remedies were not working; and the stance that there was no alternative was wearing thin. "Adjustment fatigue" is what commentators came to call it. Even Garret Fitzgerald suggested a "relaxation of budget constraints" because the gap between economic and social performance is "increasingly intolerable."[100]

SALVATION IN EUROPE?

Can European community funds, a paltry share of collective GNP, bail out Ireland? A vigorous and expensive government campaign was mounted to stave off a seconding of Denmark's nay vote on the treaty. Prime Minister Reynolds denied what was a correctly attributed remark by a government official that the government must "strike terror into the hearts" of the Irish public to win consent for the Maastrict treaty.[101] In June the Irish endorsed the treaty by a 69.1 percent *yes* vote despite many citizens admitting they didn't really know what to make of it.

There was ample room for skepticism about the portrayal of the EC as perfect boon. The Irish failed to gain ground on the affluent members. Irish GNP per capita was 59.2 percent of the EC average in 1973 and 68 percent in 1992. But this gain proves illusory when adjusted for outflow of repatriated funds; the figure then falls to 61.4 percent and may even be lower.[102] This isn't much to show, though most of the Irish Left agree that the way forward is to work inside the community for better bargains. In exchange for endorsement of Maastricht, Premier Reynolds wangled a promise of eight billion pounds for infrastructure spending over seven years. This amounts to one pound in thirteen in the economy although a large chunk derives from tariffs formerly levied by the Irish and now collected by the EC.

The problem of keeping up with the Germans came to the fore when Great Britain and Italy ditched the EC's Exchange Rate Mechanism in September 1992. The Irish punt appreciated against the British pound. This hurt exporters and affected investment via the high interest rates charged to preserve currency value in the Exchange Rate Mechanism. Under speculative pressure that the Irish pound devalued in the Spring of 1993. This experience underscores another adverse aspect of EC monetary rules, which is that the "only competitive leverage left to the states to reduce their manpower costs and improve competitiveness is a dismantling of social service systems." In Spain, Belgium, and Netherlands, "the EMU [European Monetary Union] is cited as a reason for reducing social services."[103]

THE FRAYING COALITION

The unraveling of Fianna Fail-PD (Progressive Democrats) coalition owed more to iniquities than inequities, to scandals rather than to ideologically charged conflict. The Progressive Democrats forced Fianna Fail to chastise its candidate for the presidency in 1990 because of a controversy over his past conduct, thereby damaging his run for the office. Fianna Fail was stung by the victory of the labour's Mary Robinson, who quickly became an immensely popular figure. In 1991 a succession of scandals rocked Fianna Fail. These involved allegations of inside dealing by a cattle exporter, the phone company, the sugar company, the siting of a college, and even the installation of a wind-power device at state expense on the party leader's privately owned island. We cannot delve into all the details. However, the antics of Goodman offer an instructive look at hardy Irish entrepreneurs at work within the state.

In 1987 Goodman, the largest cattle export firm, hankered to export beef to Iraq which, being at war, was a risky market. In Spring 1987 the Goodman CEO, a friend of Premier Charles Haughey and a contributor to Fianna Fail, obtained state insurance for his exports so that if Iraq defaulted Irish taxpayers were stuck with the tab. This was granted despite state reports discouraging the insurance and the fact that Goodman was under investigation for fraud at the time.

Goodman shipped 150 million pounds of beef to Iraq, much of it substandard stuff. The Iraqis—unhappy with the shipment or broke, or both—defaulted. The Irish government canceled the insurance when officials discovered that 40 percent of the beef was not even of Irish origin. Goodman went bankrupt and sued the state. It was not so slick a swindle as the Savings & Loan mess but it's the best Irish operators could do.

A second strand of the scandal was the negotiations with the IDA. "We were talking about picking winners," a former civil servant pleaded. The objective was to concentrate the cattle export industry in the hands of Goodman (with virtual monopoly power over native farmers) and one other firm. To this worthy cause the state would pitch in 90 million pounds. Haughey admitted he "pressurized the IDA to bring forward this scheme."[104] Haughey also pressed the IDA, in May 1987, to drop a "jobs performance" clause that it wanted inserted into the contract.[105]

The scheme never got off the ground but the Goodman inquiry eventually brought the coalition down. Premier Albert Reynolds, who succeeded Haughey, was involved in the deal too. Stung by attacks, Reynolds accused his coalition partner of being "reckless, irresponsible, and dishonest." The furor led to new elections.

THE 1992 ELECTION

Fianna Fail began the election determined to dump the Progressive Democrats. Labour was certain to improve its tally. So, although party leader Albert Reynolds denounced labour's plan to borrow to fund new programmes as "indefensible and irresponsible," another prominent Fianna Failer pleaded with supporters to transfer votes to labour which he said, like Fianna Fail, were "not hung up on" a fetish for "unfettered private enterprise" and had "roots in social radicalism."[106]

Keeping borrowing within parameters was a tough trick. Borrowing was not to exceed 3 percent. Labour proposed a hike from 2.4 to 3.7 percent of GNP to fund self-financing projects. Fianna Fail agreed to halt privatization and to use funds from past privatization for spending instead of debt relief. (Labour leader Dick Spring, like Neil Kinnock in Britain, softened Labour's stance on many issues to attract middle-class votes.) Labour won Fianna Fail's consent to create a state bank for investment via the merger of several existing agencies.

EC funds were to be used for an employment creation fund (which would triple over time) and for public works such as port, road, and rail investments. Mortgage relief was granted to ease pressure from rate hikes for the middle class. Child care payments were improved and there was a pledge to intensify tax-collection and enforcement procedures so as to "ensure equality between those on PAYE, the self-employed, and those with substantial investment incomes."

Special savings accounts with 10 percent tax for investment in Irish equities. Labour pressed for a tripling of housing starts to 3,500, and for an injection of funds to reduce hospital waiting lists and to help HIV/AIDS sufferers. They set up structures for safeguarding rights of consumers and helping the homeless. A National Economic and Social Forum was established to debate policy initiatives. They created three new ministries: Enterprise and Employment; Tourism and Foreign Trade; and Equality. The coalition intended to engage in family law reform and to present another referendum on divorce (which, under a Fine Gael-Labour coalition, would eventually occur in 1995, and pass). The gamble undertaken is that employment can be created via public works spending and training and wage subsidy schemes while the government and the interest groups confer in corporatist settings to devise permanent ways of alleviating the crisis and generating a more equitable scheme of adjustment.

CONCLUSION

Neither political nor economic ideas are neutral.[107] There are "implicit value positions embedded in any analysis of how social institutions operate" and which also condition the choices made in particular situations.[108] Today the "master concepts" of neo-classical economics increasingly diverge from reality: especially the relevance of standard trade theory or the relation of growth to job creation.[109] These debates have enormous policy implications. It is certain that "economic necessity does not predict the society's actual social arrangements" nor does it determine an "optimal" choice.[110]

One observer argues axiomatically that "greater politicization will reduce the coherence of policy and the speed with which adjustments can be taken" because it "reduces the flexibility of both the private sector and the state."[111] But is this the case? There is data attesting that neo-liberal nostrums have not worked well, if at all: "Argentina and Brazil, where several attempts at stabilization occurred, but also Poland and Bolivia, where stabilization was successful, show that the pursuit of the elusive criterion of 'efficiency' can be counter-productive, politically and even economically."[112] The political factors in the economic equation—democratic participation—may be essential for efficiency.[113]

In Ireland there is a strong case for building a vibrant public sector and for exploiting employment and growth potential of indigenous industries.[114] An Industrial Policy Review Group urges the state to promote a "cluster of firms" strategy to exploit sophisticated niche markets. The Central Bank, like the Industrial Review Group, predictably notes that a "radical reform of the tax system is not inconsistent with fiscal consolidation."[115] There are complex connections yet to be made of fiscal policies to industrial policy and to social welfare. But for once in the Irish Republic there is no lack of alternative schemes on the table—and there is half a chance the Irish are moving toward a "normal" pattern of European politics at last.

Notes

1. Countries commonly dubbed "newly industrialized" include "Argentina, Brazil, Greece, Hong Kong, Republic of Korea, Mexico, Portugal, Singapore, Taiwan, and [former] Yugoslavia." In J. P. Lewis and Victoria Kalleb, eds. *U.S. Foreign Policy and the Third World* (New York: Praeger, 1983). Lists vary depending on the criteria applied. Some rankings exclude OECD nations by virtue of this affiliation. In others, Israel is occasionally cited. I include the Irish Republic. In any case the list above is neither exhaustive nor indisputable.
2. Institute of Development Studies, *IDS Bulletin*, 1982, p. 2.
3. Martin Carnoy, Manuel Castells, Stephen S. Cohen, and Fernando Cardoso, *The New Global Economy in the Information Age* (University Park: Pennsylvania State University Press, 1994), p. 36.
4. John G. Ruggie, *The Antinomies of Interdependence* (New York: Columbia University Press, 1983).
5. Ibid., p. 481; also Tony Smith, *The Pattern of Imperialism* (Cambridge: Cambridge University Press, 1979), pp. 69, 77.
6. See Bill Warren, *Imperialism: Pioneer of Capitalism* (New Left Books, 1982); Anthony Brewer, *Marxist Theories of Imperialism* (London: Routledge, Kegan Paul, 1982); Magnus Bjornstrom and Bjorn Hettne, *Development Theory in Transition: The Dependency Debate and Beyond* (London: Zed Press, 1985); and Mary Ann Tetrault and Charles Frederick Abel, eds., *Dependency Theory and The Return of High Politics* (New York: Greenwood Press, 1986).
7. Fernando Cardoso, "Associated Dependent Development," in Alfred Stepan, ed. *Authoritarian Brazil* (New Haven: Yale University Press, 1973), p. 143. Cardoso was elected president of Brazil in 1994.
8. Paul Baran, *The Political Economy of Growth* (New York: Monthly Review Press, 1958) and Andre Gunder Frank, *Capitalism and Underdevelopment in Latin America* (New York: Monthly Review Press, 1969).
9. Ruggie, *Antinomies of Interdependence*, p. vii.
10. Guillermo O'Donnell, *Modernization and Bureaucratic Authoritarianism* (Berkeley, CA: Institute of International Studies, 1973); and O'Donnell's essay in David Collier, *The New Authoritarianism in Latin America* (Princeton: Princeton University Press, 1979).
11. Cardoso and Enzo Faletto, *Dependency and Development in Latin America* (Berkeley: University of California, 1979), p. 175.
12. The term "post-industrial" refers only to science-based, research-intensive industries. A "post-industrialization" strategy employs such industries as the

cornerstone of economic development. This analysis in no way subscribes to
the particulars associated with Daniel Bell's forecasting adventure, *The Coming
of Postindustrial Society* (London: Penguin Books, 1973).

13. On "complex-factor cost industries" and strategies for maximizing competitive
    advantage, see Ira Magaziner and Robert Reich, *Minding America's Business*
    (New York: Harper and Row, 1982), p. 198. Magaziner headed Telesis, an
    organization that figures in later discussion.
14. Peter Katzenstein, "The Small European States in the International Economy:
    Economic Dependence and Corporatist Politics" in Ruggie, *Antinomies of Inter-
    dependence*.
15. Theodore Moran, "Multinational Corporations and Dependency: A Dialogue
    for Dependentistas and Nondependentistas" *International Organization 32*, 1 1978;
    Aidan Foster-Carter, "From Rostow to Gunder Frank," *World Development* 4,
    3 (1976); and Thomas Biersteker, *Distortion or Development?* (Cambridge: MIT
    Press, 1979).
16. The best argument for a "statist approach" is Stephen Krasner's *Defending the
    National Interest*, see Chapter 3.
17. Stephen Haggard and Chung-In Moon, "The South Korean State in the Inter-
    national Political Economy: Liberal, Dependent, or Mercantilist" and in Ruggie,
    Antinomies of Interdependence, p. 161.
18. On the ambiguous relation between state and capital in "state entrepreneur-
    ship," see Peter Evans "Reinventing the Bourgeoisie," in Michael Burawoy
    and Theda Skocpol, eds. *Marxist Inquiries* (Chicago: University of Chicago Press,
    1982).
19. Bob Jessop, *State Theory: Putting Capitalist States in Their Place* (Oxford: Polity
    Press, 1990) and Martin Carnoy, *The State in Political Theory* (Princeton: Princeton
    University Press, 1983).
20. See John Mollenkopf, *The Contested City* (Princeton: Princeton University Press,
    1983) on political entrepreneurship.
21. Robert Keohane, *After Hegemony* (Princeton: Princeton University Press, 1984)
    and Walter Dean Burnham, *The Current Crisis in American Politics* (New York:
    Oxford University Press, 1982).
22. Antonio Gramsci, *Prison Notebooks* (New York: International Publishers, 1971),
    pp. 181–182.
23. Ibid., p. 247.
24. Ibid., p. 182.
25. Hirschman in Collier, *The New Authoritarianism*, p. 65.
26. Barrington Moore Jr., *Reflections on the Causes of Human Misery* (Boston: Bea-
    con Press, 1972), p. 144.
27. See Chapter 3.
28. Evans, *Dependent Development*, p. ii.
29. Fred Block, *The Origins of International Monetary Disorder* (Berkeley: University
    of California, 1977), p. 3.
30. Peter Lange, "Unions, Workers and Wage Regulation" in John Goldthorpe,
    ed., *Order and Conflict in Contemporary Capitalism* (Oxford: Oxford University
    Press, 1984).
31. *Interfutures: Facing the Future* (Paris: OECD, 1979), p. 336.
32. On metropole technology see Lynn Mytelka, "Technological Dependence in
    the Andean Group," *International Organization 32*, 1 (1978) and Frances Stewart
    and Jeffrey James, *The Economics of New Technology in Developing Countries* (London:

Frances Pinter, 1982). On the Indian effort to counter this problem, see Ashok Parasothi "India's Efforts to Build an Autonomous Capacity in Science and Technology," *Development Dialogue* 1, 2 (1979) and Joseph Grieco, "Between Dependency and Autonomy: India's Experience with the International Computer Industry," *International Organization* 36, 3 (1982). Wherein an antidependista conclusion is drawn from remarkably ambiguous evidence.

33. Roy Hofheinz and Kent Calder in, *The East Asia Edge* (New York: Basic Books, 1983) provides a Kiplingesque exemplification of nondemocratic "deference"—indeed a tribute to it. Noting how sparse democratic activity is in regions "where East Asian officials form a caste of oligarchs vying with one another to exercise authority over a deferential and productive society," they continue undismayed to observe "citizens of East Asia, especially the businessmen are comfortable knowing their governments do not change." The assumption seems to be they are productive *because* they are deferential. For a more critical view see Bruce Cumings, "The Origins and Development of the Northeast Asian Political Economy: Industrial Sectors, Product Cycles, and Political Consequences" *International Organization* 38, 1 (1984).

34. Raymond Duvall and John Freeman, "International Economic Relations and the Entrepreneurial States" *Economic Development and Cultural Change* 32, 2 (1984), p. 375.

35. Ibid., p. 391.

36. Desmond Greaves, *The Irish Crisis* (New York: International Publishers, 1974), p. 36.

37. Karl Marx, *Capital* (New York: Modern Library, 1906), pp. 8–9.

38. Raymond Crotty, "Capitalist Colonialism and Peripheralisation: The Irish Case" in Dudley Seers, ed. *Underdeveloped Europe* (Atlantic Highlands, NJ: Humanities Press, 1979), p. 227.

39. Anthony Orridge, "The Blueshirts and the Economic War: A Study of Ireland in the Context of Dependency Theory," *Political Studies* 31, 3 (1974), p. 353; and James Meenan, *The Irish Economy Since 1922* (Liverpool: Liverpool University Press, 1972).

40. Ibid., pp. 364–365.

41. "By 1951 state-sponsored bodies controlled 25 percent of investments and employed 5 percent of all employed workers at a wage 40 percent higher than average" according to P. Beresford Ellis, *A History of the Irish Working Class* (London: Gollancz, 1972). If so, room existed for friction with small capitalists unhappy with the comparatively generous state. Even so, "10% owned 66.7% of land and capital in 1953" by Nevin's estimates.

42. Michael Hechter, *Internal Colonialism* (Berkeley: University of California, 1975), p. 123.

43. Orridge, "The Blueshirts and the Economic War," and Maurice Manning, *The Blueshirts* (Dublin: Gill and Macmillan, 1972).

44. John Sweeney estimates that by the mid-1950s more than half of "Irish" manufacturing assets were controlled by foreign (mostly British) interests "Foreign Companies in Ireland," *Studies* 62 (1973).

45. Tom Garvin, *The Evolution of Irish Nationalism* (Dublin: Gill and Macmillan, 1981); and Erhard Rumpf and A. C. Hepburn, *Nationalism and Socialism in Modern Ireland* (New York: Barnes and Noble, 1977).

46. Sean Lemass was unable to put his most aggressive economic strategies into practice while he was Minister of Industry and Commerce. See Paul Bew and

Henry Patterson, *Sean Lemass and the Making of Modern Ireland* (Dublin: Gill and Macmillan, 1982).

47. See Kieran Kennedy and Brendan Dowling, *The Irish Economy Since 1947* (Dublin: Gill and Macmillan, 1975).

48. *Parliamentary Debates* 1961.

49. Adam Przeworski, "Material Interests, Class Compromise, and the Transition to Socialism" in *Capitalism and Social Democracy* (Cambridge: Cambridge University Press, 1985).

50. Gosta Esping-Anderson, Erik Olin Wright and Roger Friedland, "Modes of Class Struggle and the Capitalist State" *Kapitalistate* (Summer 1976), p. 183.

51. NESC *Industrial Policy and Planning* (Dublin: CSO, 1980), p. 61.

52. Ibid.

53. Robert Kaufman, "Industrial Change and Authoritarian Rule in Latin America: A Concrete View of the Bureaucratic-Authoritarian Model" in Collier *The New Authoritarianism*, pp. 212–213.

54. See J. K. Jacobsen, "Changing Utterly: Irish Development and the Problem of Dependence" *Studies* 67 (1978); Dermot McAleese, *A Profile of Grant-Aided Industry* (Dublin: IDA, 1978); and NESC *Industrial Policy and Planning* 1980.

55. NESC *Prelude to Planning* (Dublin: CSO, 1976), p. 20.

56. McAleese, *A Profile of Grant-Aided Industry*, p. 25.

57. Joe Durkan, "The Irish Economy: The Recent Experience and Prospective Future Performance" in Brendan Dowling and Joe Durkan, eds. *Irish Economic Policy* (Dublin: Economic and Social Research Institute, 1978), p. 47.

58. Interview, January 1977.

59. Raymond Carr, *Puerto Rico: A Colonial Experiment* (New York: Vintage, 1984), p. 227; Jose Vilamil, "Puerto Rico 1948–76: The Limits of Dependent Growth" in Jose Vilamil, ed. *Transnational Capitalism and National Development* (Atlantic Highlands, NJ: Humanities Press, 1978).

60. IDS Bulletin, 1983, p. 25.

61. Sean McDermott, "Multinational Manufacturing and Regional Development," *Scottish Journal of Political Economy* 26, 2 (1979), p. 304; Norman Hood and Stephen Young, *Multinationals in Retreat: The Scottish Experience* (Edinburgh: Edinburgh University Press, 1976).

62. NESC, *A Review of Industrial Policy*, (Dublin: CSO, 1982), p. 33.

63. Ibid., p. 185.

64. *Sunday Tribune*, 17 February 1985.

65. Merritt, *World Out of Work*, p. 22.

66. David Stout, "The Impact of Technology on Economic Growth in the 1980s" *Daedelus* 109, 1 (1980); Simon Nora and Alain Minc, *The Computerisation of Society* (Cambridge: MIT Press, 1981).

67. Cited in Gerhardt Freidrichs and Adam Shaff, eds. *Microelectronics and Society* (New York: Mentor Books, 1983), p. 197.

68. In this period farm income fell precipitously so that a rise in farm tax was off the agenda. The government introduced a 10 percent nominal manufacturing tax in 1981. Tax protests brought as many as half a million people into the streets, which discouraged (though not for long) a rise in "average earner" tax rates. The easiest and most tempting "way out" for a government with a thin electoral edge was to continue to borrow.

69. See Jeff Frieden "The Indebted Emerald Isle" (mimeo, 1984) for a breakdown of the debt and a more pessimistic appraisal.

70. *Sunday Tribune*, 8 January 1985.
71. David Becker, *The New Bourgeoisie and the Limits of Dependency* (Princeton: Princeton University Press, 1983), p. 329.
72. Ibid., p. 278.
73. NESC, *A Review of Industrial Policy*, pp. 232–233.
74. Peter Gourevitch, "Breaking with Orthodoxy: The Politics of Economic Responses to the Depression of the 1930s" *International Organization*, 38, 1 (1984), p. 128.
75. Milton Viorst, "Israel Faces its Economic Woes," *The Nation* 16 March 1985, p. 304.
76. *New York Times*, 11 March 1984.
77. Kaufman, "Democratic and Authoritarian Responses to the Debt Crisis: Argentina, Brazil, Mexico" in Miles Kahler, ed., *The Politics of International Debt* (Ithaca: Cornell University Press, 1986).
78. See Cumings, "Origins of Northeast Asian Political Economy"; IDS Bulletin; Gary Gereffi and Richard Newfarmer, "International Oligopoly and Uneven Development: Some Lessons from Industrial Case Studies," in Richard Newfarmer, ed., *Profits, Progress and Poverty* (South Bend: Notre Dame University Press, 1985), pp. 418–420.
79. Ennio Rodriguez, "The Endogenization of Technological Change," in Osvaldo Sunkel, *Development from Within: Toward a Neo-Structuralist Approach to Latin America* (London: Lynn Rienner, 1993), p. 226.
80. Juan Rada, "The Microelectronics Revolution and the Third World" in Tom Forester, ed. *The Information Technology Revolution* (Oxford: Basil Blackwell, 1985); Gerd Junne, "Automation in the North: Consequences for the Developing Countries' Exports," in James Caporaso, ed. *A Changing International Division of Labor* (Boulder: Lynn Rienner, 1987).
81. Carnoy, "Whither the Nation-State?" in Carnoy, *The New Global Economy in the Information Age*, p. 71.
82. Giles Merritt, *World Out of Work* (London: Collins, 1982).
83. Nathan Rosenberg, *Inside the Black Box: Technology and Economics* (Cambridge: Cambridge University Press, 1982), p. 277. On business views, see the glum survey by *Business International* (1079), p. 68. An American executive observes: "Every businessman I know is trying to run his business with the least number of people. It's understandable. And yet I don't know of a place in the world where finding meaningful employment isn't perhaps the number one problem. Now these two things are absolutely inconsistent."
84. Paul Goodman, *People or Personnel and Like a Conquered Province* (New York: Random House, 1968), p. 76.
85. Figures cited in *Sunday Tribune* (Ireland), 15 November 1992.
86. *The Guardian* (UK), 31 January 1991.
87. *Irish Times*, 29 November 1990, on growth rates; and 26 June 1991, on the ESRI report.
88. Richard Kearney, "Introduction: Thinking Otherwise," in Kearney ed. *Across the Frontiers: Ireland in the 1990s* (Dublin: Wolfhound Press, 1989), p. 7.
89. On the state of the economics discipline in Ireland see Joseph J. Lee's acerbic remarks in his *Ireland 1912–1985*. (Cambridge: Cambridge University Press, 1989).
90. *Irish Times*, 4 October 1992.
91. Ibid., 5 April 1992.
92. *Sunday Tribune*, 29 March 1992.
93. Paul Sweeney, *The Politics of Public Enterprise and Privatisation* (Dublin: Press,

1990), pp. 62–63. He continues: "Thus money was poured into Irish Steel, B&I, Great Southern Hotels and NET when on the brink, but was not given to the profitable companies such as GSH (later), Aer Lingus, Irish Sugar and Irish Life."

94. *Irish Times*, 16 December 1991, p. 8.
95. Ibid., 19 December 1991, p. 16.
96. *Sunday Tribune*, 19 April 1992.
97. *Irish Times*, 11 November 1991.
98. See Paul Bew, Ellen Hazelkorn, Henry Patterson, *Dynamics of Irish Politics* (London: 1990), p. 161.
99. Dick Walsh, "Look Forward to a New Europe but Keep Your Eyes on Home Ground," *Irish Times*, 7 December 1991, p. 12.
100. Ibid., 1 August 1992.
101. *Sunday Tribune*, 26 April 1992.
102. *Irish Times*, 8 March 1992.
103. Ibid., 31 December 1992, Supplement, p. 3.
104. *Sunday Tribune*, 22 March 1992.
105. *Irish Times*, 11 October 1992. Haughey survived a party vote of confidence in November 1991. But the coup de grace was delivered in January 1992 when a former minister attested that Haughey knew of wiretaps on two journalists back in 1982, a charge which he had denied. Under the cumulative weight of these charges, and Progressive Democrat pressure, Haughey resigned.
106. Ibid., 22 November 1992.
107. Fred Block, *Postindustrial Possibilities: A Critique of Economic Discourse* (Berkeley: University of California, 1990), p. 2.
108. Ibid., p. 12. Block criticizes the definitions and roles of GNP, capital, the market and labor; decrying, for example, "a methodology that assumes that increases in output are inherent in the equipment itself and divert attention from the centrality of organizational factors."
109. On trade see John Zysman, *Governments, Markets and Growth* (Ithaca: Cornell University Press, 1983) and Robert Kuttner, *The End of Laissez-Faire* (New York: 1990).
110. Ibid., p. 22.
111. Stephen Haggard, *Pathways from the Periphery* (Ithaca: Cornell University Press, 1991), pp. 160, 234.
112. Adam Przeworski, "Economic Reform in New Democracies: A Social Democratic Approach" (mimeo, University of Chicago, 1992), p. 1.
113. Ibid., pp. 2–3, 18. His arguments are "that (1) reforms that constitute the current standard recommendation—stabilization and liberalization—are necessary but they are not sufficient to restore the capacity to grow unless they are accompanied by active state coordination of the allocation process. (2) Since any reform package must consist of discrete steps taken over an extended period of time, without a social policy which protects at least those whose subsistence is threatened by the reforms, political conditions for their continuation become eroded. (3) Unless the representative institutions play a real role in shaping and implementing the reform policies, the consolidation of democracy may be undermined.
114. Eoin O'Malley, *The Irish Engineering Industry* (Dublin: Economic and Social Research Institute, 1987).
115. *Irish Times*, 9 December 1991, p. 18.

5

The Political Economy
of High Technology

This chapter examines the role that political management plays—and more contentiously, should play—in guiding technological change in the productive structures of advanced industrial societies. The focal point is what I dub the "microchip dilemma": the proposition that in a competitive global economy slow adoption by "firms (relative to other industrial nations) of productivity-increasing technologies is likely to cause more job displacement than the rapid adoption of such technologies."[1] The stark choice posed for citizens is that they consent to new technology and lose some jobs in the short term or else fail to adopt new technology quickly and lose most or all jobs in the long run. As the British Trades Union Congress expressed it: "rapid technological change need not be feared, and indeed a greater danger for the trade union movement is that it may not happen quickly enough."[2] In an era of Schumpeterian creative destruction, industries evidently must "automate or evaporate."

Many readers will recognize that this topic harks back to the 1950s automation debate which I will argue was premature but not preposterous. An alarmist image of technology as a "job killer" (particularly in the United States) vanished in the mid-1960s as employment expanded, living standards improved—and the Vietnam War escalated.[3] Analysts celebrated the newfound capacity of modern capitalist states to correct economic disequilibria through Keynesian means. The "violence of the marketplace" would be a sordid memory for polities that regulated the fiscal-monetary mix of macroeconomic policy, instituted welfare systems (and assorted "stabilizers"), and coordinated activities between public authorities and private actors so as to minimize market uncertainties, resource misallocation, and the underutilization of factors, particularly labor.[4] The linchpin of the "social democratic compromise"—that is, the institutionalization of class conflict—was a credible political commitment by advanced industrial states to sustain full or very nearly full employment through the turbulent patches any dynamic economy undergoes over time. Thus technological change could be viewed by all as more or less a benign phenomenon.

As many OECD economies foundered in the 1970s and 1980s, the specter of "technologically-induced unemployment" revived. The microchip-led "information revolution" ignited a fresh automation debate in which an optimist camp hails microelectronics as the "carrier" of a new "long wave" of economic prosperity while pessimists foresee erosion in job quantities and quality. But the authors surveyed here are wary of extrapolations and are acutely attentive to the *contingent* character of technical change. A French government report, for example, detected in the microelectronics revolution "a contradiction between employment and foreign trade," a succinctly stated thesis that is explored here. Even so, the report took care to identify social determinants that combined to create the alleged "contradiction."[5]

The Nora Report serves as a foil against which to gauge analytical works published a decade later in the debate. These books include: Giovanni Dosi, Christopher Freeman, Richard Nelson, Gerald Silverberg, and Luc Soete, eds. *Technical Change and Economic Theory*; Christopher Freeman and Luc Soete, eds., *New Explorations in the Economics of Technical Change*; Richard Cyert and David Mowery, *Technology and Employment: Innovation and Growth in the U.S. Economy*; Jean Claude Derian, *America's Struggle for Leadership in Technology*; Brian Oakley and Kenneth Owen, *Alvey: Britain's Strategic Computing Initiative*; David Friedman, *The Misunderstood Miracle: Industrial Development and Political Change in Japan*; Shoshana Zuboff, *In the Age of the Smart Machine*; and John Matthews, *Tools of Change: New Technology and the Democratization of Work*.[6]

The volumes edited by Dosi and by Freeman and Soete are macrotheoretical treatments of technological change interlaced with empirical studies. Derian, Cyert and Mowery, and Oakley and Owen conduct studies of the United States and Great Britain. In his case study of Japan, Friedman displays analytical concerns that overlap with Zuboff and Matthews whose books enable us to trace policy actions through to their impact at the workplace level and back again.

This cluster of studies covers the complete cycle of causes and consequences of technical change and their implications for public policy. High technology debates tend to focus on a search for the best policy mix to stimulate diffusion of microelectronics in order to hone a national competitive "edge," a concern that relegates questions regarding the impact of technology on wider social objectives to a peripheral status. Derian, Cyert and Mowery, and Owen and Oakley take this conventional approach. But other recent works "correct" or amend this approach, stressing that effective use and rapid adoption of technology requires a host of facilitating changes in managerial habits and organizational structures—and, for that matter, interests.

The Dosi and Freeman and Soete contributers argue that policy analysis must attend to "the broader societal context: including economic, but also social and ethical factors which will set the conditions within which technological change will be adapted, even selected."[7] Friedman likewise finds:

> politics shapes the context of the industrial rights and roles to which people resort in deciding how the economy should be organized; [in the Japanese machine tool industry] workers came to interpret industrial options and producers to adopt strategies to promote economic recovery in ways ultimately rooted in ideologies and power struggles affecting industrial choices.[8]

These authors, together with Zuboff and Mathews, also demonstrate how efficiency increases when linked to equity-enhancing measures. Their arguments are persuasive and in this Chapter I endorse an analytical agenda that demands a wider definition of what counts as "politics" in order to comprehend industrial choices. All these works challenge assumptions that self-equilibrating market forces or existing policy mechanisms will suffice to improve economic competitiveness and maintain social stability.[9] Beneath more obvious causes of economic shifts and shocks, they detect another "great transformation" in which Polanyi's "double movement" recurs: that is, (1) a reassertion of the market as a organizing principle (extremely so in what was formerly the Eastern bloc), legitimated by technological "imperatives" and trade pressures; and (2) political countermovements organized on the basis of the "principle of social protection."[10]

Even those scholars who reject the job "killer" or "de-skiller" arguments foresee persisting mismatches between labor skills and available employment, and acknowledge the many potential ways in which a haphazard diffusion of new technologies can aggravate social inequalities. The authors suggest with varying degrees of audacity, policy prescriptions to meet problems the microelectronics revolution poses for public administrative capacities, the adaptability of economic sectors, and the economic theories that inform policy choices. This chapter explores the rationales for and the determinants of policy responses to the "microchip dilemma" in advanced industrial democracies and argues that the dilemma can be got round under certain conditions that I identify—particularly changes in the institutional structures and in the ideas that guide industrial policies and practices.

PROMOTING HIGH-TECH: MILITARY ORIGINS AND COMMERCIAL IMPERATIVES

The high-tech label applies to industries in which "new product development involves large development costs, long lead times, and considerable technological uncertainty" and "rely in significant ways on knowledge that is close to the frontiers of present-day scientific research."[11] These industries include computers, robotics, fiber optics, biotechnology, aerospace, artificial intelligence, telecommunications and microelectronics. The list overlaps and is not exhaustive. Microelectronics is the most vital element because it undergirds, pervades, and enhances all other technological advances and promises to revitalize "lower-tech" industries like steel, autos, and even garments. The advance of microelectronics is rapid in its pace of development and extremely wide in scope of applications. These widely publicized achievements need not be repeated here.

The U.S. government, and primarily the Department of Defense, played the crucial role nurturing the industry through grants and its procurement policies, so that Rosenberg deemed it "the most outstanding success story in terms of government policy to stimulate technical progressiveness, growth and employment in the postwar period."[12] Another analyst answers with "a fairly clear "no" the question whether private interests could have developed the computer industry even remotely at the pace of the state-aided program.[13]

Military Keynesianism is often cited as a key component of a covert industrial policy. Programs linked to national security needs usually win approval of conservative legislators. In the last decade several defense programs were "sold to Congress as a response to industry's eroding technological leadership."[14] It is difficult to think of high-tech product devoid of defense applications, so this is—or was until the end of the cold war—an attractive rationale by which "free market" supporters in the United States and Great Britain can keep their consciences at bay while furnishing aid to these industries.

In the United States these implicit dual-purpose programs include National Science Foundation funding (which increasingly favors applied projects), the Defense Department's Division of Applied Research and Advanced Projects (DARPA) which in turn supported the Very High Scale Integrated Circuits (VHSIC) project, the 1983 Strategic Computing Initiative, and a share in the public-private Sematech Corporation in 1987. Anti-trust regulations were also relaxed in 1982 for formation of a pioneering industrial consortium, the Microelectronics and Computer Technology Corporation. All these measures were driven at least as much by economic rivalry with Japan as by fear of likely military rivals. In Europe Oakley and Owen observe that Japan's announcement of a "fifth generation" project "made it respectable to use public funds on a large scale" in information technology projects like France's *Plan Filiere Electronique* and Britain's Alvey, both of which had a significant defense component.[15] Ronald Reagan's startling Strategic Defense Initiative (SDI) likewise dangled before participants the seductive prospect of reaping industrial advantages.

However, in appraising the Strategic Defense Initiative, Rosenberg finds that "it reinforces the impression that the military and civilian sectors confront increasingly divergent needs because of 'unique military requirements' that are of little use or relevance to manufacturers of civilian products."[16] The urgent public policy task, which Derian argues military R & D now hinders, is to shift investment patterns to align with the upswing of a new "long wave," a concept drawn from an innovation-based theory of growth. Microelectronics is nominated as the successor to earlier "basic innovations" (steam and looms, coal and transport, steel and autos, oil and consumer durables) that propelled four previous long waves.

Despite a sharp mid-1980s industry-wide downturn, technical advances continuously decrease production costs (though the expense of chip-making equipment and laboratories soars), greater complexity and packing density per chip, product price plummets, and improvements in reliability, custom capability and power consumption. By now it is a cliche to say that the design and applications are limited only by imagination—and, as I also emphasize, institutions. If "innovations carry the Kondratiev" waves, there is no more conspicuous candidate for the role of revitalizer of first world economies.

What is to be done and who is to do it? Derian advises the United States to shift resources from "sheltered" industries—which manufacture "complex custom-made products for a few sophisticated customers" such as the Air Force—to "exposed" commercial enterprises. These two sets of firms work at "frontiers of knowledge" in distinct arenas characterized by different logics of competition; their products and processes do not cross the boundary easily. Cyert and Mowery find that since the mid-60s, and perhaps earlier, there have been "declining commerical pay-offs from military R & D." After deducting defense-related funds from total R & D they found that over 1961–1985, U.S. spending was surpassed by France, Japan, and West Germany.[17]

In 1990 U.S. nondefense R & D comprised 2 percent of GNP versus Japan's 2.9 percent ($47 billion more) and Germany's 2.6 percent ($31 billion more). The upshot is that the direction of spin-off between military and civilian applications has reversed. In the 1980s DARPA funded both the VHSIC research program and the Strategic Computing Initiative in hope of capturing know-how from commercial enterprises. In turn these firms would use the results to develop marketable products, a process that has proved unsatisfactory.[18]

Derian encourages U.S. policymakers to pursue collaborative ventures in research and in product development and marketing, such as the $1.5 billion Sematech project jointly funded by private manufacturers and the Pentagon. The United States, he says, cannot afford the "mirage" of development fostered by superiority in perfecting esoteric products with little commercial spin-off.[19] With a few exceptions defense industries perform unimpressively outside the realm of cost-plus contracts. Boeing and Grumman failed in their ventures into public transport products. Raytheon, the second largest defense contractor and manufacturer of the controversial Patriot missile systems in the Gulf War, is much less adept at making and marketing household appliances and small civilian aircraft.[20]

Among the remedies urged are more grants, tax breaks to stimulate industrial R & D and the creation of a government department, other than the de facto one of defense, devoted to the commercial technology base. Derian also wants U.S. firms to collaborate with European partners to fend off the Japanese, whom U.S. firms instead are embracing in hordes of joint ventures (Motorola-Toshiba, AMD-Sony, RCA-Sharp, Intel-Oki, Fairchild-Hitachi) and very nearly the purchase of a White House-approved stake in Moore Special Tool Co. (a manufacturer of nuclear weapons components).[21]

Joint ventures alone only allow proficient foreign firms to gain capital from weaker partners while keeping control over innovation and strategy. So there is no substitute for an active state policy in these competitive times. The pragmatic need is such that even in Britain a doctrinaire conservative government became a 'cooordinater and catalyst,' appointed a minister for information technology, and grudgingly launched (with "no new money") the five-year Alvey project. In the event, much more catalyzing than coordinating went on. Alvey's director tactfully noted, for example, how "ironic" it was that university cutbacks resulted in reducing the number of engineering and computer science personnel that the state, via other conflicting policies, wished to expand.[22] After Alvey, policies remain rigorously uncoordinated even if they improved upon an earlier attitude, recalled by Reay Atkinson of the Department of Industry's Information Technology (IT) division.[23]

> In 1979 Keith Joseph asked me and my division to produce a report on information technology . . . We put the report together which, infelicitously, we headed "A strategy for information technology." I remember Lord Trenchard, the industry minister, responding: "Atkinson, what is this bloody nonsense? We don't have strategies in this government."

Alvey intended to foster precompetitive research and a "collaborative culture" of academics and industrialists. The single and, for the authors, untroublesome issue was "How to organize Britain's effort to the best advantage of industry." What happened? Academic institutions forked out more money than anticipated. Scholars performed well while firms—Plessey, British Telecom and others—came and went pretty much as they pleased.[24] Alvey applied a thin layer of funds—a tiny fraction of U.S. allocations—in its broad mandate to build on industrial strengths and "to plug gaps." Oakley and Owen, like Derian, do offer interesting insights. The Alvey volume contains a valuable set of competing appraisals of policy guidelines for consideration whenever a United Kingdom government decided to impose some direction on an individually impressive but motley array of research institutions, science parks, training councils, and whatnot.

Still, there is nothing particularly novel in the prescriptions or in the scope of analysis of these works, which assume that once concerns about competitiveness are met everything else will sort itself out. But placing civilians, even the Business Roundtable or the Confederation of Business Industries, in control of policy is hardly likely to resolve problems in introducing and accommodating new productive technology. We next examine the reasons why.

RIDING THE FIFTH WAVE

A dominant theme in recent literature is that socio-organizational changes (institutional, managerial, legal, and educational) are essential if technical innovations are to flourish in socially benign ways. Progress is not merely a matter of finding the right promotional schemes. This view is promoted vigorously by what might well be dubbed the "Sussex School," comprising personnel within and scholars influenced by the Science Policy Research Unit at the University of Sussex. In an earlier and formative work Freeman, Clark and Soete focus on job-generating aspects of long waves, and offer radical Keynesian prescriptions for an environment in which, they contend, technical change is eroding the premises of neoclassical economics and of the demand-management version of Keynesianism.[25]

Freeman and coauthors add technical change to the usual impediments to equilibrium growth: time lags, undetermined expectations, limited factor substitution, and wage and price inelasticities due to oligopolistic practices. Thus, they raise "the possibility of technological unemployment which results from technical change but is dependent on institutional constraints to adaptation."[26]

There are many long-wave theories, all controversial.[27] The version favored by the Sussex researchers, who fill the Dosi and the Freeman/Soete volumes, posits that in a boom period new industries avidly exploit the commercial potential (or "trajectory") of interrelated "technology systems," install new capacity, stimulate associated capital goods production and secondary investments, and so create many jobs. These new and mostly small firms are labor-intensive because the technology is in a "fluid state" and production is not standardized. But "as the sustained expansion generates labor shortages and inflationary pressures on labor costs, so profitability tends to decline" and there is increasing induced demand for labor-saving technical innovation throughout the economy.

> [As] a new industry or technology matures, several factors are interacting to reduce the employment generated per unit of investment. Economies of scale become increasingly important and these work in combination with technical changes and organizational changes associated with increasing standardization. The profits of innovation are diminished both by competition

and by pressures on input costs, especially labour costs. A process of concentration tends to occur . . .[28]

Markets are saturated and surplus capacity occurs. Investment is chan-
nelled primarily into productivity-enhancing rationalization so that even when
investment expands during successive "upswings as a result of Keynesian and
other stimuli, it has less effect on employment, unless it is directed to areas
of very low capital intensity such as government and administrative services."[29] They supply data attesting that since the 1960s ever higher incre-
ments of output, growth, and investment have been required to generate a
given level of employment.[30] The trend was manifest in France, West Germany, Italy, and the United Kingdom in the mid-1960s. The United States
created 25 million jobs over 1975–85 but at a high cost of productivity and
competitiveness—and the quality of those jobs is a source of great controversy.[31] Even Japan comes under sway of the trend in the late 1970s.

The fundamental problem for researchers as well as policymakers is a change
occurring in the "techno-economic paradigm," which is "a cluster of interrelated technical, managerial, and organizational innovations, whose advantages are to be found not only in a new range of products and systems, but
most of all in the dynamics of the relative cost structure of all possible
inputs to production," with the contemporary "paradigm shift" moving from
technology based on "cheap inputs of energy to one predominantly based
on cheap inputs of information derived from advances in microelectronics
and telecommunications technology."[32] Ignoring this fundamental ongoing
change leads to flawed policy choices. How so?

The Sussex authors find that Carter's 1977–78 "reflation in one country"
strategy—repeated with similar results in France over 1981–83—exemplifies
the futility of demand-management measures that are insensitive to the uneven distribution and differential impact of technical change across sectors
and industries with varying capital, marketing, and research resources.[33] But
monetarist policies are deemed more pernicious because, apart from their
human toll, they protract periods of periods of low business expectations.
An excessive scrapping of capacity impedes the next upturn because of a
shortage of productive potential. In the United Kingdom, where the manufacturing share of GNP dropped 7.6 percent in a decade to 21.9 percent in
1987, the "leaner, fitter" survivors struck many critics as exhibiting a condition "more like emaciation."[34]

In a recessionary climate many British companies "cannot cut the work
force significantly without cutting production because they [have already]
shed so much fat."[35] Overall, the differential capacity of firms to absorb
innovations means that (1) firms with high demand-expansion potential will
exploit opportunities provided by new technology, (2) industries with low
demand-expansion potential will scrap capacity and resort to labor-saving

investment, and (3) small firms, which are either unable or unwilling to install new equipment, intensify their work processes. None of the above generates much demand for jobs or skills. Hence the authors urge governments to adopt specific microinterventionist technology policies.

In the United Kingdom, after 1973, analysts found that workplace rationalization was more important than technical change as a source of job loss.[36] This outcome was not a straightforward "response" to externally imposed influences but was as much a result of the government's adjustment strategy which changed the balance of power between capital and labour across production sites and so conditioned the calculations managers make regarding the costs and benefits of different types of investment.[37] The implication is that if a Tory (or, as in 1974–79, rightward-leaning Labour) government curbs labour's bargaining power the impact may be to diminish incentives to invest in new technologies, and there is evidence that this has been the case in the United Kingdom.[38]

In 1981 the Thatcher government dispensed 12 million pounds to promote (CAD/CAM) technology but fewer than 250 of 2000 private firms contacted installed such devices within the first three years—though the number rises after 1984 with the economic upturn.[39] Hence, the institutional foundations for low growth were laid through political decisions more than through sheer technological change. Neither macroeconomic explanations nor an abstract "logic of capitalist development" suffice to account for shifts in the forms of productive investment and their employment effects. State policy, which is the outcome of wider social contests (which in turn reflect the historically given structures shaping those contests), mediates the internal impact of economic forces all the way down to the workplace level. In short, there are distinct *political* causes of "technological unemployment."

The Sussex authors affirm Schumpeter's prediction that the largest firms would "bureaucratize" research, creating a "strong feedback loop from successful innovation to increased R & D . . . leading to increased market concentration." Small firms provide key innovations but the superior capital and marketing capabilities of large firms enable them to play "fast imitator" and buy out smaller dynamic firms as "captive suppliers," as in the exemplany case of General Motors.

Three cogent objections can be raised to the foregoing analysis. First, the authors commit the "lump of labor" fallacy wherein one neglects price and productivity elasticities that enlarge demand, output, and job totals. A National Academy of Sciences study, for example, contends that "reductions in labor requirements per unit of output from new process technologies have been and will continue to be outweighed by the beneficial employment effects of the expansion of total output that generally occurs."[40] Second, one should acknowledge that technical change can be capital-saving, too.

Third, a growing demand for customized small batch goods may undermine corporate efforts to concentrate production and maintain "Fordism." This latter term refers to a set of capitalist institutions that successfully wed mass production techniques to mass consumption in a self-sustaining growth cycle.[41] (The homely example is Henry Ford's policy of paying assembly line workers a high wage, thereby increasing both productivity and the purchasing power of the consumer.)

The Sussex School replies that "price elasticity of output" (demand) and the "productivity elasticity of prices" (the degree to which productivity rises allow product prices to fall) are weakened by trends toward concentration. On the second point, capital-saving technologies exert labor-saving effects insofar as they reduce the "depth of production," eliminating layers of service workers which indeed is an explicit goal of many industries from motor vehicles to banking.[42] This second objection also contains the crucial implication that technological *design* is a socially determined variable. The third objection stems from analysts such as Piore and Sabel who foresee that the new "flexible specialization" technologies required to meet modern consumer tastes inherently favor small entrepreneurial firms and more democratic work regimes.[43] Friedman takes his cue from Piore and Sabel in arguing that "political struggle throughout society cumulatively defines the rights that structure an economy toward either mass or flexible production."[44]

Flexible specialization is rated the potential successor to the "Fordist model" of mass production and mass consumption.[45] Friedman shows that Japanese commercial success was less the product of Ministry of International Trade and Technology (MITI) savants than of a wide range of commercial contests that were responsible for an expansion of small producers who were able to resort to small-scale general purpose machinery to build goods more flexibly and thereby enable the state to pursue "an aggresive strategy of constantly differentiating products to break up [and enter] mass markets."[46] But there is little evidence to suggest that the advent of more flexible producer goods inherently deters industrial concentration or even that they necessarily improve productivity.[47] Matthews marshals a host of examples to support his argument that democratized "post-Fordist" workplaces are superior in productivity performance to rigid mass production organization, but that is a different kind of claim, which says nothing about scale.[48]

That these counterarguments may still be judged as pertinent is very much the Sussex School's point: the direction of technical change, they say, is contingent on institutional variables which are politically shaped. Three decades is too short a span in which to assess costs and benefits because a host of facilitating changes of social and institutional structures are necessary to realize their full productive potential. In contrast to literature a decade ago, and after a good many industrial trials, the direction the debate on high technology has taken is not whether but how best to go about accomodating workplace organization to new technology—and on whose terms.

THE POLITICS OF TECHNICAL CHANGE

The key macroconcepts deployed in the Dosi volume are "techno-economic paradigm" and "regimes of regulation," the latter being "the whole set of institutions, private behavior, and actual functioning of the various markets which channel the long-term dynamics and determine the cyclical properties of the economy during an historical period for a given society."[49] This term overlaps exactly with what Gordon, Edwards, and Reich (1982) dub the "social structure of accumulation" which is the "institutional environment within which accumulation occurs (including the pattern of state involvement in the economy, the character of class conflict, interindustry relations, and the nature of the money and credit systems)."[50] Institutional reconstruction is a matter of matching organizational structure to new techniques and market conditions. It is also the object of "sharp group conflicts about the distribution of relative costs and benefits" that alternative schemes of institutional change portend.

Each long swing is associated with a distinct "social structure of accumulation." Stable growth resumes when the contest over which groups will determine the key features of this new structure or the "regime of regulation" is resolved. Ideological "habits" and traditions can impede the search for appropriate institutions and practices. There rarely is a "best way" of organizing either an economy or a workplace, and economic strategies tend to be varying amalgams of data-based designs and power-retention tactics. Hence, the struggle.[51] Where these aspects of strategy conflict, economic logic, at least in the short term, tends to get short shrift: just witness the rise of supply-side Reaganomics. This is the case the Sussex School makes against monetarist policies. In the new environment technical change is increasingly capital-using so that investment increases as a fraction of GNP to avert a shortage of productive potential, so demand (which the shortage chokes) must rise with productivity growth in order that both employment and productivity improve. This feat is judged to be beyond the reach of monetarism or standard Keynesianism. Freeman and his colleagues argue instead for a directive mix of macro- and micro-economic intervention, a targeted technology policy via exploratory subsidies (instead of "picking winners"), expanded training, diffusion of innovations in the public sector, negotiating "multilateral agreements of prices and incomes on semipermanent basis," and encourage industrial democracy because a broad responsibility for, and diffusion of the rewards of, technical change will hasten the adoption of "growth-oriented abut anti-inflationary policies."

Examining Japanese success, Freeman cautions against knee-jerk adoption of their organizational modes. In the corporatistic German and Scandinavian cases high productivity and skill formation derived from successfully pressing strategies that accorded with indigenous institutions and with their sociopolitical context.[52] German companies "faced up to competitors by concentrating on high quality goods, produced in small batches at high prices" in flexible specialization style, while British firms, because of low skills, are "forced to compete with those in the Third World, producing large quantities cheaply" and at much lower wages.[53] There are alternatives to gravitating toward the "militarized approach to social order" in Japan; ironically, the Fifth Generation project, to get the creative juices flowing, entailed establishing work zones in which Japanese researchers could "behave more like relaxed Westerners."[54]

The search for alternatives will be discouraged if citizens (1) are inured to lower expectations, (2) are persuaded there is no alternative, or (3) conclude that opposing domestic groups and/or international forces are too strong. If these conditions obtain, the "microchip dilemma"—"a contradiction between employment and foreign trade"—is depoliticized. Acute and protracted adjustment pains can provoke a policy crisis—that is, a crisis of authority for the coalition in charge of formulating the "social structure of accumulaton" in a manner that reconciles exploitation of economic trajectories with political stability.[55] But given the actual relatively gradual diffusion of technology and, in wealthy countries, a fall-off in demographic pressure, this seems a minor threat.[56]

Still, in public discourse "progress," "technology," and "market" are words that are suffused with ideologically-charged meaning, usually connoting implacable autonomous forces that compel single optimal responses. The criteria defining what is optimal (for whom and for what purposes) are a crucial concern in the political struggle to control the character of the social structure of accumulation. In the political arena contending groups strive to portray their policy preferences as logically irresistible, as practical necessities, and as immaculately attuned to the public interest. A propensity to invoke teleological concepts is not a unique fault of mechanistic versions of marxism, it is a staple tactic in policy debate. Any inquiry into the assumptions guiding technological design "appears increasingly inseparable from a scrutiny of the forces which shape them."

Shop-floor workers are no less appreciative than Ivy League economists of the value of technological change. It is not technology that is the target of criticism but rather the specific societal groups whose interests are embodied in the design stage. Remarkably, management tends to be the greater source of resistance.[57] If anything, lower-skill workers acceded easily to technological "imperatives."[58] Only if technology ceases to be viewed as an autonomously evolving "public good" can it be politicized and become the legitimate object of struggles in the workplace and at national levels to decide its purposes and limits. To what extent public debate exerts influence on policy outcomes will be conditioned by a country's institutions, political structures and channels, and economic pressures—with Sweden (and, more ambiguously, Japan) appearing at the more dynamic end of the participatory spectrum and the United States and United Kingdom at the other.

SHAPING TECHNOLOGY: A "TRICKY MATTER"

The French Nora Report characterized microtechnology as "practically an alteration of nature" and argued that the integration of computers with telecommunications ("telematics") increases unemployment while improving competitive capacity. The short term remedy is "a double policy, consolidating hyper-competitive sectors, and generating, through transfers, an increase in amenities and collective consumption . . . a tricky matter."[59] In light of world market difficulties and the diffusion of microtechnology to the service sector, the authors judge that the chances that market growth can compensate for jobs lost from productivity gains is "hardly plausible." The Nora Report acknowledges that adjustment was imperative, yet it was unusually attentive to problems the new technologies pose for the social stability. Successful adjustment implies a "massive computerization" that, as the Sussex School similarly argues, upsets orthodox assumptions about the relation of economic growth to job creation, hence a new "model of growth, aimed at stimulating new kinds of demand" must be devised.

The Nora Report's model derived from recommendations floated within Japan's Ministry of International Trade and Industry (which, incidentally, went unheeded). The state should aim to establish a "precise mix" between trade-exposed sectors, where the premium is on productivity and profit, and trade-sheltered sectors where job creation has priority. The latter can expand to the extent permitted by demand for collective amenities, import content level and a social willingness to transfer trading sector surplus.[60] This scheme would channel demand into collective goods projects guaranteeing outlets for industries using the home market as a "laboratory" to refine products for export. In effect, this is a dirigiste version of product cycle theory. But this scheme presupposed the achievement of a social consensus, a task beyond even (and perhaps especially) the most sophisticated social engineers. Intervention of this kind and of this scale tends to make the various interests at work more visible, thus mobilizing opposition. Taking the supposedly exemplary Japanese case in close-up, Friedman cites a long and unbroken litany of failures by MITI to channel investment: "the political strength of the firms involved led to a system in which bureaucrats provided financial incentives while industrialists controlled actual economic activity."[61] Nonetheless, this is indisputably a form of state-corporate cooperation. No one denies that such cooperation was crucial to Japanese success.

Regardless who controls whom, states will intervene. Few industrial democracies can permit global economic trends to dictate the pace as well as the direction of competitive adjustment and technical change and to allocate risks and losses. Even in the United Kingdom training is an issue in conservative as well as labor ranks. Researchers report huge training gaps between the British and the German (and, less so, the French and the Dutch) clothing industries, a situation that is "probably typical" of U.K. companies facing foreign competition. So the British state confronts a critical "chicken or the egg" question: do trained workers breed higher profits, or vice versa?[62] Forecasts suggest that the supply of skills does not create its own demand, at least not in a climate of low demand growth and in the absence of state provisions. British training funds, public, and private, are low. Training expenditures by manufacturers fell from 1.8 percent of total labor costs in 1981 to 1.3 percent in 1988 while those of European competitors increased.[63] In the long run (*pace* Keynes) economic competition may favor the adoption of a "high-skilled, high-wage" policy, but whenever it happens it will be cold comfort to the losers of market shares and jobs.

One policy task is to remedy a perennial collective action problem of capitalist firms: that the individual units will not and/or cannot supply resources required to promote collective prosperity. Instead of relying on employer-led Training and Enterprise councils, a prudent objective even for a "voluntarist state" is to make compulsory provisions for the funding of training that firms are unlikely to provide for themselves. The French have a minimum percentage (1.2 percent) of company payrolls set aside for upgrading skills. A rather more robust model is the Swedish Training (Renewal) Fund, enacted in 1985 and financed by a 10 percent levy on company profits. This model stemmed from centralized trade union representation in an industrial relations system embedded within a pro-labor and interventionist state.[64]

Conquering the "microchip dilemma" will demand a keen analytical appreciation of the manner in which policies enacted at state or international regime-level affect the politics of technical choice down through the shop-floor level. Nothing short of this will suffice as a dynamic political economy of high technology. But to create such a macroconceptualization is a very demanding task. No one claims as yet to have a "completely satisfactory alternative to the dominant theory."[65] The point, however, is that the microchip dilemma stems neither from pure market demands nor from "autonomous technological development." The dilemma is ultimately political. Its determinants and consequences can be grouped under the four headings: (1) automation, (2) socioinstitutional change, (3) ideology, and (4) the international dimension.

DILEMMA OR PROBLEM?

I. AUTOMATION

The authors do not underestimate how difficult it is to distinguish "technological unemployment" from job displacement resulting from other sources. All authors agree that macroeconomic factors are more important at present. One can, however, make the case that trade-displaced jobs are ultimately lost because of superior technology deployed in competitor nations.[66] Microtechnology penetrates and creates simultaneous savings in all sectors. Some early estimates of job loss were overstated, but there is scant reason to believe that losses will automatically be offset by job creation elsewhere.[67] Even a relatively optimistic scholar finds no reason to doubt that "the marginal-employment dividend of new investment in technology is low."[68]

The spread of high-tech automation is not a panacea for what ails business. The 1950s' automation debate was premature because forecasters did not account "for the long time lags in building up a capital goods supply industry and a components industry on a sufficient scale," misjudged the time needed to train personnel, and erred in estimates of the rate at which the relative costs of labor and capital begin to favor the latter.[69] The factors inhibiting investment include high software costs, aversions to investing in rapidly changing and cheapening technology, reluctance to rely on fragile equipment, skill shortages and a myriad of debugging problems. As noted above, monetarist policies negate the inflationary levels of demand, the wage pressures and the volumes of government regulation per employee that motivate firms to replace labor with machinery.

On the other hand, the abiding motives to automate include: trimming middle-management salaries, improving stock quality, economizing on inputs and inventory (including Japanese "just-in-time" techniques), increasing safety, and maximizing production flows.[70] But these factors are secondary to, and are largely derived from, the scale of profitable opportunities offered by nations' policy environments and global economic trends.

Marxists argue that a shifting threshold of profitability will hold a total automation scenario at bay. Capitalists cannot automate to the degree technology allows because "if wage earners push for full employment, production becomes more capital intensive [to avert upward wage pressure]; if workers push toward liberation of labor power, production becomes more labor intensive [as capitalists strive to avoid transferring 'surplus' via the state to unused labor]."[71] There is a "basic contradiction between the increase in fixed capital and accelerated obsolescence" imposed by continuous innovation resulting in "valorization": problems, increasing corporate debt, and in an ambivalent dependence on state resources.[72] Still, if there is one clear historical tendency in Western capitalism it is that contradictions tend to get counteracted. This never occurs automatically and will require socio-organizational changes if states are to adjust productive structures to new economic patterns in politically palatable ways.

II. SOCIO-ORGANIZATIONAL CHANGE

The good news is that the pace of labor displacement is moderated by the foregoing factors; the bad news is that laggard adoption of technology creates cumulative trade difficulties that are likely to compel countries to undertake either harsh adjustment schemes or protectionist measures, or a mingling of both. In the absence of policies geared to reconcile social needs with exploitation of technological product "trajectories" the microchip dilemma could take a corrosive hold. Are there alternatives?

There are some encouraging if not easily emulated experiences: particularly in the small European states deploying "domestic compensatory mechanisms" to complement an "aggressive marketing orientation based on specialized export production."[73] Unemployment typically has been lowest in nations with comprehensive labor market institutions: Norway, Sweden (until lately), Austria, Luxemburg—though even they are not immune to rocky economic times.[74] Industrial policy proponents say the road to prosperous growth is paved with programs that enhance the competitive advantage of skilled labor.[75]

This is the outcome engendered by the "German-Scandinavian model" in which the "rights of employees, enforced by the state make it easier for workers and unions in these countries to negotiate about change in the organization of work."[76] Marxists are skeptical about whether the "high training, high-tech" scenario is plausible because it "undermines the entire hierarchical structure of factory and economy, without which the extortion of surplus value from productive labor is impossible."[77] One need not subscribe to iron laws of capitalism (or generic industrialism) to suspect that management may not welcome the erosion of authority that an expanded, skilled work force portends.

In a study of several service industries Zuboff finds "hierarchical power" is the major barrier to the unfolding of a democratic division of labor wherein "mental" and "manual" tasks eventually blend. Although some deskilling occurs in the process of automating, technologies have the effect of transferring managerial tasks into a collective base to which employees must have access if they are to do their jobs well. In short, the workers take on managerial responsibilities—or would if managers would let them.[78] This Harvard Business School lecturer's account accords with Noble's tale of General Electric's shop floor war over control of numerically controlled tools, resulting in what appeared to be a calculated trade-off of productivity gains for control. (Other studies indicate situations in which capitalists choose more profits and less efficiency over the reverse distribution as in, for an egregious example, the U.S. health care industry.)[79] Noble also contends that technological advance is impeded by inadequate accounting of socio-organizational influences at the design stage, and at the operational level.[80] How technology is adapted to a given work environment depends on the pattern of authority and the purposes of the most powerful actors (whose plans, of course, may go awry).

Piore and Sabel admit that "computers adapt to any environment"—including presumably the authoritarian mass production mode they assert is being superseded by flexible specialization. Matthews, too, argues that in the fullness of time the Fordist mode will be surpassed by post-Fordist firms boasting multiskilled, training oriented, and partcipatory workplace regimes churning out high production and profits. But one cannot sit back and wait for it. Strategies are outlined and concrete examples cited of ways in which unions can take the initiative in putting industrial relations on a footing based on "mutual advantage that capital and labor derive from a productive and efficient enterprise that is grounded in respect for human skill and ingenuity."[81] Among the examples are Australian Telecom, Swedish Volvo, Ericcon, German Volkswagen, and ESPRIT's project in human-centered CIM systems. The catch in Matthews's cooperative model is that businesses do not always want to play. If this energetically democratic and efficient post-Fordist system is to emerge, the rub is that there is probably no substitute for having a labor-controlled party formally in charge of the state.[82] Quite a prerequisite!

State policy influences the balance of power in workplaces, so it is no surprise that socio-organizational changes—from labor markets to technology agreements—are enacted swiftly in corporatist states with centralized labor organizations and potent labor-oriented parties. Although these states are best poised to navigate prudently between social needs and economic competitiveness, their success is by no means assured. In 1985 the European Commission joined with the European Trade Union Confederation to promote a "social dialogue" document on participation in technological decisions. In 1987 the trade unions simply ratified the venerable principle that final decisions on technology belong to the employer.[83] In the case of technology agreements forged in Belgium in 1983 (under government pressure), analysts find that the national agreement, despite strict clauses, had only a "marginal impact" on choices, because the workers "still did not question management prerogatives" and because technology is "still viewed as an autonomous factor."[84]

III. IDEOLOGY

The "automate or evaporate" dilemma also stems from ideological premises. Potent notions—call them "automaticities"—can appear independent of human agency and capable of constraining human agents. The "free market" is one example; "autonomous technology" is another. When intertwined, these inherently political and cultural categories yield a "Darwinian View of technological development." If existing technologies have ever been "put to rigorous tests,"

> it has typically been only after the decisions were made to invest social surplus in their development and use, and these decisions were based not only upon mere guesses as to their technical and economic potential but also upon the political interests, enthusiastic expectations, and culturally sanctioned compulsions of those few with the power to make them.[85]

This restricts social awareness of the variability of technical change, market relations, and of their interaction—thereby imparting a sense of artificial fatedness to certain policy preferences. In other words, the microchip dilemma needs to be disentangled from a "damned if you do, damned if you don't" plight and be portrayed more accurately as a *problem* of social power and choice. If, for example, a "right-to-work" system (employing all comers at a median wage) were imposed this requirement would soon be reflected in the design of productive technologies, workplace organization, and the structure of decision making from the work site to the state level as in Sweden.[86]

A major benefit of such demystification would be a reduction in the pressure for protectionism. As the "dislocation costs" of domestic retooling rise, the distribution of costs and the regulation of the pace of adjustment predictably become political issues. Policy debate may take two not mutually exclusive forms: (1) how to allocate the social surplus generated by new technology to citizens "freed" from labor, and (2) how to restore full employment at the postwar norms of 2 to 4 percent. Whether or not domestic mechanisms (training programs, labor-market boards, etc.) can moderate the costs of adjustment, labor and labor-oriented parties would be ill-advised to press for less than full employment (vital for bargaining power) since full employment would reinforce efforts preemptively to work for introduction of technology on agreeable terms. The upshot of the argument here is not that societies are "free to choose" productive regimes or adjustment strategies as they please but rather that the range of choice of one shapes the other—and that the range of choices is wider than is usually acknowledged.

IV. INTERNATIONAL ASPECTS

Apart from the unlikely advent of a "global Marshall Plan," industrial states will determine, according to their own devices (and social divisions), their own competitive strategies and allocations of the burdens of adjustment. Certainly, the "microchip dilemma" would be exacerbated by disjointed strategies and protectionist trends by powerful states unwilling to take a global view of their problems. The Sussex School correctly, if perhaps futilely, advocates coordinating economic exchange among OECD members and between them and the Newly Industrializing Countries and the Third World regarding credit, investment, technology transfer, and trade concessions.[87]

One potentially attractive strategy for all major players is a Nora Report scenario in which each country lets a moderate expansion of high job-generating domestic sectors occur along with a brisk free trade in high-tech products, easing the political reaction to declines in unsalvageable industries and creating the effective demand to absorb enhanced production. The collective action problem, however, is that nations will be tempted to free ride, gaining a competitive edge by keeping social expenditures down.[88] This likely problem, though, depends on how public programs are applied. It is at least conceivable that public training programs and a robust industrial strategy may yield better competitive benefits than will be reaped by countries taking the "cheaper" route.

Another joker in the pack is a phenomenon that virtually all these works cite—that while there is no prospect of a stampede of foreign investors out of Third World locales, new computer integrated systems are enabling First World firms to offset cheap labor advantages abroad.[89] IBM, Motorola, Fairchild, and National Semiconductor are among the firms that returned (or remained rooted) to the United States because of new-found technical capacities to churn out small-batch customized products. "[Computer Integrated Systems] is the key to bringing factories back to the industrialized countries," Derian jubilantly predicts.[90] This transformation of old industries heralds a progressive shortening of the product cycle which diminishes the attractiveness of offshore investment and thus possibly adversely affecting Third World development overall.[91] Little thought is spared for the implications for the next band of industrializers after the "gang of four" NICs (South Korea, Taiwan, Hong Kong, Singapore) and what this might mean for Third World demand—which, after all, is supposed to absorb some of the anticipated increase in First World output.

CONCLUSION

The microelectronics revolution offers—indeed imposes—opportunities to revitalize productive bases in industrial societies. The authors emphasize that political processes shape technical innovation and economic growth, and that the "microchip dilemma" is the cumulative effect of *alterable* patterns of distributions of power, wealth, and ideas. Macroeconomic policies are not enough to mediate the social impact of technical change. Policymakers are urged to test mixes of macro- and micro-interventionism if they are to reconcile economic imperatives with social demands in the information age.

States mediate the impact of exogenous forces upon domestic interests whose political alliances in turn shape policy outcomes. The success of group's or coalition's projects is contingent upon (1) how congruent their preferences are with the structure of opportunities provided by the global economy and (2) the ability of competing groups to invoke (or refute) social beliefs and values to augment the attractiveness of their project to actors whose consent is crucial to the outcome of policy conflicts over technical choices and economic adjustment.

If "the search for productivity" is an exogenous factor dominating the "alternatives of domestic policy" in liberal polities like the United States and United Kingdom, this nonetheless is a condition subject to political change.[92] The "post-Fordist" scenerio envisions an active state, democratic vitality, and competitive industry enhancing one another in a virtuous cycle and is one of several value-laden alternatives, each implying a different distribution of benefits and costs. Japan is something of a cautionary case because there a flexible manufacturing system arose from a confluence of unintended circumstances, of a peculiar balance of domestic forces responding to global exigencies. One result is flexible team practices were developed and have been contained (so far) within a hierarchical system.[93] It is hardly what the post-Fordist scholars have in mind, but it is a possible model.

Policy analysis should extend beyond the sphere of who gets this grant or that tax break to illuminate the ways in which technical change, market forces, and policy actions are dynamically linked—tracing the effects from national adjustment actions to strategies in firms to impact in workplace and outward to the international arena again. This is an immensely ambitious task but, as these authors attest, such trail-blazing (with all attendent trial and error and disputation) is well under way. A fine example is David Friedman's study which argues that developmental choices are shaped by the political resolution of conflicts regarding worker ideologies, interfirm cooperation, and other domestic factors.[94]

Karl Polanyi observed that free trade in the nineteenth century required "an enormous increase in continuous centrally organized and controlled interventionism."[95] As a "protective countermovement arises in modern trading states, the continuation of what we call "free trade" may well depend on a recurrence of this process. Market competitiveness and at least a major ("post-Fordist") element in this "countermovement" are arguably reconcilable. I have argued that in this high-tech era "efficiency" is not opposed to "equity"—and indeed may presuppose improvements in the latter. When several organizational forms are compatible with the same economic goal, politics, not pure economic logic alone, decides the outcomes. As always, the state will be drawn into contests among social groups to determine this efficiency-equity mix in each case. Certainly, the worst policy is to let "technology" decide.

Notes

1. Richard Cyert and David Mowery, *Technology and Employment: Innovation and Growth in the U.S. Economy* (Washington DC: National Academy Press, 1987), p. 5; Stephen S. Cohen and John Zysman, *Manufacturing Matters: The Myth of the Post-Industrial Economy* (New York: Basic Books, 1987), p. 170; and Tom Forester, ed. *The Microelectronics Revolution* (Cambridge, MA: MIT Press, 1980), p. 295.
2. TUC, Annual Economic Survey, 1979.
3. Among the works generated during the 1950s early 1960s debate were Walter Buckingham, *Automation: Its Impact on Business and People* (New York: Mentor, 1965); John Diebold, *Automation* (Princeton: Von Norstrand, 1952); Charles Dechert, *The Social Impact of Cybernetics* (New York: Simon & Schuster, 1965); and Norbert Wiener, *The Human Use of Human Beings* (New York: Houghton Mifflin, 1954). There was a still earlier edition of the automation debate during the Great Depression of the 1930s; see Chapter 1 in Cyert and Mowery.
4. For example, Andrew Shonfield, *Modern Capitalism* (Oxford: Oxford University Press, 1965).
5. Simon Nora and Alain Minc, *The Computerization of Society* (Cambridge, MA: MIT Press, 1980). This originally was a commissioned report to the French president Giscard d'Estaing, composed by two inspecteurs des finances and a team of specialists. It was published in January 1978 and became a best-seller.
6. Dosi et al., eds. (London: Frances Pinter, 1988); Freeman and Soete (London: Frances Pinter, 1990); Cyert and Mowery (Washington DC: National Academy Press, 1987); Derian (Cambridge, MA: MIT Press, 1990); Oakley and Owen (Cambridge, MA: MIT Press, 1990); Friedman (Ithaca, NY: Cornell University Press, 1988); Zuboff (New York: Basic Books, 1989); and Matthews (London: Pluto, 1989).
7. Richard R. Nelson and Luc Soete, "Policy Conclusions," in Dosi, et al. eds., *Technical Innovation and Economic Theory*, p. 633.
8. Friedman, *Misunderstood Miracle*, pp. 17, 161.
9. In itself job loss is not a symptom of grave underlying problems. A dynamic economy sheds as many as one of every ten jobs each year while the labor displaced is absorbed elsewhere in more productive and profitable activities. This pleasant scenario assumes that workers' skills are at least partially transferable and/or that adequate public/private provisions for retraining exist. It also assumes that labor is quite mobile or else that capital is—but not too much so (i.e., going offshore). Unemployment becomes a policy problem when (1) the rate of displacement outruns the pace of job creation for a protracted period and (2) when public pressure is brought to bear on policymakers who are ideologically disposed and institutionally capable of responding with ameliorative measures.
10. Karl Polanyi, *The Great Transformation* (Boston: Beacon Press, 1944), pp. 140–141.
11. Nathan Rosenberg, *Inside the Black Box: Technology and Economics* (Cambridge, MA: MIT Press, 1982), p. xi.
12. Ibid., p. 236; also see Merritt Roe Smith, ed., *Military Enterprise and Industrial Technology* (Cambridge, MA, MIT Press, 1987), p. 9.
13. Kenneth Flamm, *Targeting the Computer* (Washington, DC: Brookings Institution, 1987) p. 18.

14. Ibid., p. 77.

15. Oakley and Owen, *Alvey*, pp. 178, 221.

16. Quoted in Derian, *America's Quest for Leadership*, pp. 143–144; also Richard R. Nelson, "Institutions Supporting Technical Change in the United States," in Dosi, ed., *Technical Innovation and Economic Theory*, p. 323.

17. Cyert and Mowery, *Technology and Employment*, pp. 37–38.

18. Derian, *America's Quest*, p. 143, also, see David Mowery and Nathan Rosenberg, *Technology and the Pursuit of Growth* (Cambridge, MA: Cambridge University Press, 1989).

19. Derian, *America's Quest*, pp. 106–124.

20. *New York Times*, 20 February 1991.

21. Ibid.

22. Oakley and Owen, *Alvey*, p. 60.

23. Ibid., pp. 12–13.

24. Ibid., pp. 186–187.

25. Christopher Freeman, John Clark, and Luc Soete, *Unemployment and Technical Innovation* (London: Frances Pinter, 1982).

26. Ibid., p. 16.

27. Joseph Schumpeter, *Business Cycles: A Theoretical, Historical, and Statistical Analysis of the Capitalist Process* (New York: McGraw-Hill, 1939); Joshua Goldstein, *Long Cycles: Prosperity and War in the Modern Age* (New Haven, CT: Yale University Press, 1988); Ernest Mandel, *Late Capitalism* (London: New Left Books, 1975; Gerhard Mensch, *Stalemate in Technology* (Cambridge, MA: Ballinger Press, 1979); William R. Thompson, "Long Waves, Technological Innovation, and Relative Decline," *International Organization* 44 (1990).

28. Freeman, Clark and Soete, *Unemployment*, pp. 74, 76.

29. Ibid., pp. 79, 97.

30. Ibid., pp. 153–157.

31. See Robert Kuttner, *The End of Laissez-Faire* (New York: Houghton Mifflin, 1990).

32. Freeman, "Preface to Part II, Evolution, Technology and Institutions: A Wider Framework for Economic Analysis," in Dosi, *Technical Change and Economic Theory*, p. 11. The notion of a "techno-economic paradigm" derives from theories of scientific paradigm change. For an overview of these debates see Chapter I in this volume.

33. Freeman, Clark, and Soete, *Unemployment and Technical Innovation*, p. 191.

34. *The Guardian*, 28 June 1989 and 8 January 1990.

35. *Independent on Sunday*, Business Section, 20 December 1990.

36. Doreen Massey and Richard Meegan, *The Anatomy of Job Loss* (London: Metheun, 1982), p. 225.

37. Ibid., pp. 183–184.

38. See Francis Green, ed., *The Restructuring of the UK Economy* (London: Macmillan, 1989) and Bob Jessop, Kevin Bonner, and Simon Bromley, "Farewell to Thatcherism?" *New Left Review* 179 (1990), p. 73.

39. Tom Forester, *High Tech Society* (Cambridge, MA: MIT Press, 1987), p. 180.

40. Cyert and Mowery, *Technology and Employment*, p. 2.

41. Robert Boyer, "Technical Change and the Theory of Regulation," in Dosi, *Technical Change and Economic Theory*, p. 73.

42. Giovanni Dosi, "The Nature of the Innovative Process," in Dosi, ed. *Technical Change and Economic Theory*, p. 227.

43. Michael Piore and Charles Sabel, *The Second Industrial Divide* (New York: Basic Books, 1987).
44. Friedman, *Misunderstood Miracle*, p. 25.
45. See Michel Aglietta, *A Theory of Capitalist Regulation: The U.S. Experience* (London: Verso, 1979); Alain Liepitz, *Mirages and Miracles: The Crisis of Global Fordism* (London: Verso, 1987); and, a critical appraisal from the Left, Robert Bremmer and Mark Glick, "The Regulation Approach: Theory and History," *New Left Review*, 188 (1991), pp. 45–120.
46. Friedman, *Misunderstood Miracle*, p. 13.
47. Cyert and Mowery, *Technology and Employment*, p. 29. Scott Lash distinguishes between post-Fordism, which is "a disintegration of Fordist hierarchies into a plethora of smaller firms," and neo-Fordism which entails "only the disaggregation of the functions of the firm, which remain within the physical space of the company" in "Disintegrating Firms," *Socialist Review*, 21 (1990), p. 104. What is at stake is the kind and degree of workplace control. See also Keith Pavitt, "Chips and Trajectories," in Roy McLeod, ed., *Technology and the Human Prospect* (London: Frances Pinter, 1986), pp. 31–54.
48. Matthews, *Tools of Change*, p. 180.
49. See Dosi and Orenigo, "Coordination and Transformation: An Overview of Structures, Behaviour and Change in Evolutionary Environments," p. 27; Norman Clark and Calestous Juma, "Evolutionary Crises in Economic Thought," and Christopher Freeman and Carlotta Perez, "Structural Crises of Adjustment: Business Cycles and Investment Behaviour" in Dosi, ed., *Technical Change and Economic Theory*.
50. David M. Gordon, Michael Reich, and Richard Edwards, *Segmented Work, Divided Workers: The Historical Transformation of Labor in the United States* (Cambridge, MA: Cambridge University Press, 1982).
51. David Noble, *Forces of Production* (New York: Knopf, 1985); Harley Shaiken, *Work Transformed* (New York: Holt, Rinehart, Winston, 1986); and Friedman, *Misunderstood Miracle*.
52. Freeman, "Japan: A New National System of Innovation," in Dosi, *Technical Change and Economic Theory*, p. 344. Also, Ben Dankbaar, "International Competition and National Institutions: The Case of the Automobile Industry," in Freeman and Soete, *New Explorations in the Economics of Technical Change*, p. 170.
53. H. Steedman and K. Wagner, in *The Independent*, 2 January 1991.
54. Karel von Wolferen, *The Enigma of Japanese Power* (New York: Knopf, 1989), p. 181.
55. See Chapters 2 and 3 in this volume.
56. A policy crisis occurs if a fall in the credibility of the state's commitment to full employment is compounded by harm inflicted on groups that support incumbent parties. Cuts in social spending and public employment lighten the tills of many businesses. Slack capacity raises unit costs so that export sector firms must lower profit margins or else lose competitiveness. High interest rates and overvalued currency interfere with interindustry purchasing patterns so that multiplier effects diminish. Unused "human capital" strains state budgets because fewer taxes and more compensation are paid. The discontent of declining producer groups is expressed in protectionist inclinations. All the more reason to attend to issues of technological design and workplace reforms.
57. Cyert and Mowery, *Technology and Employment*, p. 133; Forester, *High Tech Society*, p. 217; and Zuboff, *The Age of the Smart Machine*.

58. Heather Rolfe, "In the Name of Progress: Skills and Attitudes Toward Techno-logical Change," *New Technology, Work and Employment* 5 (1991), pp. 110–117.
59. Nora and Minc, *The Computerization of Society*, pp. 4–5.
60. Ibid., pp. 42–45.
61. Friedman, *Misunderstood Miracle*, p. 38.
62. *The Independent*, 2 January 1991.
63. *The Guardian*, 14 February 1990.
64. Matthews, *Tools of Change*, pp. 134–135.
65. Dosi, "Introduction," in Dosi, *Technical Change and Economic Theory*, p. 3.
66. Cyert and Mowery, *Technology and Employment*, p. 62.
67. Forester, *High Tech Society*, pp. 198, 213; also David Knights and Hugh Wilmott, *New Technology and the Labour Process* (London: Macmillan, 1988), p. 188.
68. Gosta Esping-Andersen, *The Three Worlds of Welfare Capitalism* (Princeton, NJ: Princeton University Press, 1990), p. 181.
69. Freeman, Clark, and Soete, *Unemployment and Technical Innovation*, p. 122.
70. See Dosi, "The Nature of the Innovative Process," in Dosi, *Technical Change and Economic Theory*, pp. 227–228.
71. Adam Przeworski, "Material Interests, Class Compromise, and the Transition to Socialism," *Politics and Society* 7 (1980), p. 149.
72. Manuel Castells, *The Economic Crisis and American Society* (Princeton, NJ: Princeton University Press, 1980), p. 56.
73. Peter J. Katzenstein, *Small States in the World Economy* (Ithaca, NY: Cornell University Press, 1986).
74. See Esping-Andersen, *The Three Worlds of Welfare Capitalism*; John Freeman, *Democracy and Markets* (Ithaca, NY: Cornell University Press, 1989); and Jan Fagerberg, et al. "The Decline of Social Democratic State Capitalism in Nor-way," *New Left Review* 181 (1991).
75. Matthews, *Tools of Change*, p. 113.
76. Dankbaar, "International Competition and National Institutions," in Freeman and Soete, *New Explorations*, p. 169.
77. Castells, *The Economic Crisis and American Society*, p. 56.
78. "[These organizations] . . . illustrated the need to defend and reproduce the le-gitimacy of managerial authority can channel potential innovation toward the conventional emphasis on automation. In this context, managers emphasize ma-chine intelligence and managerial control over the knowledge base at the ex-pense of developing knowledge in the operating work force. They use the technology as a fail-safe system to increase their sense of certainty and control over both production and organizational functions." Zuboff, *In the Age of the Smart Machine*, p. 390.
79. Fred Block, "Rethinking the Political Economy of the Welfare State," in Fred Block, Richard Cloward, Barbara Ehrenreich, and Frances Fox Piven, *The Mean Season: The Attack on the Welfare State* (New York: Pantheon, 1987), p. 11.
80. Noble, *Forces of Production*, p. 65.
81. Matthews, *Tools of Change*, p. 141.
82. Ibid., p. 158.
83. Dieter Frohlich and Hubert Krieger, "Technological Change and Worker Par-ticipation in Europe," *New Technology, Work, and Employment*, 5 (1990), p. 95.
84. Michel Albertijn, Bob Honcke, and Davy Wigaerts, "Technology Agreements and Industrial Relations in Belgium," *New Technology, Work and Employment*, 5 (1990), p. 6.

85. Noble, *Forces of Production*, p. 164.
86. Esping-Andersen, *The Three Worlds of Welfare Capitalism*, p. 153.
87. Kurt Unger, "Industrial Structure, Technical Change, and Microeconomic Behaviour in LDCs," in Dosi, *Technical Change and Economic Theory*, pp. 484–485; Freeman, Clark, and Soete, *Unemployment and Technical Innovation*, pp. 162–182.
88. My thanks to a referee who suggested this point.
89. Jeffery Hendersen, *The Globalization of High Technology* (London: Routledge, 1989), p. 143; Cyert and Mowery, *Technology and Employment*, p. 81; also, Freeman, "Technical Innovation in the World Chemical Industry and Changes of Techno-Economic Paradigm," in Freeman and Soete, *New Explorations*, pp. 74–92.
90. Derian, *America's Quest*, p. 229.
91. Cyert and Mowery, *Technology and Employment*, pp. 81, 126; Francois Chenais, "Industrial Structure, Technical Change, and Microeconomic Behaviour in LDCs," both in Dosi, *Technical Change and Economic Theory*, p. 491.
92. Nora and Minc, *The Computerization of Society*, p. 41.
93. A more benign view of Japanese work practices is given in Masahiko Aoki, "A New Paradigm of Work Organizational Coordination," in Stephen Marglin and Juliet Schor, eds., *The Golden Age of Capitalism: Reinterpreting the Postwar Experience* (Oxford: Oxford University Press, 1990), pp. 267–293.
94. Friedman, *Misunderstood Miracle*, p. 13.
95. Polanyi, *The Great Transformation*, p. 140, fn. 16.

6

Technology and the Politics of Trade Policy

"Free trade," like any other aspect of political economy, is valued not for its own sake but as a means to other ends. Sovereignty, economists like to point out, may be sacrificed cheerfully for the prospect of prosperity but, likewise, in hard times trade arrangements will come under severe pressure.[1] The precise blending of free trade and protectionism will depend on what is deemed fair in domestic balancing acts between elites' economic calculations and what citizens will tolerate.[2] Hence, an "irrational" fear (from the elite's view) of surrendering sovereignty to a World Trade Organization is probably a justifiable concern by economically vulnerable citizens about the future on their jobs and living standards.

At the Asian Pacific Cooperation forum in Jakarta in November 1994 President Clinton recited the usual litany of claims that opening markets "will make our service and products more competitive, and more sales abroad create more high-wage jobs at home." William Neikirk, however, noted that Clinton's free trade stance clashed with another favorite campaign theme—to make work more secure and workers less anxious about the future. "But if free trade does anything," Neikirk observed, "it increases worker anxiety and insecurity."[3] The Clinton administration ultimately opted to play a vigorous role in spreading this kind of economic insecurity throughout a proposed "Free Trade Area of the Americas" extending from the Aleutian Islands to Tierra del Fuego.

Free trade *per se* is not fair.[4] Fairness requires (1) monitoring of reciprocity by trade partners and (2) internal distributional arrangements that assure that the benefits are not captured by a privileged and well-positioned minority. Few industrial democracies, and fewer authoritarian systems, permit global economic trends to dictate the pace and the direction of sectoral changes or to determine how risks and costs are allotted. State interventionism rises in periods of a "politics of scarcity" when the influence of domestic structures in shaping foreign economic policy increases.[5] When redistributive issues arise, a key question is the scope of involvement by the public against whom

148

policymakers will install every possible insulating device, ranging from "fast track" legislation to the use of transnational organizations as arbiters.[6]

Like trade, technical innovation is a phenomenon whose social legitimation depends on the distribution of its benefits—and that there are benefits is indisputable. While technology may be the "most unknown of all the variables," a reliable rule of thumb in developmental economics is the high correlation of the technological level of industrial sectors to their competitiveness in international trade.[7] Hence technology and trade are usually mutually reinforcing forces for producing wealth and better living standards. Yet neither trade nor technology are systems that are neutral in design or in the way they are utilized by public actors or private groups.[8]

Ideas about technical change—such as technocratic ideologies espousing "one best way"—constrain options. Few people dare to promote policies that are characterized by opponents as backward or "Luddite." In the 1994 GATT vote no one "could come up with believable estimates of how much the American economy could benefit or how many American workers would lose their jobs because of increased foreign imports," nonetheless, as a senior Clinton administration official noted, "almost everyone voted on an emotion about freer trade. No one wanted to look like an economic neantherdal."[9] This response is particularly worrisome when reigning economic ideas are losing touch with reality.

The central proposition explored here derives from a French government report—discussed in the previous chapter—on the microelectronics revolution which concluded that *in the present context* the international market creates a "contradiction between employment and foreign trade."[10] This chapter examines how technical change and societal interests interact to shape foreign economic policies.

The key distinction in analyzing the genesis of competing economic strategies (e.g., high skill/high wage industrial policy versus a cheap labor path) is not "between different types of interests but among different social arrangements that generate different belief systems and different structural possibilities."[11] The creation of different social arrangements changes the interests of actors (as in the case of U.S. capitalists reconciling themselves profitably to a New Deal inflicted by FDR).[12] Otherwise one presumes that the structure of causal relations in trade policy will undergo only marginal changes (e.g., a training program here, a "quality circle" there). But it is change *in* causal relations that global markets and technical innovation bring sharply into question.[13]

I address technology as both physical apparatuses and as *images* of those apparatuses which are put to political use by actors. In this era of relentless corporate downsizing I probe the impact of the "microchip revolution" on productive structures and social agendas. Finally the chapter assesses the consequences of technological and economic "imperatives" for the trade regime.

STATES, IDEOLOGIES
AND "REGIMES OF INSTRUMENTALITY"

States mediate the internal impact of global economic forces upon domestic societal groups. The domestic structure of the state is an intervening variable "without which the interelation between international interdependence and political strategies cannot be understood."[14] But the modern nation-state rarely is the rational unitary actor of realist myth. Policymakers are housed in competing branches of the state where they develop interests distinct from those of societal groups, work out their own policy calculus on issues, and under broadly specifiable conditions, can shape the policy preferences of private actors during struggles over the content of policy.[15]

Models that treat states as unitary actors are seriously flawed. In economic transactions subnational groups may make large gains while the nation as a whole is losing, and to the degree "that such subnational gainers may have sufficient political strength to impose their preferences on the entire political system, the criteria [that analysts] use to assess how a nation's central decision makers order their preferences are probably mistaken."[16] These subnational actors are a vital influence in the policy outcomes. Analysts must delve carefully into these domestic structures in order to understand the motives driving the rush toward regional economic linkages.

Certainly, as institutionalists claim, the structure of the state and the specific "policy networks" linking states to society constrain how civil groups will define their own interests. But this is hardly a one-way street.[17] Societal groups and class-based organizations have different degrees of resources and, accordingly, of success in utilizing state channels to obtain desired "transfer costs" for economic adjustment.[18] Studies usually focus on domestic structure, coalitional formation, and policymakers' interests affecting a state's capacity to mobilize resources to cope with the global market. Ideology is usually shunted aside as epiphenomenal, that is, as identical with or a derivative of material interests. But interests flow through the filter of ideology and ideas about phenomena as inevitably opaque as the market or technology will skew preferences as to how they should operate.

The most powerful ideological notions are those that appear to be independent of human agency and to impose constraints on all agents. The market, as lionized by George Gilder, is one; technology, as demonized by Jacques Ellul, is another.[19] These "automaticities" are ideological constructs and are malleable resources wielded by societal groups for achieving their preferences during contests to guide economic strategy. These constructs are identified with an alluring unilinear depiction of progress. Indeed, didn't Adam Smith merge the two systems when he characterized markets as irresistible "machines"?

Machines, however, are tricky things. "In the technical realm," Langdon Winner argues, "we repeatedly enter into a series of social contracts, the terms of which are revealed only after the signing."[20] Technological systems embody and alter social relationships. Historical research discloses instances when the interests of dominant groups were inscribed at the design stage into the technical apparatus: the "small print," as it were, of the contract.[21] Yet technologies display a dismaying capriciousness (Weber's unintended consequences and unforeseen effects) and demand a compatible reorganization of institutions and social practices if they are to work. Winner characterizes these reorderings as "regimes of instrumentality" because they stand "parallel to and occasionally overlap the constitution of political society" and, in a variety of ways, can supersede it.[22]

Dominant groups strive to steer innovation along incremental tracks that are consistent with their perceived interests, although this isn't always possible. Technological development shapes the feasible range of policy possibilities while the social organization of power constrains the emergence of forms of technology so that they are compatible with the preservation of dominant agents. Technology systems exert a powerful aura of "automaticity" not only where markets hold sway but also where state intervention is vigorous or a socialist movement holds power.[23] One automaticity drives another; hence, global competition stimulates high-technology exports and vice versa.

FAIRNESS VERSUS "FREEDOM" IN TRADE

"Fair trade" is undeniably fodder for demagogic appeals, as witness Ross Perot's presidential campaigns. In the mid-1980s in a conciliatory retreat before Congress even President Reagan had to appoint a "swat team" to search and destroy "unfair trading practices," which grew more numerous than reds under beds in the 1950s.[24] Because the United States lacks adequate policy tools to retrain workers, redistribute income (other than upward), and coordinate economic activity, policy sentiment among an aggrieved public tends to be protectionist. If a state cannot compensate players for dislocation costs then projects for technological change, as well as adherence to a liberal trade regime, will be threatened.

In 1990 a majority of U.S. citizens and Europeans demanded restrictions on Japanese investment.[25] The new "nativism" of California's Proposition 187 was yet another angry if addled reaction to economic uncertainties. (Curiously, in seeking scapegoats, populist critics consistently overlook U.S. multinationals which are, after all, "among the external economic forces from which the domestic economy might be protected.")[26] An important determinant of these domestic responses is the economic strategy the state pursues. The United States pursued a "cheap labor" strategy which the NAFTA agreement, despite President Clinton's side payments and concessions, re-affirmed. The NAFTA battle was so fierce because economic progress is becoming difficult to portray as being synonymous with social progress. This disjuncture is partly why publics have to be coaxed to go along with European Union expansion and centralization; it offers, however faintly, the promise of mediating mechanisms that will deliver desired social benefits of economic growth.[27]

So the liberal trade regime now ironically depends upon "coordinated deviations" from market standards. These deviations increasingly take the form of regional trade blocs to promote a "competitive liberalization process." The idea is to create leapfrogging trade pacts so that "as one group lowers barriers others will be pressured to do so too."[28] In Social Democratic nations undertaking multilateral bargains, Peter Katzenstein observes, elites usually try to arrive at "policies that prevent the costs of change from causing political disruption."[29] This objective partially holds because there are conflicting motives among actors for joining trading blocs.

Free market proponents intend to use trade blocs in order to avoid policy changes at home that might endanger their power and wealth. This approach entails depleting the welfare state, subsidizing capital, weakening unions, regressive taxation, privatization, and shifting power to undemocratic transnational institutions.[30] Social democratic proponents seek to secure gains at a regional level that they no longer can obtain inside their national boundaries: workers rights, regional redistribution, progressive tax reform, industrial democracy, and economic coordination.

The prospect of "Keynesianism in one continent" was an explicit lure of European Union (EU) participation for British labour—not to mention Left Labour parties elsewhere.[31] The objective for European Union recruits Sweden, Austria, and Finland, apart from access to a large market, is to acquire an effective voice in economic arrangements that are seen as otherwise slipping out of their control. (Such a program—albeit with a democratic twist—parallels that of Friedrich List a century ago who in a pan-German context urged adoption of state subsidies within and protection without.)

The scale and pace of microelectronics change is perceived to exceed any state's scope of authority. So it is no surprise that states seek regional arrangements whose terms are hardly all they desire.[32] Should they be foiled, they can always cheat, temporize, or defect. In the meantime the "supply," as it were, of adjustment is sorely strained. In an era of intensifying rivalry, rapid technical change, and slow growth, the United States is particularly handicapped by its institutional legacies and a well-financed right-wing.[33] The corrosive result is an intensifying domestic demand for protection. The way out for corporate elites is to promote regional blocs.

ACTIVIST STATES AND LIBERAL TRADE

The new trading blocs form in a global economy that operates at variance with textbook theories of comparative advantage and product cycles.[34] New industrializing countries pursue policy-induced "competitive advantage" strategies to upgrade their production. They disregard the theoretical strictures of Ricardian and Hecksher-Ohlin factor endowment theories for directive industrial development that intensifies competitive pressures.[35] Western corporate executives may plead for "a restructuring of the world economy with the United States, Western Europe, and Japan competing in the high-technology capital goods area and the Less Developed Countries (LDCs) with low technology, labor-intensive products," but they rushed to the periphery to exploit the advantages available there anyway.[36]

Many analysts advise market economies to draw lessons from democratic corporatist states that devised institutional mechanisms, a repertoire of policy instruments, and managed to mesh economic liberalism with domestic compensatory action so as to streamline the adjustment process.[37] Robert Kuttner urges "social brokering policies" together with a neo-Listian protectionism designed to "incubate" rather than merely protect industries, but he may underestimate the extent to which new technologies disrupt standard economic wisdoms.

There is evidence of a widening ratio between investment and output increases on one hand, and job creation on the other.[38] The democratic corporatist cases hiked investment and used new technologies to avert falls in trade performance, but technological transformation exerts a steady strain even on "flexible, reactive" political structures. Despite high investment rates and compensatory policies, West European job growth was nearly nil through the 1980s. So there was the temptation to try the "recapitalization path of maintaining free trade for export expansion" which[39]

> beggars a nation's citizens by changing the tax structure and decreasing public expenditures so as to transfer income from consumers to potential manufacturing investors; and it beggars other nations by trying to increase domestic production and employment and by invading other countries' markets.

In the absence of multilateral agreements for allocation of production niches, the fallacy of composition argument would come into play. The domestic price of these policies in democracies should motivate states to resort to an uneven meshing of sectoral upgrading and selective trade closure. But these practices can get out of hand as domestic forces subject policymakers to an intensifying tug-of-war.

HIGH TECHNOLOGY: PANACEAS AND POLICY

All advanced industrial societies support high-tech development to revitalize their productive structures. Since the late 1980s promises of full employment have been conspicuous by their absence. The Clinton administration tacitly accepted the Reagan-Bush redefinition of full employment at 6 percent, but there is a growing concern that a market-based society cannot spread prosperity widely enough to secure legitimacy. After all the self-congratulatory hoopla in the west over the communist collapse in 1989 Hungary, Poland, and the Czech Republic have backed away from their first giddy embrace of the market as cure-all.

High-tech strategies alone are no solution to domestic difficulties. Nor is increased trade. Trade actually reduces the labor requirement for a given level of consumption because the labor required to produce 1 billion dollars of exports falls below the labor required to produce an additional 1 billion dollars of imports. "In this sense trade closely resembles technological change."[40] Capital intensive export industries utilize less labor while the imports drawn in by an export push will threaten domestic producers. In these circumstances, free trade and technical change are job-eroding. A lack of incentive structures to guide capital movements and labor-management relations simply exacerbates the plight, increases anxiety, and become self-reinforcing. The problem then is defined perversely as the solution—e.g., less labor, lower pay, lower tax on capital and wealth—so that no escape is allowed. Conservative parties, conservative wings of labor-oriented parties and their corporate allies persuade an increasingly demoralized public that, in Margaret Thatcher's words, "there is no alternative."

New industrializers hasten the cycle by which "advantage based on innovation gives way to advantage based on labor costs"; rapid standardization exerts downward pressure on workers' wages and rights in advanced nations.[41] The tempting response for policymakers in the First World is to impose "rice bowl economics" at home, which is a foolish long-term policy. On the contrary, new "high volume flexible production" must be "developed through far reaching and painful organizational change." So-called "lean production" techniques promise to use half the material, half the space, half the time, and half the labor. "More and cheaper capital, less and cheaper labor will not restore European competitiveness," Stephen Cohen observes. "We are dealing with a new mode of production [that requires] "a fundamental reorganization of the production process."[42] Obviously, this realization alone cannot dissuade dominant economic actors in the United States or United Kingdom from their cheap labor courses.

Productivity increases, which require less labor per unit of output, historically have been offset by more than proportionate rises in demand. In the late twentieth century. Job loss still stems less from automation than from macroeconomic policy measures. (Fritz Scharpf, for example, argues that financial market deregulation forces states into policies of industrial cost reduction in ways that favor capital.)[43] But employers always use recessions to install productivity-enhancing technologies or to rationalize production. Less than 60 percent of the manufacturing jobs lost in the United States in the 1980–82 recession were regained.[44] Recessions also enable excessive scrapping of capacity so that less productive potential is available to meet surges in demand during the upturns.[45] Semiconductors and machine tool industries in the United States exemplify this process of self-inflicted loss of markets.[46]

CHEAP LABOR AND ECONOMIC POWER

Political pressures and a declining share of labor in production costs mean that the advanced societies could be poised to engage in "a new wave of automation that can 'melt' the LDCs cheap labor advantage."[47] Junne, Rada, and Sabel all have noted a 1980s trend by multinational corporations (MNCs) to relocate new production units on home soil.[48] This trend was spearheaded by democratic industrial states sensitive to imports that endanger a more than proportionate share of jobs at home.[49] In the 1990s multinationals still located their management-intensive, high value-added activities close to home. However, firms like Ford and Honda found that their need for quality control did not force them to "go North." Instead they applied management-intensive programs in Third World sites; Ford's most productive engine and final assembly plants are in Mexico operating at a fraction of U.S. labor costs.[50] NAFTA's "leveling down" orientation can only exacerbate this clash of interest between First World and Third World work forces.

Western workers who want work time reductions must resort to supporting protectionist measures if they are to stave off damage to competitiveness.[51] So, accordingly, there has been a surge in the north of adjustment strategies that blend *benign* mercantilism (to promote domestic welfare and stability) and *malevolent* mercantilism (to promote state power or else the collective power of First versus Third Worlds states).[52] Meanwhile, Third World debt repayments stanched investment when restructuring was most urgent, especially in Latin America. In Brazil, GDP growth fell from 9.0 to 2.7 percent.[53] The East Asian NICs (including China and India) have done well but "with absolute costs of labor becoming less and less important (versus low labor costs relative to a certain level of technological sophistication and economic integration in the world conomy), many countries and regions face a process of rapid deterioration that could lead to destructive reactions."[54] The analyst cites an explosion of criminal activity (especially drugs), anomic violence, and psychotic forms of fundamentalism that are becoming as widespread in the ghettos of the United States as in slums surrounding La Paz or Lima.

ECONOMIC PROGRESS AND SOCIAL DECLINE

The image of a "coolie America" resonated vividly in the Reagan-Bush era. In the 1980s European elites looked to the United States for market solutions to accelerate technical change, increase investment, create "flexibility" in labor markets and reduce disincentives for productivity.[55] Of the much-envied 21 million U.S. jobs in the 1970s, the vast bulk were in service activities paying less than half an average industrial wage. In that decade a 30 percent rise in demand in the manufacturing sector yielded a 1 percent job growth.[56] Slow productivity growth and stagnant wages in the United States were attributable to a demographic upsurge in which employers used labor instead of equipment investment so that a rising ratio of capital equipment to labor was difficult to sustain. The increase in fast food jobs in the 1973–80 exceeded employment in steel and auto industries. Four such jobs for two people just might enable raising a family decently.

The price of free trade is to impose restrictive domestic policies to generate positive trade balances that increase the share of profits in the economy, and which are presumed to increase investment levels in industries and create jobs—if not better wages. U.S. wage levels relative to capital fell 37 percent over 1972–1983; under such conditions employers could utilize cheap labor and automate at the same time.[57] An aggressively regressive tax system together with rollbacks of regulation and of labor protection also harmed median income-earners. Noting that 350,000 new jobs in 1994 were accompanied by a fall of two cents in the wage rate, even the *New York Times* had to conclude "the job bounty, one suspects, is concentrated in dehumanizing minimum wage dead-end jobs."[58]

In the 1990s a new trend was trumpeted: two and a half million new jobs appeared that paid three-quarters more than the national average. But on inspection these turned out to be mostly managerial and professional posts; the hourly wages of the lower half of employees continued to slip. The "great financial houses, insurance companies, and real estate firms provide low paid and increasingly insecure employment"; their nonsupervisory employees earn less than production line workers.[59]

In U.S. manufacturing 660,000 full-time jobs were lost in 1993; one-third disappeared and the other two-thirds were filled by temps. One quarter of all American full-time workers toil at or below the poverty line. Since 1973 American children in poverty rose by half; 22 percent are raised in poverty. One in three of the twenty million part-timers want full-time work. Overall, seventeen million Americans were looking for full-time work. The "declining middle" in the occupational structure augurs serious consequences for the level and the structure of demand and for the political agenda.

Even the bulk of high-tech jobs are low wage. High technology capital goods manufacturers are themselves liable to be automated. Chip designers ironically are threatened by "silicon compilers" (chips that design other chips according to producer specifications). The buzzword is "connectivity" a project to shear layers of jobs by tighter organization of office systems. The Office of Technology Assessment anticipates a decline in office work an office worker organization says jobs "are disappearing now."[60] IBM, ATT, General Motors, Sears, and GTE announced 325,000 layoffs in the early 1990s.

The largest MNCs automated zealously as have smaller import-sensitive firms in response to trade exposure. Retailing, nondurable foods manufacturing, and various service industries, largely free of competition, are in the forefront of the low-wage economy. "At present," John McDermott notes, "various service industries, light manufacturing, and retailing are at the core of the legislative and political coalition that maintains the low wage/high unemployment economy."[61] What makes this degenerative domestic process possible is a high skill/low wage work force available abroad to which NAFTA and GATT will increase corporate access.

The worst case scenario for the United States and United Kingdom, where the free market coalitions are strongest, is an export platform experience "writ large"—a dynamic sector with fewer good jobs plus a sheltered sector with mostly substandard ones.[62] Restrictive policies in these conditions can only depress demand so that automation of workplaces must result in similar outputs made with less labor.[63] This has a familiar ring. "Technological unemployment in a climate of global competition and slow growth is just a variation on the Keynesian theme of insufficient purchasing power and the maldistribution of demand."[64] Yet it is one thing for this to unfold in authoritarian states and another in democracies, especially in Europe where labor is still an institutional force with which to reckon.[65] A balancing act between manpower reductions and market increases must be still worked out.

PERILS OF LIBERALIZATION

As international competition drives advanced nations into high-tech paths, the reinvestment rate is raised, job levels are eroded, and the Social Democratic compromise is scuttled.[66] James Alt notes that conversion costs hinder the reallocation of production, and the greater the magnitude of reallocation required the greater will be the strain on state resources and on social stability.[67]

> Government subsidies or public investment will not have aggregate effects unless differences over the distributional costs of adjustment can be resolved and agreements implemented and sustained across the board, which would require a government disposed to provide subsidies and either a

large state share in employment, or labor and other interest organizations centralized and sufficiently monopolized to prevent the benefits of subsidies being frittered away through sectoral wage competition.

The supply of the means of adjustment is best increased through a blend of labor market and investment policies to facilitate sectoral shifts and make the costs of adjustment equitable.[68] To the extent that adjustment pressure is moderated and demand boosted, each nation can conduct an orderly accommodation of new technologies to its social goals rather than focus exclusively on staying a fraction ahead of rivals in productivity. Such a policy mix is consistent with trade liberalization. Jobs and living standards need not be jeopardized in order to reap the payoff of a dynamic modernized economy.

Managerial goals and attitudes shape the application of new technologies so that a premium is placed on manpower reductions and intensified monitoring of the remainder of the work force. Case studies document alternative designs that are both labor-using and skill-enhancing and are equally or more productive than those in place. Whether labor is released into a more rewarding existence or is consigned to the dole is a result of social decisions, not technological determination or the tender mercies of the marketplace.

In these deliberations the central actor is still the state as both strategist and as the strategic field which private actors vie for power. Despite propaganda about the decline of the nation-state, competitiveness is "highly dependent on the political capacity of national and supranational institutions to steer the growth strategy of these countries or areas under their jurisdiction, including the creation of comparative advantage in the world market for these firms which are considered to represent the interests of national and supranational collectivities."[69]

Voluntary agreements can be worked out among First World nations and between them and aspirant industrializers over trade, capital, credit, and production allocation. Is this a utopian prospect?[70] It unavoidably touches sensitive terrain: the internal political and industrial relations arrangements of trading partners. This constitutes a potential bind because First World states can only ultimately win domestic consent by encouraging processes of political liberalization in authoritarian antilabor states.

The passage of NAFTA was a setback for labor, but one that poses a new set of issues, including "questions of how countries act within their borders—like labor conditions, environmental standards and human rights—rather than simply how they interact with other states."[71] The key concern—most acute in NAFTA—is establishing terms that assure "leveling up" rather than "leveling down." Without trade rules with a "leveling up" bias there will be precariously thin domestic backing in advanced countries for free trade. "[W]e are going to have to create more and more credibility for trade," acknowledged trade representative, Mickey Kantor. "If the rules are not fair, the playing field not level, we will not have the credibility among the American public that free trade is to our benefit."[72] Here is an abiding contradiction and a source of possible progressive activity.

The Clinton administration, pushed rightward by Republican tactics, backed off from linking domestic issues to trade. Clinton waived concern about China's human rights status with regard to trade essentially because China is the second only to the United States as a site of foreign, including U.S., investment. Indonesia and Singapore likewise bridled at possible infringements on their domestic set-ups as interference in, as Lee Kwan Yew majestically put it, "Asian values," including a "national right to economic development that supersedes most individual rights."

Clinton gained a minor concession for a "fig leaf" appellate panel to review World Trade Organization decisions and the scope of GATT agreement (whose authority is implicitly conceded). A *New York Times* editorial claimed that the United States would be "protected in the future, as it is now, by the unwillingness of countries to engage the United States in a trade war."[73] This far from soothing judgment presumed that a phalanx of domestic conservatives weren't eager to import "Asian values" into the United States. Clinton, a protege of the conservative Democratic Leadership Council, has obliged them with regressive welform reform, interest rate hikes, and pursuit of free trade at almost all costs.

The high-tech export rout will exacerbate internal dislocation costs and generate domestic demands for new social contracts and forms of protectionism. Regional trade blocs are only a temporary route out. But in the absence of creation of domestic cushioning devices—which we witness the British Tories battling tooth and nail—even these blocs will be afflicted by the "contradiction between free trade and employment." There is, however, a dangerous inbuilt complacency in the United States where productivity still surpasses trading rivals, a fact which in the Gingrich era is bound to be attributed to free markets and niggardly welfare policies.[74] Nonetheless, in the long run, regional blocs are the new terrain for struggle over the conditions of conducting trade, managing production, and distributing benefits.

This global situation would seem to call for proliferation of what Richard Rosecrance calls "mediative states" that "reshape international forces to make them more hospitable to domestic needs, but at the same time building understanding at home for the intransigent international factors that cannot be altered."[75] However, the line between the two is not clear. The problem is that societal groups arrive at divergent interpretations about which international factors are "intransigent" and which aren't.

CONCLUSION

The scale and depth of microelectronics revolution exceeds any single state's authority. So it is no surprise that they seek regional arrangements. Trade pacts are what states enter in order to avoid redistributions of power and wealth. But this gambit doesn't always work as Britain, for example, found in December 1994 when it was forced by the EU to observe the rights of part-time workers. The attraction of joining the EU for many states is that they gain some control and access to coordinating mechanisms and are thereby permitted to attain domestic goals.

Technology shapes policy outcomes in two senses: (1) social reorganization is required for efficient exploitation of a technology system, and (2) prevailing ideas about technical change are weapons in policy debate over economic strategies. If mystiques about technology and the market fade, public questions arise regarding who determines policies and who ought to in the future.

Finally, economists correctly laud the historical gains that workers derived from a liberal trade system, but it is likewise correct that in exposed economies "the evident need to protect the balance of payments . . . serves to reinforce the capitalist resistance to reforms that might damage its interests."[76] The social democratic bargain established a balance between these imperatives.

A failure of the EU to move to full monetary union would be a defeat only for technocrats. In that event German leader Helmut Kohl suggests a "Europe with a variable geometry" with Germany, France, and Benelux going ahead whilst others lag behind. But John Kenneth Galbraith is correct to observe that a monetary union in the European Union can be achieved only "after there is an alignment of internal social and economic policies, including in particular fiscal, budget and employment policies."[77] If a liberal trade regime is to survive, a reconstitution of the social democratic compromise at regional level is not only possible but necessary.

Notes

1. See, for example, Richard Cooper, *The Economics of Interdependence* (New York: Prentice-Hall, 1966).
2. Words mean a great deal in these matters. Note the uproar when Secretary of Labor Robert Reich in November 1994 used the term "corporate welfare" to describe the pampering of business with tax breaks.
3. William Neikirk, "Job Worries at Root of GATT Fears" *Chicago Tribune*, 27 November 1994. Also see Ralph Nader, "GATT Hypocrisy" *The Nation*, 5 December 1994.
4. There is of course a large literature on "free trade imperialism" which, while important and provocative, is not directly relevant to this essay.

5. Peter Katzenstein, ed., *Between Power and Plenty* (Madison: University of Wisconsin, 1976).

6. Ibid., p. 11.

7. Ennio Rodriguez, "The Endogenization of Technological Change: A Development Challenge" in Osvaldo Sunkel, ed., *Development from Within: Toward a Neostructuralist Approach for Latin America* (London: Lynn Rienner, 1993), p. 223.

8. On technocratic ideology see Jürgen Habermas, "Science and Technology as Ideology" in Habermas, *Toward a Rational Society* (Boston: Beacon Press, 1969). Technological systems, like institutions, "are created as instruments of action and their organization reflects the political fights that established them and the goals of the leadership that animates them." John Zysman, *Governments, Markets and Growth* (Ithaca, NY: Cornell University Press, 1983). Also, see Dan Clausen, *Bureaucracy and the Labor Process: The Transformation of U.S. Industry* (New York: Monthly Review Press, 1980).

9. *New York Times*, 4 December 1994.

10. Simon Nora and Alain Minc, *The Computerization of Society* (Cambridge: MIT Press, 1980), p. 41.

11. Fred Block and Margaret Somers, "Beyond the Economistic Fallacy" in Theda Skocpol, ed. *Vision and Method in Historical Sociology* (Cambridge: Cambridge University Press, 1984), p. 62.

12. The story of U.S. politics since the 1960s is the implacable counter-attack on the New Deal. See, e.g., Steven Fraser and Gary Gerstle, eds., *The Rise and Fall of the New Deal* (Princeton: Princeton University Press, 1992).

13. On divergence between growth rates and employment see Barry Jones, *Sleeper Awake* (Oxford: Oxford University Press, 1984); Fred Block, *Postindustrial Possibilities* (Berkeley: University of California, 1991); and Bob Rowthorn and Andrew Glyn, "The Diversity of Unemployment Experiences Since 1973" in Stephen Marglin and Juliet Schor, eds., *The Golden Age of Capitalism* (Oxford: Oxford University Press, 1991).

14. Katzenstein, "Introduction," in *Between Power and Plenty*, p. 3.

15. Mary Furner and Barry Supple, "Ideas, Institutions and State" in Furner and Supple, eds., *The State and Economic Knowledge: The American and British Experiences* (Cambridge: Cambridge University Press, 1990), p. 34. There are well-known exceptions where states cede to private groups authority to devise policy in certain areas. Sometimes formally and explicitly as in corporatist arrangements, sometimes informally.

16. Timothy McKeown, "The Limitations of Structural Theories of Commercial Policy" *International Organization* 40, 1 (Winter 1986).

17. On Japan see David Friedman, *The Misunderstood Miracle* (Ithaca: Cornell University Press, 1988); on France, see Stephen S. Cohen, *Modern Capitalist Planning* (Berkeley, CA: University of California Press, 1975).

18. Katzenstein, *Between Power and Plenty*, p. 11.

19. George Gilder, *The Spirit of Enterprise* (New York: Simon & Schuster, 1984); Jacques Ellul, *The Technological Society* (New York: Vintage, 1965).

20. Langdon Winner, *The Whale and the Reactor: A Search for Limits in an Age of High Technology* (Chicago, IL: University of Chicago Press, 1986), p. 45.

21. See Harley Shaiken, *Work Transformed* (New York: Holt, Winston, Rinehart, 1985); Winner, *The Whale and the Reactor*; and David F. Noble, *Forces of Production* (New York: Knopf, 1984).

22. Winner, *Whale and the Reactor*, pp. 54–55.

23. Technological optimism is a powerful element in socialist thought. Note Mitterand's high-tech promotionalism in the 1980s or British Labour's slogan on the "white heat of a technological revolution" by which the United Kingdom escaped being seared, or Lenin's formula "Electrification plus soviets equals communism."

24. Neo-protectionist devices had "reached 30% of the total consumption of manufactures in the industrial countries in 1983, up from 20% in 1980." *Wall Street Journal*, 7 January 1986, p. 60.

25. Martin Carnoy, "Multinationals in a Changing World: Whither the Nation State?" in Carnoy, Manuel Castells, Stephen S. Cohen, Fernando Cardoso *The New Global Economy in the Information Age* (University Park: Pennsylvania State University Press, 1993), p. 94.

26. Evans, "Transnational Linkages and the Economic Role of the State," in Skocpol, et al., eds., *Bringing the State Back In* (New York: Cambridge University Press, 1984), p. 210. American multinationals collectively form the third or fourth largest economy in the world and account for 67 percent of U.S. merchandise exports and 41 percent of U.S. imports in 1988.

27. In the 1990s, the North American Free Trade Agreement was enacted among Canada, the United States, and Mexico. Mercosur was formed by Brazil, Argentina, Paraguay, and Uruguay while Chile, Bolivia, and Colombia considered entry. Among the other Latin American pacts are Caricom, the Andean Pact, and the Central American Common Market.

28. *New York Times*, 11 December 1994, p. 4.

29. Katzenstein, *Small States*, p. 25.

30. See Jeremy Brecher and Tim Costello, *Global Village or Global Pillage: Economic Reconstruction from the Bottom Up* (Boston: South End Press, 1994) and Richard Barnet, *Global Dreams: Imperial Corporations and the New World Order* (New York: Simon & Schuster, 1994).

31. Martin Kettle, "Dragon the Press Slayed," *The Guardian*, 17 December 1994.

32. "Left parties must turn the European Union and the Social Charter from the gimmick it is into a real instrument of defense for working people." Daniel Singer, "The Triumph of Euro-Americanism" *The Nation* 12 December 1994. There is a long way to go on the financial front too. Stephan Leibfried and Paul Pierson note that in 1990 Germany spent as much on child allowances as the EU devoted to the European Social Fund and European Fund for Regional Development. "Prospects for a Social Europe," *Politics and Society* 20, 3 (September 1992).

33. The United States believes that "our own developmental experience is a useful guide to productive economic policies." George Schulz quoted in *New York Times*, 28 (May 1986).

34. See Alice Amsden, *Asia's Next Giant* (New York: Oxford University Press, 1989): Stephen Haggard, *Pathways from the Periphery* (Ithaca, NY: Cornell University Press, 1992); Gary Gereffi and Donald Wyman, *Manufactured Miracles* (Princeton: Princeton University Press, 1990); Robert Wade, *Governing the Economy: Economic Theory and East Asian Industrialization* (Princeton: Princeton University Press, 1990); and James Fallows, *Looking At the Sun: The Rise of the East Asian Economic and Political System* (New York: Pantheon, 1993).

35. See Ira Magaziner and Robert Reich, *Minding America's Business* (New York: Harcourt Brace Jovanovich, 1982) on "comparative" versus "competitive" advantage.

36. David Dickson, *The New Politics of Science* (New York: Pantheon, 1984), p. 214.

37. Katzenstein, *Small States*, and *Corporatism and Change: Austria, Switzerland and the Politics of Industry* (Ithaca: Cornell University Press, 1985); and Robert Kuttner, *The Economic Illusion* (Boston: Houghton Mifflin, 1984) and *The End of Laissez-Faire.*

38. See Freeman, et al., *Technical Innovation and Unemployment*, p. 134.

39. S. M. Miller and Donald Tomaskovic-Devey, *Recapitalizing America* (London: Routledge Kegan Paul, 1982), p. 19.

40. Lee Price, "Growing Problems for American Workers in International Trade," in Thomas A. Kochan, ed., *Challenges and Choices Facing American Labor* (Cambridge, MA: MIT Press, 1985), p. 141.

41. Zysman, *Governments, Markets and Growth*, p. 46.

42. Stephen S. Cohen, "Geoeconomics: Lessons from America's Mistakes" in Carnoy, *The New Global Economy in the Information Age*, p. 108.

43. Fritz W. Scharpf, *Crisis and Choice in European Social Democracy* (Ithaca: Cornell University Press, 1991).

44. Robert Z. Lawrence, "Is Trade Deindustrializing America?" *Brookings Papers on Economic Activity* I (1983).

45. See Chapter 4.

46. The machine tool industry is a paradigmatic case of the "productive potential" shortage argument advanced by Freeman and associates. Capital goods imports rise from 8 percent of U.S. purchases in the mid-1970s to 18 percent by 1985; imports captured 45 percent of the machine tools market (up from 17 percent in 1978) while almost 200 of 850 U.S. machine tool firms folded.

47. Juan Rada, "The Microelectronics Revolution: Implications for the Third World," in *Development Dialogue* 2, (1981).

48. Gerd Junne, "Automation in the North" in James A. Caporaso, ed., *A Changing International Division of Labor* (Boulder: Lynn Rienner, 1987).

49. Ibid., p. 17.

50. Carnoy, "Whither the Nation-State?" in Castells, *The New Global Economy in the Information Age,* p. 72.

51. Ralph Kaplinsky, *The Impact of Electronics on the International Division of Labour* (London: Frances Pinter, 1982).

52. See Barry Buzan, "Economic Structure and International Security: The Limits of the Liberal Case," *International Organization* 38, 3 (Autumn 1984).

53. Manuel Castells, "The Informational Economy and the New International Division of Labor," in Carnoy, *The New Global Economy in the Information Age*, p. 34.

54. Ibid., p. 37.

55. See, for example, Robert Boyer, ed., *The Search for Labour Market Flexibility* (Oxford: Oxford University Press, 1988).

56. S. M. Miller and Donald Tomaskovic-Devey, *Recapitalizing America*, pp. 103–104.

57. Lester Thurow, "Jobs Versus Productivity: The Euro-American Dilemma" *Technology Review* 2, 9 (October 1984).

58. *New York Times*, 4 December 1994.

59. Richard Barnet, "Lords of the Global Economy," *The Nation* 19 December 1994.

60. OTA, *The Automation of America's Offices* (Washington, GPO, 1985); and Karen Nussbaum of National Association of Working Women, quoted in *Chicago Tribune*, 22 November 1985, p. 2.

61. McDermot, ibid.

62. Peter Evans, ibid.

63. Nora and Minc, *Computerization of Society*, p. 196.
64. Kuttner, *The Economic Illusion*, p. 178.
65. See Frederic C. Deyo, *Beneath the Miracle: Labor Subordination in the New Asian Industrialism* (Berkeley, CA: University of California, 1989). More recently, see Stephen Haggard's conclusion in *Pathways from the Periphery*. James North perceptively suggests that a crucial element in success was a "courageous and principled opposition in Korea which eventually pressured reforms. All along, South Korea's shipbuilders and auto workers felt that they were working those long hours for a potentially different and democratic future." *The Nation*, 13 June 1994, p. 842.
66. See Charles Sabel "The Internal Politics of Trade Unions" in Susanne Berger, ed., *Organizing Interests in Western Europe* (Cambridge: Cambridge University Press, 1982), pp. 218–221.
67. James Alt, "Political Parties, World Demand, and Unemployment: Domestic and International Sources of Economic Activity," *American Political Science Review* 79, 4 (December 1985), p. 1020.
68. On the notions of "supply" and of "demand" for adjustment, see David K. Stout, "The Impact of Technology on Economic Growth in the 1980s," *Daedelus*, 109, 1 (Winter 1980).
69. Carnoy, in *The New Global Economy in the Information Age,* p. 23. In 1988, U.S. multinationals had 78 percent of assets, 70 percent of sales, and 74 percent of employment at home. The Japanese figures are nearly 90 percent, p. 53.
70. Ronald Muller, *Revitalizing America* (New York: Simon & Schuster, 1979).
71. *The New York Times*, 4 December 1994.
72. Ibid.
73. *The New York Times*, 22 November 1994.
74. Henry Nau, "Making U.S. Trade Policy Truly Strategic," *International Journal* XLIX, 3 (Summer 1994), p. 532.
75. Richard Rosecrance, *The Rise of the Trading State* (New York: Basic Books, 1986), pp. 40–41.
76. Fred Block, *The Origins of International Monetary Disorder* (Berkeley, CA: University of California, 1977), p. 3.
77. John Kenneth Galbraith, "The Larger World Economy" in Colm Keane, ed., *The Jobs Crisis* (Cork, Ireland: Mercier Press, 1993), p. 172.

7

Is Peace a Rational Choice in Ulster?

Few conflicts have generated more cynicism and ritualized despair among onlookers than the Northern Irish "troubles." Pundits rarely have been able to resist the temptation to pronounce the Ulster plight insoluble.[1] Only a week before the 1994 ceasefire a noted British columnist berated his government for its "breathtaking" naivete: the Provisional Irish Republican Army (PIRA) "was playing with [British politicians] like a cat toying with two wounded mice."[2] Even if a cease-fire were announced, the IRA would only split and continue the fight. "Nobody conversant with Irish politics has any hope" for a rational dialogue.[3] Indeed, the day of the cease-fire only 30 percent of Catholics and 9 percent of Protestants surveyed believed it would be permanent.[4] On 9 February 1996, after seventeen months of fragile peace, the IRA with what it said was "great reluctance" bombed London's Docklands, and that commentator at last seemed correct, though for all the wrong reasons.

"Rational" may not be the first adjective that commends itself to investigators of Ulster's strife; nonetheless, most analysts recognize that contending groups there do try to relate means to ends in light of changing circumstances. If so, the unspoken premise behind the pessimism is that peace really was not a rational choice for the contestants. The credible incentives on offer could not induce all the necessary parties to explore, let alone enter, an accord.

I must mention at the outset that I use "rational" in its everyday meaning (as "able to reason, sensible, sane, moderate") rather than in the severely constricted sense commonly employed in rational choice models.[5] In ordinary usage "rational" is virtually synonymous with "reasonable." *Webster's Dictionary* informs us that with regard to policies, projects, or acts, "rational" means "satisfactory to the reason or actuated by reason," while "reasonable" implies a "weaker" application of guidance by reason, "applying to actions or decisions or choices that are practical, sensible, just or fair."[6] Why a need to be just or fair in human affairs weakens the rationality of analysis is a question no one has answered satisfactorily.[7] Indeed, critics are well aware that the artificial context and narrow criteria needed to sustain elegant rational choice frameworks usually yield results that in practice are neither practical, nor sensible, nor just, nor fair.[8] Perhaps we really are in need of "reasonable choice models," but here I take the less ambitious tack of challenging the unduly restrictive use of "rational" in academic discourse.

Yet who can blame nay-sayers?[9] British Ulster for twenty-five terrible years was a perfect paradigm of irreconcilable interests. The IRA wanted a British withdrawal and Irish unification; Loyalists wanted to restore their customary domination; the British, reluctant to pressure the Loyalist majority, wanted to crush the IRA or, failing that, keep the lid on at "acceptable levels" of costs; and the Irish Republic, fearful of a spillover, wanted to stay out of the way as much as possible. As long as any one side believed it benefited more by fighting than by the likely outcome of negotiations, the war continued.

The toll of the "low intensity" war has been high. From 1969 until the Provisional IRA's cease-fire, Northern Ireland suffered more than 3,100 deaths (equivalent to 100,000 in mainland Britain), 38,600 injuries and 10,000 bomb blasts. More than 100,000 people emigrated. Unemployment rose from 6 percent in 1968 to 12 percent in 1978 and is now at about 13 percent. Despite remedial measures, Catholics to this day have borne the brunt of joblessness with rates consistently double those of Protestants. Few working-class families, especially Catholics, escaped systematic intimidation and surveillance in a small society of one and half million in an area the size of Connecticut.[10]

Northern Ireland is patrolled by three times as many police per capita as on the mainland; the security bill exceeds health and education spending combined. Ulster drew a net surplus over revenue of four billion pounds, not including defence, from the United Kingdom treasury last year. Since 1969 Britain spent twenty-five billion pounds coping with Ulster—funds that politicians dearly would love to have put to better use elsewhere, such as tax cuts for wealthy Tory voters.[11] The IRA bombing campaign struck London spectacularly hard in recent years (so hard that a major Japanese investor made veiled threats to pull out if the British could not protect their property). Ulster-related killings were committed as far away as Gibraltar and Germany. For twenty-five years every peace feeler and initiative has quickly crumbled.

What changed to enable the start of a peace process? Key influences include the initial euphoria over political settlements in the Middle East and South Africa, the end of the cold war, the clear inability of any side to prevail in the foreseeable future, sheer war weariness, and perhaps an intangible yearning by leaders to write themselves into history books. The diminished influence of Britain in U.S. policy circles in the post–cold war era arguably exerted a positive effect too. President Clinton, in granting Gerry

Adams a U.S. visa last year, reportedly overruled the CIA director, FBI director, secretary of state, and U.S. ambassador in London—not to mention brushing aside angry British protests.

Loyalists are only too well aware that their peculiar brand of "loyalty" is not warmly reciprocated in mainland Britain where 67 percent favor options other than keeping Ulster and a majority want troops withdrawn.[12] The British, who declare they have "no selfish or strategic interest" in Ulster any longer, also have incurred continual embarrassments over alleged "shoot-to-kill" policies, the wrongful jailing of Irish prisoners, and an erosion of civil liberties. Feature films such as *In the Name of the Father* or *Hidden Agenda* publicized this seamy side. The European Union was no comfort either. A month prior to the cease-fire, for example, a pro-Sinn Fein pressure group submitted to the European Court of Justice a challenge to an exclusion order against Gerry Adams under the United Kingdom Prevention of Terrorism Act 1989 which the group argued breached European law and was "a misuse of antiterrorism laws."

MEDDLING THROUGH

For all these cumulative pressures nothing was more crucial for kickstarting the peace process than unorthodox initiatives taken outside formal channels. One must strain now to recall that at first John Hume was vilified for inaugurating talks in 1988 with Sinn Fein, the political wing of the IRA. Only a decade ago Margaret Thatcher had scolded U.S. House Speaker Tip O'Neill who had the temerity to suggest that Britain "bears heavy responsibility for the failures in recent years on the political front."[13] Yet it was private diplomacy by an ad hoc U.S. delegation, led by former Congressman and Clinton confidante Bruce Morrison, that tapped U.S. government influence to play a vital role in reassuring both Ulster communities sufficiently so as to break the deadlock.[14] Eventually, all groups—except Ian Paisley's Democratic Unionist Party—were induced to take necessary chances.

The IRA overcame bitter memories of a 1975 cease-fire that leaders believed with some justice was only a British ploy to lure the organization into the open to be crushed. The new cease-fire is in part a result of a changeover to a new leadership emphasizing a "diversified struggle on many fronts." As long ago as 1980 Sinn Fein's Gerry Adams admitted that "there can be no military victory."[15] The new political emphasis stemmed from a "long war" strategy that the IRA adopted in the late 1970s when it became clear that "one big push" would not drive the British out.

Sinn Fein abandoned political abstention in 1986 and contrived as best as it could to distance itself from—without ever repudiating—unpopular IRA actions.[16] In 1989 Gerry Adams stressed the urgent need to "take political risks" to achieve peace. That same year Britain's Northern Ireland Secretary Peter Brooke significantly stated that it was "difficult to envisage a military defeat of the IRA" because the tactics required only seemed to breed more republican recruits. Indeed, the IRA long has expressed its willingness to engage in "a *negotiated* settlement, not an immediate withdrawal" so long as the British are willing to put everything—particularly the Loyalist veto—on the table.[17]

Provo supporters—especially in the United States—have a dismaying tendency to regard the million Northern Protestants as nothing more than pawns who must come to their senses once the British leave. In 1991 Sinn Fein recognized the obvious at last by stating they "cannot and should not ever coerce the Protestant people into a united Ireland." However, a Sinn Fein's official unwisely asked that the "British should play a crucial and constructive role in persuading the Unionist community to reach a democratic accommodation with the rest of the Irish people," which only demonstrates that not all Provos fully appreciate that the Protestants loyalists are an independent force and have reasons to be extremely wary.[18]

Today one can hardly avoid concluding with many apprehensive loyalists that the IRA campaign succeeded insofar as it achieved recognition and reached the threshold of negotiations from a degree of strength, that particularly the bombing campaign in London—such spectacular strikes as Bishopsgate, the Baltic Exchange, and Downing Street—"forced the British to the negotiating table." The British can just as plausibly deny it. They conceivably could continue the war indefinitely but appear to have grasped that the only long-term solution lies in disengagement—the only question being the terms and the timing.

The IRA ceasefire at first had backed both the astonished British and the befuddled loyalists into a conciliatory corner. They then quickly scrambled to recover a fragment of the moral high ground by imposing the retroactive condition of "decommissioning" of arms on the IRA alone—a dangerous delaying tactic—through the first year of peace. This tactic only suggested that the Tory government valued its links to the own extreme right-wing, the military, and the loyalists more so than a negotiated peace settlement inclusive of republicans in Northern Ireland. Hence, U.S. diplomatic pressure and international opinion (which feed each other) needed to be wielded to force the Tories to break from their internal game of coalition maintenance and to incur the risks involved in undertaking a redistribution of power in the larger field of conflict in Ulster.

The IRA ceasefire at first backed both the loyalists and the British into a conciliatory corner. Now the respective "bottom lines" are that loyalists will not abide Irish unity, the British cannot be seen to cut and run, and nationalists can neither turn in their arsenal nor accept a solution that lacks an

"Irish dimension," (i.e., some sort of institutional avenue that may in time facilitate unity). For all their public posturings to the contrary, all opponents do understand these parameters. They also understand that whoever is seen gratuitously to ruin the peace process will pay a very high price. Of course, this may only mean that the "blame-allocation" publicity machines on all sides of the conflict are working at a supersonic clip to compete to put the right spin on events to support their ends.

Moderate politicians face the exceedingly delicate task of persuading their own hardliners to agree to settlement terms in such a way as to enable moderates in other groups—the IRA, Britain, the loyalists—to mollify their own hardline factions. Accordingly, everyone exaggerates positions and their gains to certain audiences and minimizes these to others. This inevitable double-talk aspect is not quite the same as behaving duplicitously. A judicious "shading" of interpretations is entirely tolerable so long as each side believes the process is harmless or even advantageous. But any outright duplicity—exposure of secret deals, sudden switches, or lies—would demolish the fragile chances for peace for years to come. Still, as all seasoned hands realize, some disruptive episodes of political expediency are bound to occur over a long-term process. All parties tacitly acknowledge the internal pressures with which negotiating partners cope and the short-term concessions they will be tempted to make.

The British Tory leadership contest on 4 July 1995 was such an occasion. The day before the vote reaffirming him as Tory leader and Prime Minister, Major, as a sop to far right-wingers, paroled a British paratrooper who was serving a life sentence for killing a teenage carjacker in Belfast. This rash act ignited demonstrations in nationalist areas and some dismay in working-class loyalist areas too, because of the contrast of special treatment for a British soldier as compared with the issue of early release of Irish prisoners. (Treatment of republicans in British mainland jails reportedly had worsened since the cease-fire.) Still, a beneficial side effect of the paratrooper's release was that it pushed prisoners to the top of the agenda so that ameliorative action became likely.

MANEUVERING TOWARD PEACE

The progression of events toward the breakthrough seems, in retrospect, almost eerily rapid. In 1991–92 Sinn Fein was excluded from three-stranded talks between Britain, the Irish Republic, and other Northern parties for its refusal to renounce violence. In April 1993 Sinn Fein began a new round of talks with Hume and soon also met with representatives of the Irish Republic's Fianna Fail-Labour government. The British Foreign Office had conducted exchanges with Sinn Fein representatives since 1990 to explore truce possibilities.

By 1993 these mainly epistolary contacts soon evolved into intermittent secret talks. The "leak" of news of these talks in 1993 (soon after an IRA bomb in Warrington killed several children) created an uproar in the House of Commons when Northern Ireland Secretary Patrick Mayhew was found to have misrepresented the nature of these extensive contacts. Mayhew survived the flap, which however may have delayed progress toward the cease-fire by a year.[19]

The Hume-Adams statement, expressing a consensus of militant and constitutional republicanism, rejected purely internal solutions and requested that the British undertake (reciprocal) demilitarization and to aid the "search for an agreement on Ireland by encouraging the process of national reconciliation."[20] In December 1993 British and Irish governments published a "joint declaration"—listing, among other things, conditions for Sinn Fein participation. (Sinn Fein sources believed the original declaration was meant to divert attention from the Hume/Adams discussions, restore control of the process to the two governments, and to score propaganda points against the IRA by offering extremely vague terms for peace.)[21] The British finally responded in May to persistent Sinn Fein requests for "clarifications" about the declaration. Then came the stunning announcement in August of "a complete cessation of military operations"—without conditions. Only a few days before virtually all experienced observers expected any cease-fire to be highly conditional and of a limited duration.

The Ulster Unionists, the largest loyalist party, were cajoled into the process through entreaties, enticements and assurances by Hume, the British and the U.S. officials (even as the Democratic Unionist Party (DUP) shunned what Paisley called a "black, dark conspiracy"). National security adviser Tony Lake assured Ulster Unionist Party (UUP) leader James Molyneaux that the United States would be even-handed. Lake earlier also had met Adams. Indeed, Americans were doubtless the key catalyst only because they had the power and credibility to assure republicans that the British would not treat peace overtures as signs of weakness or later renege on bargains. The United States, primarily though not only through the ad hoc delegation, has since played the benign role of guarantor so deftly in these bracing events that today nationalists and republicans consider the U.S. dimension "a permanent part of the Northern Ireland equation."[22]

British, Irish, and U.S. governments must work with extreme care and sensitivity to allay unionist fears without at the same time alienating the nationalists. (Sinn Fein representatives were only admitted to an International Investment conference in Belfast in December when U.S. pressure induced the British to reverse their foolish initial decision.) There is an inherent paradox operative here that this kind of extreme care requires a great deal of coordination which can appear to suspicious loyalists to resemble exactly the sort of conspiracy they are so inclined to find arrayed against them. The "British link" surely will stay in place for the foreseeable future—but will not rule out dual citizenship and other concessions for northern Catholics. Anyway, even if loyalists quite cheerfully agreed to unification, it would only inflict ruinous expenses on the Republic which simply cannot match United Kingdom subventions. The best interim ideal is installing vigorous legal and political reforms, reviving the economy and instituting, however vague, an "Irish dimension."

THE ROLE OF RATIONALITY

An analysis of Ulster must attend to shifts over time in the distribution of *relational* power among the combatants. The purpose is to identify points of leverage which can be used to enhance specific strategies and strengthen certain groups so as to increase likelihood of a progressive peaceful outcome. (Of course, one can guess erroneously, as the British did in conducting "criminalization" in the late 1970s and 1980s.) A related objective is identifying the means by which physical circumstances may be arrayed to alter the context within which the contending actors will deem their choices rational or not. This focus, of course, can be overdone and result in massive follies.

Cost-benefit accounts cannot encompass all relevant factors that shape the actors' preferences because not every factor that counts in a conflict is "countable." Morale and ideology, for examples, are not very amenable to meaningful measurement and manipulation.[23] "Social engineering optimism" is rightly distrusted. However, an action is rational where the ends and means are aptly related within a specific political context. The context is itself an object of political conflict because it determines what is rational. If the context can be changed so too should the criteria by which actors determine choices of actions in their self-interest. But this is not a process where Skinnerian lab rats automatically respond to environmental stimuli. All the actors are acutely aware of the ongoing manipulation of circumstances and images in the conflict. Structure isn't everything.

In this regard Margaret Archer usefully warns that "systemic influences are only part of the story about how cultural situations are made up for actors. The other part is made up of the casual relations operating between groups and individuals at the sociopolitical level. Such relationships have their own dynamics, rooted in different material interests, producing various forms of stratification and different ideal interests, such as ethnic, religious and linguistic divides . . . they influence what actors do on the spot. They form the other part of the interface and thus are codeterminates (with system conditioning) of what actually takes place."[24]

The overarching objective is to seek the maximum feasible concession of each negotiating party consistent with the self-interest of their support base. One needs to illuminate short-range policy options and to identify the actors who can be induced to implement them. The "interplay between structural possibilities for action and the actual behavior of social groups and leaders" obviously "do not always coincide."[25] The question then is why they have come to coincide in the fall of 1994 and whether the peace process can resume despite the bombings in 1996. Any useful analysis of the six counties, portrayed in the media as a gruesome backwater where the Irish pursue purely medieval vendettas, requires a sober sifting through the past.

COLONIALISM AND THE "MERE" IRISH

Ireland posed a grave security problem for English colonizers. Since the Anglo-Norman invasion of 1169, Spanish, French, and Papal troops arrived at various times to aid Irish insurgents. After English forces completed the conquest in 1607 the plantation of Ulster was conducted so as to discourage Scottish Presbyterian settlers from falling into "the barbarous customs of the Irish."[26] Previous settlers had a distressing tendency to become, according to the cliche, "more Irish than the Irish themselves."

The plantation coincided with the Protestant reformation so that the population divided neatly into colonizing Protestants and colonized Catholics. Here is the source of misleading media portrayals of a "holy war." As Geoffrey Bell observes, "the ancestors of the present-day loyalists were planted not to convert Ireland to Protestantism but to hold Ireland for England."[27] By 1775 only 5 percent of the land was owned by Catholics who were two-thirds of the population.

An Anglican aristocracy ruled imperiously over Presbyterians, too, but the "Ulster custom" conceded advantages that kept lower-class Protestants a rung above Catholics. In the 1790s a nonsectarian movement, influenced by the French Revolution, became alarmingly influential. An English officer informed his superior[28]

> I have arranged . . . to increase the animosity between Orangeman and the United Irish. Upon that animosity depends the safety of the centre countries of the North, were the Orangemen disarmed, or put down, or were they coalesced with another party, the whole of Ulster would be as bad as Antrim or Down.

British troops plus a sectarian-based *divisa et impera* strategy defeated the United Irishmen of 1798 who joined a dismal recital of bungled uprisings. A blend of bribery and coercion forged the Union of 1801 wherein few Irish industries withstood free trade.[29] Linen manufacture, which did not compete with English goods, provided an attractive base for investment and diversification.[30] So Ulster industrialized and there began an imbalanced development between North and the rest of the Island.

The radical Presbyterian of the United Irishmen was eclipsed in mid-nineteenth century by a fire-breathing Calvinism supported by landlords and a nascent bourgeoisie. Sectarian tendencies were exacerbated by intensifying competition for urban work and rack-rented land. By century's end, a class alliance of Protestants was consecrated through the Orange Order.

Over 1885–1913 Charles Stewart Parnell's Irish parliamentary party championed home rule bills that sparked resistance in Ulster. Parnell had planned a high-tariff autarkic strategy to develop the whole island. Ulster therefore feared market losses from retaliatory duties, tariff-induced higher prices for imported materials, higher taxes to subsidize the South and the prospect of becoming a minority within a vindictive Catholic state.

In 1912–13 when a home rule bill passed, British Tories stoked defiance in Ulster that was so fierce that the United Kingdom edged to the brink of civil war. One hundred thousand Ulster Protestant volunteers were quite prepared to kill British soldiers to retain the right to fly the British flag. After the "Curragh Mutiny" when British officers declined to fight their Ulster brethern, the Liberal government backed down. For Tories the partition of Ireland was not an end in itself but part of a larger power struggle.[31]

The British responded to the Anglo-Irish War of 1919–21 with an act partitioning six of nine Ulster counties from the other twenty-six. (In all Ulster home rulers held a majority of one.) The loyalist regime shed Catholic counties Monaghan, Cavan, and Donegal to assure a two-thirds Protestant majority. When Britain signed a treaty with republican forces in 1922, the Irish civil war erupted over the terms. But the "immediate cause of the South's bloody civil war was the Provisional Government's determination, under British pressure, to stamp out attacks by the IRA on the North."[32]

Ulster handily fended off the Southern upheavals with the aid of the British Army and U.K. funding. A 25 percent unemployment rate provided recruits for sectarian violence. The draconian Special Powers Act of 1922 was passed. Twenty-five nationalist (of a total of eighty) Ulster local councils were dissolved. The Unionist Party created desired political arrangements by gerrymandering, a restricted property-based franchise, and abolition of proportional representation voting.[33] These measures were designed to prevent power flowing to splinter groups that might divert Protestant workers into economic issues.[34] From 1929 until 1969 46 percent of Ulster seats went uncontested and the Unionists never lost a seat in Stormont or Westminster.[35]

CRACKS IN THE MINI-STATE

Rising unemployment for all denominations—30 percent in 1932—ignited a fragile nonsectarian movement. Many industrialists and landowners were born again as loyalists.[36] The nascent threat was snuffed by a blend of concessions, sectarian demagoguery and repression. In 1931 the United Kingdom agreed to fund shortfalls in social spending so that British taxpayers effectively subsidized a sectarian state that could not pay its own way. The ruling class thrived on high productivity, cheap labor, and low strike rates (a third the U.K. rate into the 1960s).[37] British governments otherwise ignored the province's internal problems.

In the 1950s shipbuilding, textile, and heavy engineering industries slipped against competition and sheer obsolescence. Unemployment fluctuated between 6 and 10 percent (the mainland rate was 2 percent). The Northern Ireland government took a technocratic-sectarian tack. A "forward-looking" fraction of the Ulster elite adapted the ongoing internationalization of capital to local circumstances.[38] Of 217 new firms in Ulster in 1945–66, 20 were sited in Catholic areas; Derry, two-thirds Catholic, was even bypassed as a site of a new university.[39] Foreign firms couldn't create enough jobs to soften a zero-sum sectarian environment anyway.[40] The new firms "on balance [seem] to have widened the gap between Protestant and Catholic workers— still leaving both susceptible to the uncertainty endemic to the international conditions of the textile industry."[41] In the late 1970s many firms, despite receiving state grants, would threaten to pull out rather than let the Fair Employment Agency examine their records.[42]

The nationalist community alternated between futile participation in the Stormont parliament and undertaking feeble IRA activities.[43] After the "border war" fiasco of 1956–62 a new chief of staff led the IRA from the nationalist physical force tradition toward social and political agitation. Avowals of marxism had alienated some members who had other dogmas to uphold.[44] By 1967 a new left-wing IRA had sold off its arsenal and supported the reformist aims of the Northern Ireland Civil Rights Association whose slogan was "British Rights for British citizens."[45]

The British welfare state gave the province a standard of living higher than in the Republic and provided many Catholics with educational opportunities and entry to the professional middle class.[46] Catholics in the mid-1960s were less nationalist and more assertive. But their demand for reforms, given the logic of the sectarianism, were unavoidably an assault on the core values and practices of the state. Moderate unionists like Premier Terence O'Neill were unable to appease Catholic and British pressures without incensing their party base. "To the vast majority of the Unionist Party," O'Neill recollected, "the activities of the Civil Rights movement appeared to be almost treasonable."[47] Loyalists reacted by splitting the heads of civil rights marchers and attacking Catholic neighborhoods.

ARMALITES AND BALLOT BOXES

The bombs that propelled O'Neill from office in April 1969 were loyalist devices disguised as republican explosives.[48] The IRA, caught empty-handed, rearmed. (At one point southern businessmen offered the IRA funds for weapons in exchange for a pledge to confine military activity to the North and to shed socialism.)[49] In August 1969, the British army entered Ulster "in aid of the civil power" and thus were fatally compromised. The army would humor Unionist paranoia about imminent Fenian blitzkriegs and so was at odds with politicians trying to push through credible reforms.

A Tory Party victory in June 1970 brought about a crackdown solely on the Catholic community.[50] While the army's enormously provocative arms sweeps netted less than 200 weapons of various vintages and lethality, the Protestants, undisturbed, possessed 100,000 licensed weapons, including two machine guns licensed "to kill otters."[51] In 1970 a Provisional wing, scorning the marxism of the "Official" leadership, broke away. This sequence cannot be overemphasized if one is to understand the escalating conflict. It was only when reformist hopes were extinguished that the Provos arose as a lethal symptom, not a cause, of Northern nightmares. But the "Provos" (and, later on, splinter groups) then added their own deadly dynamic.

On 9 August 1971 internment began by netting 342 Catholics and nary a Protestant. The result of this repressive masterstroke is that, while just 34 killings occurred from January to August, from that day to the end of the year 139 people died. The Compton report later attested to the "ill-treatment" dealt out in the internment camps. The Social Democratic and Labour Party (SDLP) withdrew from Stormont in protest. In January 1972 on "Bloody Sunday" British paratroopers killed thirteen unarmed demonstrators. After a horribly misfired reprisal the Official IRA called a cease-fire, committed itself to socialist parliamentary politics (as the Workers Party and most recently the breakaway Democratic Left) and ceaselessly condemned the Provo campaign.[52]

Britain began "direct rule" in March 1972. In abolishing Stormont the British fulfilled the Provisional IRA's intermediate goal. Decrying this evident "sellout," loyalist paramilitaries stepped up their random killing of Catholic civilians. In July, when the army reached a peak of 23,000 (proportionally higher than the United States forces in Vietnam), a truce with the IRA quickly foundered. The army first smashed nationalist "no go" areas and soon did likewise in some Loyalist neighborhoods. Loyalist paramilitaries declared war on the British, killing several erstwhile defenders over 48 hours before calling a halt.

In 1973–74 the British attempted to install a weak power-sharing government along with a proposed Council of Ireland in which the South was to
participate. The Executive, critics charge, was too hamstrung in resources
and authority to alleviate the Catholic community's plight while the "Irish
dimension," which was meant to be an empty promise, only served to antagonize loyalists.[53] Loyalist extremists mobilized a campaign of intimidation
that culminated in a province-wide strike that demolished the political experiment. The army declined to oppose the strike and what was, for all its
defects, the best chance thus far for a political breakthrough evaporated.[54]

MILITARY INITIATIVES AND POLITICAL INERTIA

Britain then attempted to destroy the nationalist—and only the nationalist—
paramilitaries. In 1977 Northern Ireland Secretary Roy Mason bragged that
the IRA was being squeezed "like a tube of toothpaste." Peace was at hand.
But the IRA reorganized; an intensified bombing campaign, assassinations of
"prestige targets" Christopher Ewert-Biggs, Airey Neave, and Lord Mountbatten,
and the killing of eighteen British soldiers in a single day at Warrenpoint
attested to their ferocious resilience. A captured British army document judged
that the Provos could wage war into the "foreseeable future," that members
were not the mindless thugs decried in tabloids but were genuinely politically motivated, disciplined, and formidable, assessed the new active service
units as virtually impenetrable and saw no end to conflict so long as the
British army stayed in Northern Ireland.[55] The apparent failure to stamp out
the IRA stirred no fresh political initiatives. Meeting British officials in 1978,
Senator Daniel Patrick Moynihan beheld malign neglect.[56]

> I came away absolutely dazed; [They] had no intention of doing anything
> except keeping the British there. The question of Northern Ireland never
> even came up at the conferences of the two leading British political par-
> ties. There is no political will to settle.

New prime minister Thatcher intensified the "Ulsterization" and "criminalization" policies in place since 1976. Ulsterization, like Vietnamization,
relied on indigenous security forces—a 93 percent Royal Ulster Constabulary (RUC) and 98 percent Ulster Defense Regiment (and a multitude of
covert British operatives).[57] "Police primacy" put the army under the direction of a professionalized and itself highly militarized RUC. These measures
diminished both public pressure and media coverage of Northern Ireland
because of fewer British casualties and inevitably enhanced the sectarian character
of the war because most corpses in army [The Ulster Defense Regiment] or
RUC uniforms thereafter had to be Protestant. "Criminalization" explicitly
intended to submerge or erase the political dynamics driving Ulster's con-

flicts, so it was no wonder that Senator Moynihan detected no trace of a "political will to settle." Nonetheless, the Provisional IRA campaign continued—joined by fierce splinters: the Irish National Liberation Army and the Irish People's Liberation Organisation.

Carrots accompanied the stick. Britain increased public spending to alleviate zero-sum struggles and to encourage support for moderates.[58] This paid dividends by enlarging the middle class but such spending was little help for working-class communities where repressive forces were most keenly felt. Pleas for new political initiatives went ignored. The "Peace people" of 1976–77 briefly arose but sputtered out. The abiding question for the Catholic community was, peace on what terms? Unfocused yearnings for peace couldn't alter institutions that reproduce sectarian power and attitudes.[59]

Great Britain ended internment and abolished the "special category" status originally granted the IRA (and extended to loyalist paramilitary prisoners) in 1972. In March 1976 the first men went "on the blanket." In 1981 ten republican prisoners starved to death for a status that need only have connoted recognition of the abbreviated legal system that Catholics dubbed the "conveyor belt."[60] Margaret Thatcher claimed that the strike was the IRA's "last card" at a time when the IRA was turning away 80 percent of recruits.[61] In June 1981 two hunger strikers were elected to the Republic's parliament, annihilating the image the British had tried to construct of the Provos as nothing more than a collection of thugs and lunatics.

The Anglo-Irish Summit of 1980 was more a matter of having to be seen to be doing something than actually doing anything to bring parties to the negotiating table. The Irish premier intensified border security (costing three times more per capita than in the United Kingdom), was discreet during the hunger strike and curbed his republican wing in exchange for "study groups." Still, this was an admission of an "Irish dimension." New premier Garret Fitzgerald, weathering riotous protests, was unable to alter the hard stance of British leaders. The hunger strike ended and three days afterward the British granted lesser demands of the prisoners.

In 1982 a woefully inadequate Assembly election was held. The SDLP boycotted it but Provisional Sinn Fein shockingly reaped a third of the Catholic vote. In Westminster elections the next year Sinn Fein attained a high of 42 percent of the Catholic vote and 13.4 percent overall (versus 17.9 percent for the SDLP; 34 percent for the Ulster Unionist Party and 20 percent for Paisley's Democratic Unionists). The SDLP argued that the Sinn Fein result expressed "the frustration that the people feel against the totally inadequate proposals of the British Government" which led "many to express it in the most vehement way open to them in constitutional terms."[62] The SDLP then took institutional refuge in 1983 in the New Ireland Forum in Dublin.[63] Thatcher bluntly rejected the three options the Forum offered but, after an IRA assassination attempt and U.S. pressure was brought to bear on her by O'Neill, Moynihan, and Ted Kennedy she began negotiations that developed into the 1985 Anglo-Irish agreement.[64] This time the British weathered furious loyalist protests and the RUC's behavior impressed even some nationalists.[65]

Meanwhile the Ulster Defence Association (UDA) offered its own program for an Independent Ulster with a new constitution, a bill of rights, proportional representation, and safeguards for the minority. But power-sharing with fixed ministerial seats and an Irish dimension was unacceptable. Still, the UDA and Ulster Volunteer Force (UVF) had edged teasingly close to a class politics perspective. The Provisional IRA found the proposals "encouraging."

As the "material bases of consent" of the Protestant hegemony eroded through economic decline and direct rule, segments of the Protestant working-class groped for new designs to accommodate their conception of Catholic needs with their own interests. There also have been ongoing contacts on matters of cross-community interest.[66] Likewise there are a plethora of reports of surprise by both these working-class communities at their wide range of agreement on issues other than constitutional arrangements. But such contacts cannot flourish in the absence of durable democratic institutions.

THE CHANGING CONTEXT OF COSTS

In 1981, in the disheartened aftermath of the hunger strike and a stillborn plan for "rolling devolution," British Labour Party members began to grumble openly about the obstructive veto the Northern majority held over constitutional change. A spokesman on Northern Irish affairs addressed a Protestant audience impatiently:

> the fact that there seems to be no serious political movement taking place means that people are seriously asking the question that the guarantee seems to be one-sided. They are asking what part of the guarantee comes back to them, and there are suggestions in many quarters that if the guarantee is backed by the U.K. then there is an obligation on the politicians of Northern Ireland to come up with a solution.

However, prodding loyalists leaders to solve the problem is disingenuous because they do not determine their own destinies. The Loyalists have felt aggrieved and abandoned when Britain shut Stormont, negotiated with the IRA in 1972 and 1975, were called "spongers" in 1974 by prime minister Harold Wilson, and over the signing of the 1985 Anglo-Irish Agreement granting consultative status to the Republic on Northern affairs.

The "leverage" lay elsewhere. The power to allocate power among the various sites (the Loyalists, militant republicans and the Irish Republic) is in

British hands. The British determine the value of the resources that other players hold and they control the form the bidding may take on the Ulster gameboard. British politicians long have denied their own contributing role to the conflict—posing as "peacekeepers"—and thus denied their ability to influence bargaining outcomes. The "political will to settle" stems from how the context of cost and benefits is constructed (and reconstructed)—and that is determined by the internal balance of political forces, international pressures, and the rank of Ulster in British policy priorities.

While the British link is in no imminent danger of snapping, most Unionists know they cannot wrap themselves in some political form of amber forever. Conciliation of some kind must occur. In the early 1980s a formerly vehement loyalist politician, for example, praised then-Premier Garret Fitzgerald's tabling of the claim on the North in the Irish Republic constitution's Articles 2 and 3 (an "unnecessary affront to the majority") and expressed respect for the "long-term aspirations of the Catholics" in the North.[67] Protestants "would find it easier to envisage some institutional relationship such as a community of the British isles in social and economic terms." Here were early signals of acknowledgment of potential common ground.

The IRA campaign aimed to raise the costs of British "occupation," not to shift the calculus of the Loyalists. Indeed, nothing short of a republican cease-fire could have accomplished that. Sinn Fein under Gerry Adams and Martin McGuinness had to stress that side of the ledger. The problem was to demonstrate to major loyalist parties and factions that the cost of standing pat does not outweigh the best bargain that can be struck with the Republic and United Kingdom over transition to a democratic governing structure and an unspecified consultative arrangement with the Republic.

Must Protestant hardliners respond with scorn? Paisley—who promised to wreck any new Assembly—echoes the SDLP on most social and economic issues and earlier had opposed internment. He has in the past ventured (and retreated from) several startlingly conciliatory messages, for he cannot move faster than his followers will allow. British policies can alter the price of intransigence relative to benefits of a power-sharing framework, which is the maximum feasible concession for Protestants.

DELICATE LINKAGES

The theory of linkage helps to clarify the structure of the strategy of inducing agreements. The recommended route is not punitive "blackmailing" but "back-scratching." That is, the British refrain from a policy regarded as in the interest of both parties (direct rule) and threaten to behave in their own interest (eventual disengagement) unless Loyalists comply.[68] The "worst case scenario" must be considerably outweighed by incentives to comply, e.g., rises in social expenditure, investment, and joint cooperation. What matters in back-scratching is that the welfare of *both* parties is improved if compliance is forthcoming. This presumes, of course, that they both value the good in question.

> Under backscratching, the linkee is at worst will be as well off as he would have been without the offer, and can be better off than if the offer had not been made. Were it not for the linkage, the other actor would simply go ahead with the action threatened. By joining issues, the linker offers the linkee the option of weighing interests in each issue and compensating for the foregoing an action the linker would otherwise undertake.[69]

In Ulster one must demonstrate that the linkage, if accepted, will increase "the level of satisfaction of both the linker and linkee can attain."[70] This distinction would certainly have been lost on most beholders had the IRA campaign continued. It has always been in the interest of Loyalist leaders to portray any potential bargain as blackmail (as they did after the Anglo-Irish Agreement in 1985). Loyalist attention must be drawn to the mitigating aspects of entering negotiation and to the task of maximizing gains there.[71]

PEACE FORUM AND AFTER

John Major's government, despite reliance on Unionist votes, initially modified its demands for preconditions for talks with Sinn Fein. In a meeting with Sinn Fein held at Stormont (called "historic" because it was done openly), the British demanded not the destruction but the ambiguous "decommissioning" of IRA weapons. Major skillfully played to the Unionist audience while allowing enough latitude in language for the IRA—which its own constituency would think insane for disarming—to appear to comply. Adams replied that this demand was agreeable if it included British Army, loyalists, and RUC weapons. As one republican remarked, "the IRA campaign is not the only campaign of violence" in Ulster. Over the years 1969–89 loyalists inflicted 25 percent of all Ulster killings and three-quarters of these were innocent Catholics, not paramilitaries.[72] In the three years up to the cease-fire loyalist squads killed more people than the IRA.

The Unionists had reason to welcome new Irish prime minister John Bruton of Fine Gael, known for his pro-Unionist views, and, more ambivalently, the fiercely anti-IRA Democratic Left. All partners in the Fine Gael-Labour-Democratic Left coalition formed in December 1994 agree that Articles 2 and 3 (which claim the whole territory of the island) can be amended to convert a territorial claim into an aspiration for unity. However, there is the quid pro quo that all parties must accept equal legitimacy of the two allegiances in Northern Ireland. The Irish government also desires a bill of rights and a three-stranded approach to negotiations. Any new North-South institutions should have executive powers. The Irish Republic can be of little help economically.

At the Forum for Peace and Reconciliation in Dublin business groups, who are not reliable at such projections, spoke of 75,000 new jobs. The European Union at Essen pledged support of 300 million ECUs [231 million British pounds] over three years and the U.S. ambassador to Ireland reaffirmed U.S. promises of aid of about 100 to 150 million dollars. Northern Ireland Secretary Patrick Mayhew had plans to redirect 180 million pounds in security spending over three years to economic and social purposes. Such funding would help the British "backscratch." For "unless economic regeneration gives jobs and hope to the unemployed, such people would not interconnect with the peace process," the Irish Congress of Trade Unions warn. This regenerative project requires community involvement, a halt to privatization, cross-border projects, a long term unemployment program, transparency in operation of programs, fair employment measures, retraining of displaced workers, and reform of policing.[73]

At the forum a Sinn Fein spokesman asked the British to "tilt the balance away from the negative power of the [loyalist] veto towards the positive power of consent, of negotiating consent." The British are the key card— but they are not omnipotent either. The Loyalist veto cannot suddenly be deleted without a ferocious reaction. An expert on loyalism found that "anything a Unionist might describe as progress is ruled out, and unless Loyalist paramilitaries increase their killing rate, "peace process" means conceding to republicans enough to persuade them to end their terror."[74] Major made a referendum pledge to the Unionists to assure them there will be no unity without their consent. Whatever the IRA envisions, not all Northern Catholics are eager to join the Republic anyway.[75]

The best interim ideal is legal and political reforms, a revived economy, and a good deal of time for healing. Then, under demographic and other benign pressures, Ulster may in the next century join the rest of the Island—or may not. This time frame, and the risk that it may be wrong, is understood by the Provos. So this is the terrain where all the crucial "shading" will take place. What is certain now is that there will be no United Ireland and no return to local government except in the context of a political settlement acceptable to the nationalists.

As of New Year's Day 1995 British troops were off the streets of Derry and west Tyrone but still in full gear in Belfast and regarded there as "highly provocative"—even more so in South Armagh.[76] The British, despite SDLP appeals and warnings, sent in the notoriously aggressive Paratroop Regiment, which was responsible for Bloody Sunday shootings. Concerned about the "negative impact on nationalists of the continued militarization of security in conditions of peace," former Irish premier Garret Fitzgerald cited mounting evidence that some British soldiers are now "more active than previously in harassing and assaulting young people in nationalist areas."[77] Encouragingly, the British responded to the complaints by pulling day patrols off the streets of Belfast in mid-January 1995.

The RUC too remain unacceptable in nationalist areas. (The RUC have 8,500 regulars, 3,200 full-time reserves, and 1,400 part-timers—and there are still 18,500 soldiers in the North.) The SDLP criticized the RUC chief Hugh Annesley for a dismissive response to their report on measures necessary to reform the police so as to be acceptable to the entire community.[78]

The approach of the cease-fire's anniversary was heralded by a spate of tit-for-tat arson attacks on Catholic churchs and Orange lodge halls. Republican street demonstrations and pressure from the Irish government barely prodded the British into the most miserly concession of remission of sentences—from 30 to 50 percent—for Irish prisoners. Even Mayhew said that this measure, which only restores procedures in place in 1989, would be shelved if "serious doubts start to arise about the continuation of the violence."[79] These niggardly concessions may only demonstrate that British officials still are prone to behave according to historical form in Irish matters—that is, at their very worst. But the more economical explanation is that Major has a thin majority and the Unionists supply thirteen votes. Even allowing for the need to mollify Loyalists, British tactics as of the Fall of 1995 seem geared to assure that the first anniversary of the cease-fire would be the only one.

Headlines declared "IRA Blasts Peace Process" and news anchors intoned daily that the IRA "holds the peace process hostage." Yet the underlying reality is that the Tories and the two main Unionist parties could hardly have done any more to provoke a resumption of hostilities than if they had donated the explosives that the Provos eventually detonated. How can a peace process that is not in motion be "derailed," a process already paralyzed by Unionist intransigence and British short-term electoral calculations?[80] What the *New York Times* called a "cautious" British approach to negotiations had dwindled long ago to a strategy of slow but certain sabotage of the peace process.

The last straw for the IRA was Prime Minister John Major's rejection of recommendations by former Senator George Mitchell's International Commission that Britain relax its demand that the Republican guerrillas surrender their arms in advance of the all-party talks for which the IRA had called its unilateral cease-fire in order to enter in the first place! This demand was no part of the original conditions required for talks.[81]

The explanation for the blast is simple enough. The Tory government majority dwindled to three by January 1996 and so became increasingly reliant on Unionist votes in Westminster. This cynical (if understandable) move may only have worked to strengthen the hand of those in the Republican movement who expect nothing from Britain except treachery. In this conflict, as during the cold war, hard-liners need one another in order to manufacture self-fulfilling prophecies. The Canary Wharf bombing was solely the IRA's decision, but it was also made inevitable because of unnecessarily provocative British tactics.

CONCLUSION

There certainly is political space available where common goals overlap so that each side may be coaxed to consider conceding their ideal objectives ("not an Inch" or "Irish Unity now") in order to enjoy common goals. Polls indicate that the Protestant community is amenable to "power-sharing within the United Kingdom with guarantees for Catholics."[82] Consenting in addition to an institutional link with the Republic is surely not more noxious a prospect for Protestants than turning Belfast into another Beirut or a Sarajevo.

In the context of a political climate created by what hopefully is only an interrupted IRA cease-fire, Britain can alter, in part because of useful U.S. "meddling," the value of intransigence by each party relative to other political and economic benefits that they can realistically secure. The objective of negotiation is to extract the maximum concession from each party that is consistent with their support base—and so a good deal of interpretive double-talk doubtless will take place. The margins, however, are set: no united Ireland (at least not right away) and no return to local government except through a settlement acceptable to the nationalists. Major—or soon Tony Blair—is not so likely to forget that now.

Notes

1. Among the exceptions are Jack Holland *Too Long a Sacrifice* (New York: Dodd, Mead & Company, 1983); Tom Hadden and Kevin Boyle, *Northern Ireland: A Positive Proposal* (London: Penguin, 1990); and Brendan O'Leary and John McGarry, *Explaining Northern Ireland* (Oxford: Basil Blackwell, 1995).
2. Simon Jenkins, in *The Times* (London) 24 August 1994.
3. Ibid.
4. *Irish Times*, 3 September 1994.
5. *The Pocket Oxford Dictionary* (Oxford: Clarendon Press, 1969, 5th ed.), p. 680.
6. *Webster's Third New International Dictionary* (Springfield, MA: G. & C. Merriam Co., 1964), p. 1885.
7. Regarding Ulster John McGarry and Brendan O'Leary pertinently note that it is "usually conceded that opposition to discrimination is not exclusively materialist but rather is rooted in norms about justice and fair play—which is why well-to-do Catholics are as incensed about discrimination as those without jobs and why

it is difficult to separate complaints about economic discrimination from those about political or cultural oppression." *Explaining Northern Ireland* (Oxford: Basil Blackwell, 1995), p. 283.

8. See, as an early example, Jürgen Habermas, *Knowledge and Human Interests* (Boston: Beacon Press, 1973).

9. John Hume said he was disturbed that certain commentators and politicians seem to "have a vested interest in the peace process not working, so that they can be proved right." *Irish Times*, 23 July 1994.

10. See Rona Fields, *Society Under Siege* (Philadelphia: Temple University Press, 1978); Frank Burton, *The Politics of Legitmacy: War in a Belfast Community* (London: 1978) and Fionnula O'Conner, *In Search of a State: Catholics in Northern Ireland* (Dublin: Blackstaff Press, 1993). On loyalists, see Sarah Nelson, *Ulster's Uncertain Defenders* (New York: Syracuse University Press, 1984).

11. *Evening Standard*, 31 August 1994.

12. Only 16 percent said they were concerned by the lack of human and civil rights in Northern Ireland. *Irish Times*, 3 September 1994.

13. Ulster was an "issue for the people of Northern Ireland, this government, this parliament, and no one else," Thatcher thundered. *The Guardian*, 22 March 1980.

14. The ad hoc delegates include Niall O'Dowd (Irish Voice and Irish America, publisher), Chuck Feeney, of General Atlantic group; William Flynn, chief executive of Mutual Life, and Joe Jameson of the AFL-CIO.

15. *Hibernia* 17 January 1980.

16. The relationship between Sinn Fein and the Provisional IRA is extremely complex. See J. Bowyer Bell, *IRA: Tactics and Targets* (Dublin: Poolbeg, 1990) and Martin Dillon, *The War Within* (London: Transworld Publishers, 1994).

17. Dillon, *The War Within*, p. 258.

18. *Irish Times*, 10 December 1994.

19. *Irish Times*, 26 November 1994.

20. *Guardian*, 29 August 1994.

21. Dillon, *The War Within*, pp. 247–249 and conclusion.

22. Frank Millar, "Major's Crisis Could Carry Crucial Implications for Peace," *Irish Times*, 31 December 1994.

23. On "rationalistic" misjudgments in the Vietnam War see, for example, William James Gibson, *The Perfect War* (New York: Random House, 1991).

24. Margaret Archer, *Culture and Agency* (Cambridge: Cambridge University Press, 1989), p. xx.

25. Fernando Cardoso, in David Collier, *The New Authoritarianism in Latin America* (Princeton: Princeton University Press, 1979), p. 56.

26. Liam De Paor, *Divided Ulster* (London: Penguin, 1970), pp. 19–20.

27. Geoffrey Bell, *The Protestants of Ulster* (London: Pluto Press, 1976), p. 13.

28. De Paor, ibid., p. 40.

29. Emil Strauss, *Irish Nationalism and British Democracy* (London: Methuen & Co., 1951), p. 15.

30. Liam O'Dowd, "Shaping and Reshaping the Orange State," in Liam O'Dowd, et al., eds. *Northern Ireland: Between Civil Rights and Civil War* (London: CSE Books, 1980), p. 6.

31. "I was only a puppet," Lord Carson, leader of the Ulster resistance, later said, "and so was Ulster, and so was Ireland in the political game that was to get the Conservative Party into power." Quoted in Desmond Greaves, *The Irish Crisis*

(London: International Publishers, 1974, 2nd ed.), p. 38.

32. Michael Farrell, *Northern Ireland: The Orange State* (London: Pluto Press, 1976), pp. 39–69.

33. Tom McGurk, "Agony of the Thirties," *Irish Times*, 6 September 1980.

34. De Paor, ibid.

35. O'Dowd, ibid., p. 10.

36. McGurk, ibid.

37. Over 1928–1939 "55% of the capital covered was invested abroad. In 1950, the surplus of Northern Ireland capital abroad over foreign capital in Northern Ireland was 330,000,000." D. R. O'Connor Lysaght, "British Imperialism in Ireland" in Austen Morgan and Bob Purdie, eds. *Ireland: Divided Nation, Divided Class* (London: Ink Links, 1980), p. 23.

38. On the "modernizing ideology," see Paul Bew and Henry Patterson, *The British State and the Ulster Crisis* (London: Verso, 1985), pp. 15–18; and Belinda Probert *Between Orange and Green: The Political Economy of Northern Ireland* (London: Pluto Press, 1981), p. 127.

39. Richard N. Lebow, "Ireland" in Gregory Henderson, et al. eds., *Divided Nations in a Divided World* (New York: David McKay, 1974), p. 210.

40. In synthetic textiles, for example, "between 1960 and 1973 employment fell by 29% and output increased by 175%; output per head had increased 287%." Norman J. Gibson and John E. Spencer, *Economic Activity in Ireland* (Dublin: Gill and Macmillan, 1977), p. 50.

41. O'Dowd, ibid.

42. "Dirty Tricks in the North's Fair Employment Agency," *Hibernia*, 21 December 1979.

43. On the IRA see Tim Pat Coogan, *The IRA* (London: Harper/Collins, 1987, rev. ed.); J. Bowyer Bell, *The Secret Army* (Dublin: Poolbeg, 1989, rev. ed.); and Eamonn Mallie and Patrick Bishop, *The Provisional IRA* (London: Heinemann, 1987). On the Irish National Liberation Army, see Jack Holland and Mary McDowell, *INLA: Deadly Divisions* (London: Hutchinson, 1990). On Protestant Paramilitaries, see Steve Bruce, *The Red Hand* (Oxford: Oxford University Press, 1992).

44. Personal interview in Dublin.

45. Ironically the voting rights act in 1965 was the crest of the U.S. Civil Rights movement.

46. Garret Fitzgerald estimated "the average living standards in Northern Ireland are over one-quarter higher than in the Republic." See his *Toward A New Ireland* (Dublin: Torc Books, 1973), p. 82. The gap closed to about 17 percent by 1983.

47. Terence O'Neill, "1968," *Hibernia*, 21 December 1978.

48. Coogan, ibid., p. 232.

49. Mallie and Bishop dispute this, but also see Henry Patterson, *The Politics of Illusion: Republicanism and Socialism in Northern Ireland* (London: Hutchinson Radius, 1990), pp. 122–124.

50. Arriving in Belfast the British Army was issued by Protestant officials with copies of an alleged IRA oath. The prose bespeaks Orange invention.

"I swear by almighty God . . . by the Blessed Virgin Mary . . . by her tears and wailings . . . by the Blessed Rosary and holy beads . . . to fight until we die, wading in the fields of Red Gore of the Saxon tyrants and murderers of the Glorious cause of nationality. And if spared, to fight until there is not a single vestige and a space for a footpath left to tell that the holy Soil of Ireland was trodden by the Saxon tyrants and murderers, and moreover, when the English Protestant Robbers and Beasts in Ireland shall be driven into the sea like the swine that Jesus Christ caused to be drowned, we shall embark for, and take, England . . . So help me God."

London Times Insight Team, *Northern Ireland: A Report on the Conflict* (New York: Vintage, 1972), pp. 152–153.

51. Coogan, p. 233.
52. All paramilitary groups in both communities have fought one another at some time.
53. The [Northern Ireland Office] never had any intention of giving the new regime the power to implement "vigorous policies." See Bew and Patterson, *The British State and the Ulster Crisis*, pp. 65–67.
54. Bew and Patterson take the view that the army in 1974 decided not to waste its energy on the already lost cause of the power-sharing executive. For a different account of army motives see Eamonn McCann, *War in an Irish Town* (London: Pluto Press, 1980), pp. 144–145.
55. *Hibernia*, 17 May 1979.
56. Moynihan quoted in Bernard Crick, "The Pale Green Internationalists," *The New Statesman*, 22 January 1978.
57. On security forces' covert operations, see Mark Urban, *Big Boys' Rules: The Secret Struggle Against the IRA* (London: Faber and Faber, 1992), and Martin Dillon, *The Dirty War* (London: Hutchinson, 1990).
58. Ed Moloney, "How Thatcher is Helping the IRA," *Hibernia*, 17 May 1979.
59. See Nell McCafferty, "A Cross of Wasted Suffering," *Magill*, August 1980.
60. The category can be viewed as an acknowledgment not of "political status" but of the plight of prisoners convicted by juryless Diplock courts on evidence obtained in interrogation or by the word of a policeman or informer.
61. J. K. Jacobsen, "Stalemate in Northern Ireland," *Dissent*, Summer 1982, and "Provo Support Not Based on Program," *In These Times*, 14–20, October 1982.
62. *Belfast Telegraph*, 22 October 1982.
63. The New Ireland Forum convened in March 1983 with the objective of formulating a constitutionally republican consensus about desired courses of action. The three main options considered were "a federal tri-partite system" among Belfast, London, and Dublin for Governance; "joint sovereignty" in which Ulster is administered by a Dublin and London committee with some European Community assistance; and a "unitary approach" that sets in motion a process leading ultimately to a Dublin-based government in a united Ireland.
64. Wim Roefs, "New Agenda, Old Hands" *Fortnight* 335 (January 1995), p. 16. Former Ambassador to Ireland William Shannon recalls that "it was pointed out to her that if she could not find common ground with Fitzgerald and Hume, she was unlikely to find any Irish politicians with whom she could negotiate the Northern Ireland problem."
65. By 1980, thirty-four UDR members were convicted of murders or other terrorist-type activities. *Sunday Tribune*, 5 February 1984. Two UVF men who murdered a Catholic music band in 1975 were UDR members. There is little doubt that information often passes from some UDR and RUC members to Loyalist paramilitaries. See Urban, *Big Boys' Rules*, p. xviii.
66. Bell, *The Secret Army*, p. 425.
67. *Irish Times*, 7 November 1981.

68. On the strategic distinction between blackmailing and backscratching see Kenneth Oye, "The Domain of Choice" in Kenneth Oye, et al., eds., *Eagle Defiant* (New York: Longman, 1979). The problem is to make this distinction matter to the protagonists.

69. Ibid., p. 15. Our diagnosis leads us to focus on the asymmetrical relations of linkees rather than between them both and the linker.

70. Ibid., p. 16.

71. On the distinction between sensitivity and vulnerability see Robert Keohane and Joseph Nye, *Power and Interdependence* (Boston: Little, Brown, 1978). The Loyalists are sensitive to British policy on non-constitutional issues but are not entirely vulnerable because there is much that they can do (and have done) to diminish impact of British decisions on political and constitutional arrangements.

72. Urban, *Big Boys' Rules*, p. 276.

73. *Irish Times*, 17 December 1994.

74. Steve Bruce, "Faulty Shades of Orange," *The Guardian*, 14 September 1994.

75. Surveys consistently indicate that a third of Northern Catholics prefer a credible democratic power-sharing arrangement within the United Kingdom.

76. Dick Grogan, "Policing the Nationalist Areas is a Critical Issue for Peace," *Irish Times*, 17 December 1994.

77. Garret Fitzgerald, "Security Tactics in North Endangering Peace Process," *Irish Times*, 31 December 1994.

78. *Irish Times*, 19 November 1994. Annesley became more receptive.

79. *Irish Times*, 26 August 1995.

80. "Derail" was the verb of choice in *New York Times*, Reports on 10 and 11 February 1996.

81. As Bertie Ahern, leader of Fianna Fail, the largest party in the Irish Republic, had pointed out to the British all along. See his remarks in *Irish Times*, 24 April 1995. Irish foreign Minister Dick Spring also repeatedly said that "decommissioning" was an impossible precondition.

82. See *Irish Times*, 10 October 1981. Also, see Richard Rose and Ian MacAlister discussion of Moxon-Browne's data that Protestants and Catholics are 38 to 1 percent for restoring Stormont; 35 to 39 percent for power-sharing within the United Kingdom; and 6 to 39 percent for Irish Unification. "Can Political Conflict be Solved by Social Change?" *Journal of Conflict Resolution*, September 1983.

8

Are All Politics Domestic?: Rethinking the National-International Connection

Theory is good, but it does not prevent
things from existing.
— Jean Martin Charcot

Are international relations scholars recognizing the truth of the maxim that "all politics is local"?[1] Political scientists in other fields observe with some justification and much disapproval that "theories of International relations typically treat individual nation-states as sovereign systems whose internal politics can be safely ignored."[2] But lately no word—apart from "rethinking"—seems to appear more often in IR titles than does "domestic."[3] The heyday of models that depict the state as a rational unitary actor, billiard ball and black box apparently is drawing at last to a close.

The perception that domestic and international politics are interdependent is hardly new. A dissident minority in IR argued for decades that it is essential to study causal links between domestic politics and foreign policy.[4] In the early 1980s, Robert Keohane called for "better theories of domestic politics, decision making, and information processing, so that the gap between the external and internal environment can be bridged in a systematic way, rather than by simply adding catalogs of exogenously determined foreign policy facts to theoretically rigorous structural models."[5] Even Kenneth Waltz hedged that someone "may one day fashion a unified theory of internal and external politics"—until which time this theoretical separation need "not bother us unduly."[6] What is new is the emergence of a cross-disciplinary enterprise in which scholars explore the intersections of IR and comparative politics in order to devise comprehensive explanatory frameworks.

188

The theory-building implications will hinge upon whether one judges that systems-level analysis (usually termed neorealism or structural realism) is intrinsically flawed, or is growing tenuous because the world has changed, or remains as powerful as ever.[7] This is an old, frequently heated and perhaps interminable debate.[8] Nonetheless the abrupt end of the cold war sparked another fierce round of reappraisals of IR theory.[9] Here a caveat is in order: realism is a highly variegated tradition in which freshly prefixed versions seem to proliferate.[10] While all realists are criticized—sometimes unjustly— for neglecting domestic factors, neorealists make a methodological virtue of it and so are the primary target. Yet some IR scholars avidly are working to incorporate domestic politics into realist-based explanations. One must ask whether these integrative endeavors concede so much analytical power to other fields, such as comparative politics and historical sociology, that IR no longer warrants its status as a separate discipline.

This chapter evaluates recent studies of the interdependence of domestic and international politics are evaluated here in light of two related but distinct perspectives. First, there is the familiar argument that internal factors require attention when we set out to explain policy responses to international stimuli.[11] The second proposition, however, audaciously asserts the *primacy* of domestic politics, a primacy that would seem incompatible with systems-level theory. Domestic primacy denies that the international dimension generates effects in the national realm which are wholly independent or immune to domestic mediating influences. This perspective pervades the books in review so strongly that even two-level games proponents, who want to insert domestic influences in a subordinate way into realist theories, must underplay the radical thrust of their analyses.[12] If upon closer scrutiny the levels of analysis often "collapse into one another," they invariably collapse to the domestic level where Waltz's first image and second image explanations hold sway.[13]

These authors argue that all politics are domestic politics. I would stress that there is no conceptual backpeddling involved in noting that this statement differs from asserting that *only* domestic politics matter, or that all politics are products of domestic forces. The prime contention here is that international forces acquire social meaning and political muscle only as they are factored into national politics in ways that accommodate the interests, strategies and ideologies of dominant local players. Domestic actors may not make foreign policy just as they please, but usually are adept at adapting external constraints to suit the exigencies of local contests over the distribution of power and wealth. It can hardly be otherwise because every state deploys diplomats, lobbyists, and a host of agents whose only task is to compete to accomplish this end (at whatever cost to less well represented citizens).

The current turn to domestic aspects of international politics stems as well from a steady infiltration of comparative politics research into IR which is just discovering, for example, that the "standard view" of government-business relations in France—that the state pushes business around—is far off the mark.[14] Systems-level explanations may be deemed so powerful that misapprehensions at the domestic level do not matter. However, the books in review (and this chapter) contend that IR theory obstructs an appropriately intricate understanding of the international system precisely because it eschews sociological inquiry into, and an historical view of, the state. In particular, the disciplinary dominance of neorealism, Doyle charges, left its "own implicit politics unexplored" and deprived IR of "insights focused on competing political values and differing institutions."[15]

By now it is virtually a truism elsewhere in political science that national leaders and "enfranchised" domestic actors are neither pawns nor ciphers for international forces—or at least not always.[16] This proposition opens space to explore the question of agency which critics complain is underplayed in IR models that are far too content with ahistorical and abstract formalizations. This chapter includes British contributions to the search for a framework spanning intra- and inter-state conflict.[17] British scholars obviously are not tied to our research agendas, methodological preferences, and professional reward structures.[18] So, with impish impunity they may chide American IR's curious coincidental focus "upon the issues which U.S. policymakers deem most vital."[19] More to the point, British IR never relinquished a concern with the nature of the dynamic interaction of national-international connections.[20] They readily acknowledge that their agenda is "British" only in the relative sense that a minority presence in U.S. IR comprises the mainstream over there.

I probe the historical origins and political stakes at the core of debates over the "national-international connection." Next I critique two-level games analysis, which is the prime realist candidate for a synthesis of domestic and international spheres. I then examine differences in impact that domestic politics, and especially mass publics, exert upon policy in the issue-areas of trade and security. Finally, I identify points where British concerns converge with U.S. proclivities and can be combined for the benefit of both.

"ENFRANCHISEMENT" AND THE PERILS OF PARSIMONY

Gabriel Almond reminds us that the impact of national factors on international politics was a thriving research program in the nineteenth century until German scholars—Leopold von Ranke, Freidrich Meinecke, Otto Hintze, and others—dispelled this "fixation."[21] Hintze thought little of democratic prospects because "the spirit and essence of internal politics is dependent on the external conditions of a states."[22] Germany, as he beheld it, was caught in a perpetually perilous squeeze.[23] But were the challenges of foreign powers and the demands of the international economy so plain and so irresistable?[24] English counterpart Sir John Seeley also divined that the "liberty a country can allow itself is in inverse proportion to the pressure on its borders."[25] These harsh "laws," Almond observes, were history-bound generalizations; they were bound, Fred Halliday detects, by a blend of *machtpolitik*, racism, and social Darwinism. (pp. 11, 48)[26]

The "primacy of domestic politics" attributes foreign policy choices to the ramifications of internal conflict while the "primacy of foreign policy" assumes that foreign policymakers must respond crisply to unambiguous external situations.[27] These clashing approaches implied drastically different distributions of political advantages for domestic groups.[28] In Wilhelmine, Germany, Paul Kennedy notes, political circles with "differing conceptions of the international order related their interpretive programs to the domestic political scene, and did not 'compartmentalize' their politics according to the categories of later scholars."[29] Chancellor von Bulow insisted that "everything, including domestic politics, be subordinated to Germany's unity and position as a European power which in turn would serve as a powerful integrative force at home."[30] Weimar era historian Eckart Kehr adumbrated two-level games when he argued that the analytical issue was[31]

> the extent to which prewar foreign policy was determined all along by the social structure of the Reich. An assessment of German foreign policy is inadequate not only when it fails to take account of English policy. A foreign policy has—this may sound trivial but it is often overlooked—not only an antagonist in front of it but a homeland behind it. A foreign policy is contending with the adversary and also fighting for its own country; it is guided by its opponents moves, but also—and even to a larger extent— by the will and needs of the homeland, whose concerns are primarily domestic.

The primacy of foreign policy affirmed authoritarian rule; the expansionist policies that accompanied this rule were easy to depict as nothing more than balance of power maneuvers (Mueller and Risse-Kappen in *The Limits of State Autonomy* (LSA), 42). Germany's naval buildup over 1892–1907 only maximized tensions with Britain even as domestic conditions minimized chances of financing a genuine challenge.[32] Elites endorsed expansion only to the degree that the added costs could be shifted to a resistant citizenry. (D'Lugo and Rogowski in *The Domestic Bases of Grand Strategy* (DBGS), 89–92)[33] What bears emphasis is that a realist orientation ("primat der aussenpolitik") was articulated within and inflected indelibly by the triumph of an authoritarian domestic agenda.

Realism relies for its explanatory power upon what Evans terms "dispro-portionate enfranchisement."[34] (An enfranchised actor is one who is politi-cally privileged to participate in the ratification process of an agreement or whose consent is required to implement it [*Double Edged Diplomacy* (DED), 371].) New enfranchised actors are a nuisance; an informed and active "people" is inconceivable.[35] Not surprisingly, realists believe elites should perform their complex tasks unencumbered by a citizenry "unable to make fine distinc-tions" because, as Walter Lippman so flatteringly phrased it, the "ability to act upon the hidden realities of a situation in spite of appearance is the essence of statesmanship."[36] The criterion of parsimony and an inbuilt tilt toward elites coincide quite nicely.[37] A managerial attitude is so thoroughly ingrained that most IR analysts hardly notice this bias, or would think it such if they did.

Nonelites who dare to intrude in high politics obviously only make mat-ters worse. So, a *de rigueur* realist distrust of the distempered public rarely is matched by concern that leaders too fall prey to ideological obsessions, be-have with blind self-regard, and crave insulation from public scrutiny in order to cloak internal policy rivalries, conceal undertakings, and stave off rumblings among the rabble. Elites, especially in the absence of scrutiny, are as likely as not to indulge their own ideational obsessions or to allow their formal roles to determine their views rather than to try to arrive at a dispas-sionate view of reality and to make pragmatic adjustments.

Can bargaining in the international sphere be growing more transparent and more salient to mass publics? It is easy to deride this notion. Modern states assiduously work to legitimate foreign policy choices through a pano-ply of techniques of perception management. (The Third Reich in 1939 had to repel invading Poles and the United States in 1964 to punish North Vietnam for attacking perfectly peaceful U.S. war ships.)[38] The rally-round-the-flag effect stirred by sudden military initiatives still is reliable, as the Gulf War demonstrated, but so too is dissipation of support as costs are counted.[39] Miroslav Nincic compiled cogent evidence that ordinary people can and do "deepen their judgment and [calibrate] their understanding on the basis of relevant experience, even if their grasp of specific events remains hollow." The U.S. public "may not understand what[40]

> the Contras or the Sandinistas stood for, but it may have had at least as accurate a common sense appreciation of how much a victory for either side would matter to the United States and of whether the stakes merited the costs and risks of military entanglement. Similarly the average person will rarely have an informed opinion on the ultimate efficacy of a space-based defense shield against ballistic missiles but his appreciation of Murphy's Law and estimate of the ultimate consequences of a porous shield may be approximately as good as those offered by the government.

The intrusion of new or formerly powerless players should alter the nature of the game unless, as neorealists insist, all domestic configurations eventually respond similarly to international exigencies. Michael Doyle in *Domestic Bases* scours the plight of European Socialists in 1914—a favorite piece of neorealist evidence—and discerned what many historians already knew, that their behavior was neorealist only when it corresponded with socialist precepts: when "the two differed, the marxists followed a marxist strategy. (DBGS, 46)[41] This *contingent* quality at the root of neorealist propositions cannot be exposed unless one is willing to take seriously the study of the interplay of domestic interests with potentially malleable international influences.

Still, we may accuse IR theory of inadequacy because it ignores "domestic groups, social ideas, the character of constitutions, economic constraints (sometimes expressed through economic interdependence), historical social tendencies and domestic political pressures." (Richard Rosecrance and Art Stein in DBGS, 5) But how is such inclusion to occur? This is extremely tricky terrain. In the comparativist camp, for example, Almond long has urged a search for a new interactive model but is perplexed that pioneers in "cross-disciplinary work should now be insisting on the reintroduction of the concept of the state, in the 'black box' sense of the state, as a unitary actor that may be either strong or weak." There is nothing surprising about it. This tendency afflicts any model that tries to preserve the primacy of the international sphere, and so it pervades two-level games.

JANUS-FACED OR JUST TWO-FACED?

No image is evoked so often as the state in the figure of the Roman god Janus. *Double Edged Diplomacy* treats "Janus-faced" chief executives (COGs) as responsible for balancing domestic and international concerns. (Moravscik in DED, 135) Janus, guardian of gateways, also was the god through whom prayers were relayed to all other deities, which seems to be the precise metaphoric note that two-level theorists want to strike.[42] But the case studies rarely uphold this image of supreme arbiter. To start with, if domestic actors construct their own two-level games to circumvent or exploit states, as they are often shown to do, the Janus image pretty much crumbles.[43] What two-level games do is reinvent systems-level theory by attaching a rung beneath the unitary state to incorporate a set of private agents as dominant constraints. Analysts see through the "eyes of the executive" so it is no wonder that these studies wind up offering us a stale form of statist theory. (DED, 23, 429 n. 6)[44]

Double Edged Diplomacy does provide a game-theoretic language: "winsets," suasive bargaining, "tying hands," positive and negative reverberations—even though all these concepts are familiar by other names. An undoubted advance for IR theory is that the black box metaphor is thrown, if not overboard, at least continuously into question. Snyder in *Domestic Bases* admonishes that if international variables are measured "in terms of the leaders' own subjective assessment of them, the 'international level' can explain all the outcomes. But the leaders assessments [were] often driven by strategic ideologies, which were shaped in part by domestic or alliance policies, and which sometimes differed markedly from an objective, Martian's eye view of international realities."[45]

The trouble with Martians, as we know from *New Yorker* cartoons, is that they never are interested in you, they want to be taken to your leader. Two-level games fanciers ask only how incumbents with given interests are to manage the policy plight besetting them. This analytical bent—fair enough for policy consultants—is disturbing because it makes a fetish of agreements which, no matter what their distributional terms and consequences, are good things. More agreements imply more international cooperation, which is always a good thing. Shared diagnoses among elites also are good things—if by chance they are correct. Only Evans is concerned that this absorption in international elites encourages "marginalization of domestically-oriented economic interests [which] while it increases the probability of successful agreements, may be a negative trend from a welfare point of view. . . ." (DED, 426) Two-level games analysis preserves realist precepts.

Double-Edged Diplomacy subscribes to the notion that the more autonomy elites enjoy, the better the quality of policy. It is utterly baffling why anyone outside inner policy circles should humor this notion. Evidence to the contrary abounds. President Johnson in February 1964 hastened contingency planning on Vietnam because of a "steady deterioration of pro-American governments in Laos and South Vietnam," which was "concealed from Congress and the public as much as possible to provide the Administration with maximum flexibility to determine its moves as it chose from behind the scenes."[46] Deceptions accumulated but the flexibility thereby secured for policymakers did not improve anything we or some of those policymakers today would care to call the "rationality" of their decisions.[47]

As for the primacy of the international sphere, one must strain to find a single case made for the determining force of this dimension either in the form of market forces or external agents. Andrew Moravscik's study of European arms manufacturers concludes that policy "reflects industry preferences. Since industry preferences are based on the global market position in that sector, and industry tends to get its way, there is little need to invoke an independent theory of domestic politics.[48] A pure 'second-image reversed' approach, in which domestic conflicts mirror global market opposition, provides an adequate explanation." Yet the study offers ample evidence to support different conclusions: i.e., COG acted as feeble guardians of economic rationality versus industrialists who mustered clout to oppose production arrangements that were more efficient but not more profitable than their desired schemes. There was more pertinent political activity at the domestic level than at least this "second image reversed" approach encompasses.

Japanese firms predictably balked at MITI concessions to U.S. trade demands, but Somalia, a weak petitioner confronting the IMF, also managed to call its own tune.[49] Brazil resisted U.S. threats to its computer policies although the European Union capitulated quickly to the United States regarding an agricultural issue.[50] In these studies nonstate actors, contrary to realist expectations and those of most two-level gamers, always try and frequently succeed in shaping governments' preferences and even the international market system, too, because, in some cases, they *are* the international market system.[51]

International forces require states to respond, but the specifics are the stuff of domestic politics. Actors interpret "external events in different ways to build support for policies they favor," Matthew Evangelista also notes.[52] "Some actions by foreign countries support the positions of particular domestic forces over others, but many are ambiguous because they are subject to divergent interpretations." When we refer to an international realm we actually refer to politicized interpretations of aspects of it—a politicization constructed domestically or with targeted domestic audiences in mind. Systemic elements rarely determine policies because multiple routes to any single objective usually exist and because political incentives operate more potently at domestic than at international levels so that most often it is the "best interest of the leader" that drives foreign policy. (Thomas Skidmore and Valerie Hudson in LSA, 3)[53] By abandoning the unitary state concept we avoid some of these habitual analytic hazards; by going further and suspending belief in the irresistable force of the international sphere we free up analysis for a fundamental rethinking of the ways domestic and external realms interpenetrate. Yet there is no question that it is difficult to ascertain causal paths from domestic group actions to policy responses. If so, the future will be much harder to chart. Why do British IR scholars, in particular, welcome this problem?

DOMESTIC POLITICS BY OTHER MEANS

The United States and United Kingdom are divided not only by a common language, as Oscar Wilde observed, but by a common discipline, too.[54] British IR, according to Steve Smith, stresses "uniqueness of the foreign policies of states and the need to use different approaches and methodologies for the analysis of each one. Rather than . . . creation of falsifiable hypotheses and testable evidence, the British approach emphasized intuition and insight. The divergence reflects fundamental division over epistemology and methodology.[55]

Thus, whereas a British analyst looks for specific historical knowledge to explain a state's foreign policy, the American will search for regularities, believing these to be inherent in the material. While the British analyst will be cynical about theorizing, the American will point to weaknesses of the "common sense" view of foreign policy, and refer to the often mutually exclusive assumptions contained in such works. To this extent the two are not participants in the same scholarly enterprise.

Dichotomizing can be carried too far.[56] It is "tempting to use stereotypes" a British observer admits. Halliday, for one, finds when one gets past the Waltzian line of fire that U.S. IR is quite diverse so that some facets of it are compatible with his argument. (pp. 28, 253, n. 2) In *Rethinking International Relation* his objective is to explain sociopolitical systems in terms of domestic and international determinants which each have a "partial autonomy" although insulating levels is counter-productive. (p. 20) Halliday works the same seams as two-level games analysts but with a different conceptual kit and for different purposes.

Because marxism is absent or excluded in U.S. IR, Halliday and other British critics infer that it became difficult "to examine not only how bureaucratic and constitutional factors affected policy outcomes but also how these are themselves shaped by broader historical and social and economic factors, including class factors, within the country concerned." (p. 18) The omission is regrettable not because marxism—typically more concerned with anarchy of the market than of state systems—offers us all the answers but because IR, lacking such a challenger, failed to generate competing paradigms that sought to encompass the same range of phenomena.

Waltz sensibly asserted one cannot understand world politics "simply by looking inside of states," but this differs from arguing that "internal processes of states can be excluded altogether from a theorization of IR." The concept of the state normally used in IR assumes "that states are equal, that they control their territory, that they coincide with their nations, that they represent their peoples, there could indeed be few concepts less 'realistic' than that of the sovereign states in its conventional IR guise." (Halliday, p. 81) Rosenberg charges that the assumption of anarchy "blocks consideration of how much interstate behavior is determined by—and is concerned with managing—domestic political processes."[57] The remedy advanced is to recast IR as the study of the relations, not between sovereign territorial states, but between "social formations":

> Thus the state is no longer an embodiment of national interest or of judicial neutrality, but rather of the interests of a specific society or social formation, defined by its socio-economic structure. How far classes control the states, or are separated from it, has been one of the main issues of dispute within the field. Sovereignty equally becomes not a generic legal

concept but the sovereignty of specific social forces. Its history is that of forms of social power and attendant legitimisation within a formation. (Halliday, 60–61)

Palan and Gills likewise view the state as "an articulation of class interests within a given territorial context," so that the state is "placed within a wider sociological context transcending discrete states boundaries." (p. 6) One highly attractive benefit is that the tiresome debate whether the state is losing power to transnational actors completely changes character. The question becomes; How do private actors, who *always* have powerfully affected the activities of states, act in a given state and set of circumstances? An investigative imperative for researchers is that the billiard ball impermeability of domestic politics is an "appearance which conceals a permanent, underlying internationalization of political and economic factors." (p. 64) Analysis is trained on a spectrum of interactions where vertical (interstate) security calculations and horizontal (intrastate) security concerns are sorted by domestic players who "deploy international resources to contain domestic threats."[58] Domestic comes first. However, Halliday, Rosenberg, Palan, and Gills and others flesh out Gramsci's advice that the "national and international should be construed as two aspects of an internally related whole."[59]

> the internal relations of any nation are the result of a combination which is "original" and (in a certain sense) unique ... To be sure, this line of development is toward internationalism, but the point of departure is "national" ... Yet the perspective is international and cannot be otherwise.
>
> Do international relations precede or follow (logically) fundamental social relations? There can be no doubt they follow. Any organic innovation in the social structure, through its technical-military expressions, modifies organically absolute and relative relations of international field too. Even the geographical position of a nation states does not precede but follows (logically) structural changes, although it reacts back upon them to a certain extent ...

Prioritizing politics inside nations therefore need not entail embracing crude reductionism.[60] The political process "not only reacts to external stimuli—military threat, economic competition, economic hierarchy—but in reacting, internalizes these stimuli. The 'outside' becomes 'inside' and inside becomes inseparable from the outside. The problem of causation [therefore] is 'misdirected.'" (Palan and Gills, 61)

Alexander Wendt similarly argues that interests and identities of actors cannot be assumed to form exogenously prior to the interaction of states with external situations and institutions.[61] Wendt wants to endogenize "identity change to systemic theory" and tends to impute excessive power to "intersubjective structures" because by definition these structures "give meaning to material ones, and it is in terms of meaning that actors act." This analytic move invites a detaching of material interests from ideas about them, and consequently reifiying those ideas. That is, one easily slips from a measured appreciation of the role of cognitive factors into idealism.

The British commend historical sociology as a well-grounded, if labyrinthine means to ferret out reciprocal relations of vertical and horizontal dimensions of power.[62] They reject forms of marxism that privilege "conflicts in production and class arenas over other political arenas"—so for that matter do many marxists. Andrew Linklater stresses studying "endogenous realm of strategic interaction and how it conditions the exogenous struggles," a project requiring a complex sociology to parse out the interacting logics at work; class, war, state-building, culture, and ideology.[63] In sum, the "international" is not something "out there," an area of policy that occasionally intrudes in the form of invasions or higher prices. "The international predates, plays a formative role in shaping, the emergence of the states and the political system." (Halliday, 77) So historical sociology and international relations "are looking at two dimensions of the same process: without undue intrusion or denial of specificity of the other, this might suggest a stable and fruitful relationship." (p. 85) This relationship, however, still needs to be spelled out. Before discussing how the British agenda can merge with U.S. IR concerns, I first address the different impacts that domestic politics—particularly public opinion and protest—exert on trade and security.

HIGH POLITICS AND THE HOI POLLOI

Systems-level analysis, it is less contentious to say, underrates the role of domestic factors in determining trade policy. Daniel Verdier argues that the trade policy process should be seen as itself a variable "whose value is determined by electoral competition." (p. xviii) Political power in private hands accumulates "at the tolerance of the voters, typically as a result of voter indifference" which only in a highly formalized sense is likely to be true. (p. xix) His thesis conjures an implausible universe populated by cunning voters and passive special interests. If high electoral participation will impede rent-seeking, low turnouts by definition will encourage rent-seeking and thus are logically if oddly construed as approval of the status quo. Why then do the most disadvantaged citizens, who have the least of which to approve, record the lowest turnouts?[64] Perhaps policy structures shape the pattern of turnouts, not vice versa. If equitable political outcomes depend on a "balance of power between the cartelized and democratic forces," one can interpret NAFTA, for example, as a victory in a highly politicized campaign to reduce the ability of nonelite actors to resist cartelized forces.[65]

Beth Simmons found that when in a domestic crisis, leaders want foremost "to maintain some semblance of control" so that international "imperatives" were invoked or ignored depending on whether they met leaders needs.[66] The gold standard was justified "among the narrow enfranchised classes as a necessary condition for the conduct of international trade and investment" but depended on labor bearing the burden of adjustment—until labor literally became enfranchised.[67] Verdier extends this dictum to security when he urges inquiry as to whether a foreign policy augurs "costs that are not borne by the people who mandate policy" because if costs "are borne by disenfranchised or misinformed individuals" a government is apt to start wars. (p. 294) Informed *and* vulnerable citizens tend to shy away from military adventurism because their blood and treasure is most likely to be squandered. Herbert Muller and Thomas Risse-Kappen contend that any differences in the impact of domestic politics upon the economic and security realms stem less from intrinsic qualities of those issue-areas than because security is less politicized than economic problems—so far. (LSA, 38) Public opinion, they believe, affects policy by influencing the coalition-building process among elites while nebulous policy networks adjust differences between elites' designs and the public. (pp. 510, 511) Yet, this formulation is too conciliatory to realism. The anti-Vietnam War and nuclear freeze campaigns were grass roots movements that imposed constraints *and* unwelcome goals on resistant policymakers.

It is now obvious even to many IR practitioners that international coercive bargaining depends on domestic public support.[68] The White House made a point of pretending that the peace movement exerted no effect on the Indochina War, except to prolong it; however, a swarm of memoirs and studies attest otherwise.[69] (In Israel, too, in 1978 Peace Now campaigners exercised an influence that then premier Menachem Begin much later admitted "rendered him somewhat more compliant" in negotiations with Sadat and Carter.)[70] Institutional structures provide "different opportunities for coalition-building among elites and allow for different degrees of grassroots influence upon them." (Muller and Risse-Kappen in LSA, 130) The antiwar movement interwove with broader forces—enemy resilience, a faltering economy, Saigon's corruption, and a concern about the big picture of superpower relations—so that it is difficult to detect through what routes leaders were swayed. Richard Helms testified that rather than specific tactics or actors "it was the totality of the [opposition activities] that [put] the pressure on officials"; McGeorge Bundy wearily called it "all part of the same ball of wax."[71] H. R. Haldeman in December 1970 scribbled that it was "very hard for our guys to keep their balance because they are beat on by the kids, by the press, by the people they meet socially, etc."[72]

The more a "guns and butter" resource base was squeezed (note Johnson's reluctance to raise taxes or mobilize reserves), the more domestic political calculations figured in every facet of the war. Bombing pauses in 1965 and 1968 were designed to persuade domestic audiences that the "enemy has left us no choice" except escalate.[73] The lesson here is that leaders often do tailor foreign policy positions to suit short-term political ends and at the cost of national needs. Hans Morgenthau, who once urged putatively wise leaders to shape the opinions of the feckless public and ignorant legislators, came to reject this characterization during the Vietnam War.[74] Johnson's aversion to bad tidings was communicated throughout the ranks so that it encouraged distorted and eventually disastrous estimates of enemy strength.[75] Presidents Kennedy and Johnson feared reactions by domestic rightwingers unable to make fine distinctions between peace with honor and cutting and running—except if a republican were at the helm.[76] Policymakers operated in a crusading paradigm replete with intense institutional and interpersonal incentives to conform.[77] The curative sequence was one of grass roots protest emboldening critics in the administration and in the media, not the other way around, though a mutually reinforcing dynamism soon was at work.[78]

Realists ardently believe that the "restraints of domestic politics" especially in vulnerable democracies interfere with sound decisions and bring about a dangerous lack of political direction. When the Nazis rose in the 1930s, however, Western elites were no more perceptive than the public and often were rancorously split: a notorious example being the slogan of a segment of the French upper class proclaiming a preference for Hitler over Leon Blum's more repugnant Popular Front. As a historian pointedly understates: "One should not unquestioningly assume that France was one nation in this period."[79]

The key military policy response to skeptical citizens in democratic polities is resorting to technology-driven "quick war" strategies. U.S. strategy, accordingly, was designed to be "expensive in dollars, cheap in lives" (and, especially in Vietnam, to spend the "cheapest" lives).[80] In the 1930s the British devised a "cheap, technological war" in large part because of the public's memories of trench warfare; this latter factor ("*kriegspsychose*") made *blitzkrieg* all the more attractive to the Nazi military whose war effort would be hampered by Hitler's care to keep Aryans on the home front content.[81]

Can the public prove to be too gun-shy in the face of mortal threats? The United States and Great Britain in the 1930s are usually cited as egregious examples of unpreparedness. Rosecrance and Steiner find instead that it was an apprehensive British populace that forced leaders out of appeasement.[82] Roosevelt secretly promised Churchill that the United States would "force an incident with Germany" and by 1941 pursued an undeclared war in the North Atlantic.[83] Roosevelt was, as he told a youth group in 1940, in a ticklish plight of maneuvering around the threat of "blindly selfish reaction" at home to deal with the mounting menace of aggressive dictatorships abroad.[84] Yet, this "selfish reaction" stemmed from a numerically small, if economically potent, portion of U.S. society.

Roosevelt, despite ever widening public support, resorted to ill-disguised deceptions—a course that arguably later encouraged "scaring the hell out of the public" (Arthur Vandenberg) and making matters "clearer than the truth" (Dean Acheson).[85] One likely cost was a concomitant McCarthyism silencing Asian experts who might well have helped avert Vietnam. In that sense, the Indochina War may have been lost because of politics on the home front *before* the United States ever dispatched troops.

Stein presses the realist line that democratic politics create disjunctures between commitments and capabilities, although any "disequilibrium generates pressures that return the state to equilibrium regardless of institutional structures." (DBGS, 98, 122) Domestic politics are a source of "stickiness" interfering with imputed needs to respond to changes in the balance of power. But what most concerns Stein is disparities between capabilities and, not commitments, but *intended* commitments. He assumes that the intentions of policy elites—further assumed to be in consensus—ought to equal commitments. Did "growing worries" about Soviet intentions luckily match "growing needs" of private industries and of statesmen for new capabilities, or did these "growing needs," as revisionists reply, shape the degree of the "growing worries"? (p. 116) The debate, despite regularly being declared won by all contestants, is not resolved. Even for some realists it *is* questionable that "the Soviet threat grew through the 1940s." (Stein in DBGS, 121)[86]

John Mueller takes the cross-disciplinary tack that it was not the distribution of capabilities but "ideas and ideology as interpreted in domestic politics" which were responsible for the dynamic of the cold war.[87] In bringing down the (iron) curtain on the cold war the Soviets made a number of military and ideological concessions but what mattered was not their behavior, but what relevant Western audiences wanted to make of it. (p. 58, and Evangelista, 154–178). Hardliners were compelled to capitulate by the public. In this vein Wendt declares the cold war "was fundamentally a discursive, and not a material, structure."[88]

SALT II and the nuclear freeze examplify the quirky dialectical interaction between policy elites and public opinion. Conservative organizations organized a well-financed campaign that swung public opinion from favoring the treaty in March 1979 to opposing it within six months.[89] In 1984, when formal U.S.-Soviet relations were still acrimonious, Americans overwhelmingly urged arms control talks—balancing firmness with a willingness to seek better relations in a sober blend notably lacking in administration officials.[90] Superpower tensions subsided in large part as a result of mass demonstrations in Europe and the United States which tapped the political potential of "unofficial realms of collective action" and rendered Reagan rhetorically more accommodating.[91] Rosenberg observes that ignoring domestic nonstate processes "makes it impossible (or irrelevant) to conceive other global structures of power apart from the political—because the only visible agents are other states. Also, with so much of the substance of international politics canceled at a stroke, it is little wonder that theories of indiscriminate power-maximizing and endless security needs of anarchy step into the breach."[92]

POST-REALISM AND INTERACTIONS

Why should IR scholars pay sustained systematic attention to domestic factors, or Americans heed Brits? Because there are interesting points of convergence. In order to work, realism assumes permissive domestic conditions so that, in their absence, states will under- or overbalance against threats. (Rosecrance and Stein, p. 21) A reciprocity strategy, Evangelista argues, facilitates benign superpower relations because states "exert leverage over other states whose policies are subject to internal debates" including "not only changes in the external environment and economic conditions but internal debate between hard-liners and moderates too." (DBGS, 156) Rosecrance and Stein point out that *symmetrical* domestic conditions among the Great Powers is a "major determinant of the viability of grand strategy." (DBGS, 6) Obviously tit for tat cooperation will fail if behavior is "driven by domestic sources that bear little objective relation to each others' actions."[93] For both analytical and practical reasons a mixed mode "post-realist" approach is worth developing and a number of U.S. scholars are tackling it. How do their models compare to the British recommendations on how to proceed?

Snyder argues that the quarry is "interaction effects wherein some variables may have different consequences depending on the condition of others" and are "conditional on other contextual factors." (DBGS, 181) Because external stimuli interact with internal conditions we must disentangle feedback loops between elites, states, private interests, and the public in order to predict the effects of any single variable. (DBGS, 199) This dovetails precisely with the British schemas.

Inquiry should not halt at the study of these interactions of variables. Scholars who already are investigating interactions overlook the importance of distinguishing objective causes from subjective reasons and exploring how they relate inside this sphere. These interactions, if we are not primed to probe further, will only be found to contain another bunch of impervious billiard balls bumping but not affecting the internal states of one another. The goal should be integrating intrastate conflict into interstate relations in a way that sensitizes us to how actors weigh their range of choices. Halliday points out that by "focusing only on the systemic Waltz's model paradoxically downplays the force of the 'systemic.' Following interstate competition and its impact within society, changes occur that then lead to further interstate conflict . . . this is the formative interaction that has shaped so much of international history." (pp. 135, 139–140)

Domestic structure so far is a terribly vague and static concept that is invoked in U.S. IR as if the invocation alone sufficed to explain residuals.[94] This palliative use of the term enables IR to continue to privilege systems-level explanations so that an independent variable—the international realm—is pictured as impacting upon the dependent variable—domestic structures—whose components lack any means or inclinations to resist, transform or bend external demands to their own purposes. The circularity inherent in using domestic structure as a variable, must be pried into so that we can explore "the extent to which the structure itself derives from the exigencies of the international system" and vice versa.[95] The term can be put to better use inside a wider framework.

British critics in this spirit insist on a balanced inquiry into how global processes interact with "processes of state/societal transformation" and how "state/society transformation at one level is affected by and in turn affects the transformations at levels B and C, and so on" so that the upshot is that it is "the transformative processes themselves that are placed at the center of analysis." (Palan and Gills, 3) This is a more promising path—one compatible with a number of analytic approaches, including some variants of realism—out of the "evolutionary dead-end" that critics otherwise see IR as having struck. (Doyle in DBGS, 25)

Such an approach is not without drawbacks. Ironically, practitioners deploy a terminology that mirrors the excessive abstraction that they deplore in structural realism. Another affliction is that while they aim to understand how human agency works within and/or arises from interacting dimensions of conflict, this objective tends to get overridden in schematic treatments of this sphere of interaction.[96] Yet the proof is in the putting of formulations to work. Here is the point where Americans can flesh out the abstract schema. This analytical agenda fastens attention on the micropolitics and domestic arrangements underlying systemic explanations of international politics. Realist propositions are treated as contingent ones and the exploration of the roots of this contingency open a very wide space for analyzing structure and agency.

CONCLUSION

Pure domestic or international stimuli—each untainted by the other—are conceptual will-o'-the-wisps and deeply misleading ones at that.[97] Although even Waltz allows that someone "may fashion a unified theory of internal and external politics," neither he nor those who heed him will produce candidate theories. This is regrettable. "It is one thing to test a fruitful line of investigation," as Mannheim observed, "and another to regard it as the only path to the scientific treatment of an object."[98]

Waltz and Robert Gilpin confess to be unable to comprehend apparently abstruse and confused critiques of realism and neorealism—critiques which British scholars of at least equal eminence have no such difficulty deciphering.[99] This divergence suggests that quality is not the decisive criterion at work and that Americans need not be dissuaded from exploring "fringe" critiques, which happen to comprise British mainstream IR. British scholars, as I have taken pains to note, certainly are not alone in attempting to "rehistoricize" IR.

New enfranchised actors are a threat to parsimonious explanations. The problem intensifies when mass publics burst into the arena. So there is a legitimate scholarly concern that we may be compelled to deal with an infinity of idiosyncrasies from which no explanation can be extracted.[100] One way to reduce variables is to focus on "domestic structures" although not by treating them as fixed and reactive, but rather by examining them within a wider sociological space. A historical sociology approach offers a fertile and open-ended network of paths. In this hybrid field of inquiry "it is the task that commands attention, not the disciplines" so that no single approach confers "privileged theoretical access."[101] So, as this integrative enterprise proceeds, will IR exhibit a desirable "disciplinary interdependence" or else dissolve? The answer, one suspects, will depend on more than purely scholarly criteria.

Notes

1. Lately the title of a political memoir by former U.S. House Speaker Tip O'Neill.
2. Paul E. Peterson, "The President's Dominance in Foreign Policy," *Political Science Quarterly* 109, 2 (Summer 1994), p. 228.
3. See Ronald Rogowski, *Commerce and Coalitions: How Trade Affects Domestic Political Alignments* (Princeton: Princeton University Press, 1989); Jack Snyder, *Myths of Empire: International Ambitions and Domestic Politics* (Ithaca: Cornell University Press, 1992); Bruce Buena De Mesquita, *War and Reason: Domestic and International Imperatives* (New Haven: Yale University Press, 1992; Friedrich Kratochwil, *Rules, Norms and Decisions: On the Condition of Legal and Practical Reasoning in International Relations and Domestic Affairs* (Cambridge: Cambridge University Press, 1993); Charles Kegley Jr. and Eugene Wittkopf, eds., *The Domestic Sources of American Foreign Policy* (New York: St. Martin's Press, 1986); James W. Lamare, ed., *International Crisis and Domestic Politics: Major Political Conflicts in the 1980s* (New York: Praeger, 1991); the *International Organization* issue on "Explaining American Foreign Economic Policy," 42, 1 (1988) edited by John Ikenberry, Michael Mastanduno, and David Lake; Thomas Risse-Kappen, "Public Opinion, Domestic Structure and Foreign Policy in Liberal Democra-

cies," *World Politics* 43, 4 (July 1991); Zeev Maoz, *National Choices and International Processes* (Cambridge: Cambridge University Press, 1990); Patrick James and Athanastos Hristoulos, "Domestic Politics and Foreign Policy: Evaluating a Model of Crisis Activity for the U.S." *Journal of Politics* 56, 2 (May 1994); Peter Cowhey, "Elect Locally—Order Globally: Domestic Politics and Multilateralism," in John R. Ruggie, ed., *Multilateralism Matters* (New York: Columbia University Press, 1993); James D. Fearon, "Domestic Political Audiences and the Escalation of International Disputes" *American Political Science Review* 88, 3 (September 1994): Jack Levy, "Domestic Politics and War," *Journal of Interdisciplinary History* 43, 4 (1988); Randall L. Schweller, "Domestic Politics and Preventative War: Are Democracies more Pacific?" *World Politics* 44, 2 (January 1992); Michael Barnett, "High Politics is Low Politics: The Domestic and Systemic Sources of Israeli Security" *World Politics* 42, 4 (July 1990); Matthew Evangelista, "The Paradox of State Strength: Transnational Relations, Domestic Structures, and Security Policy in Russia and the Soviet Union," *International Organization* 49, 1 (Winter 1995); and Bruce Russet, "Processes of Dyadic Choice for War and Peace," *World Politics* 47, 2 (January 1995).

4. Wolfram Hanrieder, "Compatibility and Consensus: A Proposal for the Conceptual Linkage of External and Internal Dimensions of Foreign Policy" *American Political Science Review* 61, (1967) and "Dissolving International Politics: Reflections on the Nation-State," *American Political Science Review*, 72, 4 (1978); James. N. Rosenau, ed., *Linkage Politics: Essays on the Convergence of National and International Systems* (New York: Free Press, 1969); and Richard Rosecrance, *Action and Reaction in International Politics* (Boston: Little, Brown, 1963).

5. Robert Keohane, "Theory of World Politics: Structural Realism and Beyond," in Keohane, ed., *Neorealism and Its Critics* (New York: Columbia University Press, 1986), p. 1.

6. Waltz, ibid., p. 340.

7. Waltz concedes "the state is not a unitary and purposive actor. I assumed it to be such for the purpose of constructing a theory." In ibid., p. 339.

8. Rosecrance and Stein testify how exasperating it has been for critics to pin down particularly structural realist propositions in order to test them. "Beyond Realism: The Study of Grand Strategy," in *The Domestic Bases of Grand Strategy*, p. 6.

9. John Lewis Gaddis, "International Relations Theory and the End of the Cold War," *International Security* 17 (1992); Paul Schroeder, "Neo-Realist Theory and International History: An Historian's View," *International Security* 19 (Summer 1994); and *The Domestic Bases of Grand Strategy*.

10. Jack Snyder refers to neorealists as "truncated realists" (because they view states as "irreducible atoms") in contrast to the "broader" realist approaches of Morgenthau, Machiavelli, and Thucydides. He adds "aggressive Realism," as exemplified by John Mearsheimer, and "defensive Realism," as rendered by Stephen Walt, to the fold. See *Myths of Empire*, pp. 12, 19. Ole Waever labels Mearsheimer a "modified neorealist," in "Identity, Integration, and Security: Solving the Sovereignty Puzzle in E. U. Studies," *International Organization* 49, 1 (Spring 1995), pp. 396, 397. One could go on and on.

11. Peter Katzenstein, *Between Power and Plenty* (Madison: University of Wisconsin, 1976); Peter Gourevitch, "The Second Image Reversed: The International Sources of Domestic Politics," *International Organization*, 31, 1 (1978) and *Politics in Hard Times* (Ithaca: Cornell University Press, 1989).

12. Andrew Moravscik, "Integrating Domestic and International Theories of International Bargaining," in Evans, *Double Edged Diplomacy*, p. 12.
13. Ibid., p. 33.
14. Daniel Verdier, *Democracy and International Trade* p. xix. Also, see Stephen S. Cohen, *Modern Capitalist Planning: The French Model* (Berkeley: University of California Press, 1977); Michael Hayward and Jack Walker, eds. *Planning, Politics and Public Policy: The British, French and Italian Experiences* (New York: Cambridge University Press, 1975). Andrew Shonfield in *Modern Capitalism* (New York, Oxford University Press, 1965) refers to "conspiracies in the public interest" between state and private actors.
15. Michael W. Doyle, "Politics and Grand Strategy," in *Domestic Bases of Grand Strategy*, p. 25.
16. An "enfranchised" actor in two-level games is one who is politically privileged to participate in the ratification process of an agreement, or whose consent is required to implement the agreement. See Evans, "Building an Integrative Approach," in *Double Edged Diplomacy*, p. 371.
17. Regrettably I can be criticized for confinement to English language works. Keohane regrets this "Americanocentrism" in *Neorealism and Its Critics*, p. 200, n. 1. Also, see Stanley Hoffman, "An American Social Science: International Relations," *Deadelus* 106, 3 (1977). Two scholars chide that "a greater degree of transnational communication with European [not to speak of Japanese] scholars would probably have relieved Americans from their intellectual obsession with realism earlier on." Muller and Risse-Kappen, "From the Outside in and from the Inside Out: International Relations, Domestic Politics, and Foreign Policy," in *Limits of State Autonomy*, p. 48.
18. This is not to imply that the British are free of all fetters or are bolder; they may only be responsive to the distinct set of incentives and constraints in their very different "mainstream."
19. Linklater, "Dialogue, Dialectics and Emancipation," p. 128. Also, see Halliday, *Rethinking*, p. 127; and Justin Rosenberg, *The Empire of Civil Society* (London: Verso, 1994), p. 32. E. H. Carr skewered this practice by British enthusiasts during their imperial heyday. *The Twenty Years Crisis 1919–1939* (London: Macmillan, 2nd ed., 1946), pp. 80–88.
20. F. S. Northedge judged "the nature of the state and its attitudes toward other state-members of the international system will elude us unless we have done something to penetrate its unique cast of mind, the product of quite unique historical experiences." *The International Political System* (London: Faber and Faber, 1966), p. 175. Wight also analyzed connections between domestic politics and the international system in *Systems of States*.
21. Gabriel Almond, "The National-International Connection," in Almond, *A Discipline Divided: Schools and Sects in Political Science* (London: Sage, 1990), p. 264.
22. Ibid., p. 266; Otto Hintze, "Military Organization and the Organization of the State," in Felix Gilbert, ed., *The Historical Essays of Otto Hintze*, (New York: 1975).
23. Charles S. Maier, *The Unmasterable Past* (Cambridge: Harvard University Press, 1990), p. 35.
24. In Berlin's Volksmuseum an exhibit of pre-World War I cloth maps of Europe portray countries by national caricatures who fill and animate the space within the borders. A typical scene is Europe pictured as a brawl in the middle of which an intrepid, spike-helmeted German soldier elbows a dandified French-

man to his left, kicks a depraved mustachioed Italian beneath him, and on the
right fends off a slavering Russian bear (or fiendish Cossack) twice the size of
all other foes on this quarrelsome, congested continent. No better graphic depiction
of the popular mentality exists—but was it not largely contrived? On SPD
leader Eduard Bernstein's analysis of, and efforts to dispell, this belligerent view
see Peter Gay, *The Dilemma of Democratic Socialism* (New York: Collier Books,
1952), pp. 274–276.

25. Maier, *The Unmasterable Past*, p. 116. On Bismarck's hostility toward parlia-
mentarians and the working class see Peter Gay's, *The Cultivation of Hatred*
(New York: W. W. Norton, 1993), pp. 252–265.

26. On social Darwinist rhetoric in Germany and Britain, see Paul Kennedy, *The
Rise of Anglo-German Antagonism 1860–1914* (London: George Allen & Unwin,
1980), pp. 308–316. On imperialist motives as represented in popular American literature, see H. Bruce Franklin, *War Stars: The Superweapon and the American
Imagination* (Oxford: Oxford University Press, 1988), pp. 19–53.

27. Eckart Kehr, *Economic Interest, Militarism and Foreign Policy* (Berkeley: University of California Press, 1977). "Sparta affords [a strong example] of the primacy of domestic politics since her interstate policy [was based on] the conduct
of a permanent war of the Spartiates against the subjugated majority of her
population, and this preoccupation governed every other aspect of policy."
Martin Wight, *Systems of States*, p. 57.

28. Maier, *The Unmasterable Past*, p. 24.

29. Kennedy, *Rise of Anglo-German Antagonism*, p. 321. It was "upon [economic
performance] that advocates rested their case, and it was from their interpretation of the [data] that they received a confirmation of their standpoint"—
which hardly can be more circular, self-interested and politicized. (Atlantic
Highlands, NJ: Humanities Press, 1987) p. 306.

30. Katherine A. Lerman, "Chancellor von Bulow and the National Idea, 1890–
1918," in John Breuilly, ed., *The State of Germany* (London: Longman, 1992),
pp. 109, 117–126.

31. Kehr, *Economic Interest, Militarism and Foreign Policy*, p. 23. He quotes Tirpitz's
1895 letter hailing fleet-building because the "great new national undertaking
and the economic gains connected with it will serve as potent palliatives against
educated and uneducated Social Democrats," p. 12.

32. David D'Lugo and Ron Rogowski, "The Anglo-German Naval Race and
Comparative Constitutional Fitness," in *Domestic Bases of Grand Strategy*, p. 79.

33. German conservatives thwarted moves toward higher income taxes so that "ar-
maments continued to be paid by consumers, in indirect taxes, and [through
growing debt]. In Britain, by contrast, the panoply of income, super-, estate-,
and death-duties, which obtained by 1914, virtually paid for defense expenditure." Kennedy, *The Rise of Anglo-German Antagonism*, p. 358.

34. Peter Evans, "Conclusion," in *Double Edged Diplomacy*, p. 400.

35. See R. B. J. Walker, *Inside/Outside: International Relations as Political Theory*
(Cambridge: Cambridge University Press, 1993), p. 153. Halliday pointedly
reminds us that even in the United States and United Kingdom full formal
democracy was achieved only in the 1960s. *Rethinking International Relations*,
p. 223.

36. Ronald Steel, *Walter Lippman and the American Century* (New York: Vintage
Books, 1981), p. 4.

37. See Chapter 2.

38. See Phillip Knightley, *The First Casualty* (New York: Harcourt, Brace, Jovanovich, 1975). Opportunistic exaggerations include Eisenhower's "rollback" threat and "bomber gap," Kennedy's "missile gap," Johnson's promise that "we're not going North and drop bombs" in Vietnam, and Reagan's "window of opportunity." (Nincic, pp. 120–121). Franklin recalls that as a SAC intelligence officer in 1957–1958, one of his duties was "helping to conceal from the American people, particularly our own SAC crews, the almost certain knowledge that the Soviets still had neither operational intercontinental bombers nor missiles." *War Stars*, p. 181.

39. Before the Tonkin Gulf resolution 42 percent of Americans supported intervention in Vietnam and afterward 72 percent; 7 percent supported action in Cambodia before the 1970 "incursion" and 50 percent afterward. A majority opposed invading Panama,; afterward, a majority supported it. Nincic, *Democracy and Foreign Policy*, p. 44. After Grenada, Reagan's approval rose from 35 to 53 percent. James Lamare, "International Intervention and Public Support: America during the Reagan Years" in Lamare, *International Crises and Domestic Politics*, pp. 16–17.

40. Nincic, ibid., pp. 38–42, 54–55.

41. Also, see Stephen E. Bronner, *Moments of Decision* (London: Routledge, 1992); Kennedy, *The Rise of Anglo-German Antagonism*, p. 38; and Gabriel Kolko, *Century of War: Politics, Conflicts and Society Since 1914* (New York: New Press, 1994) who argues that in the prelude to World War I that it was the leaders' "unwarranted optimism that they would be free from domestic pressures that made possible their embarking on war." See pp. 16, 41.

42. Helene Adeline Guerber, *Greece and Rome: Myths and Legends* (London: Bracken Books, 1986), p. 177.

43. "Domestic actors appear to have understood more clearly than their government whether agreements were ratifiable" and are more able to disguise preferences and information." *Double Edged Diplomacy*, p. 159.

44. There still is much to quibble with. "Suasive reverberation," for example, implies a one-way, top-down flow of influence which close study does not often confirm. See Judith Gross Stein, "The Political Economy of Security Agreements: The Linked Costs of Failure at Camp David," In *Double Edged Diplomacy*, p. 87.

45. Jack Snyder, "East-West Bargaining over Germany: The Search for Synergy in a Two-Level Game," *Domestic Bases of Grand Strategy*, p. 122.

46. Neil Sheehan, *The Pentagon Papers* (New York: Bantam Books, 1971), p. 241.

47. See Robert S. McNamara, *In Retrospect: The Tragedy and Lessons of Vietnam* (New York: Times Books, 1995). In May 1962, McNamara expressed confidence because every "quantitative measurement we have shows that we're winning this war." Neil Sheehan, *A Bright Shining Lie* (New York: Random House, 1988), p. 290. On his "disenchantment" by autumn of 1966 when he privately called for a "coalition government in Saigon that includes elements of the Viet Cong," see Sheehan, *Pentagon Papers*, pp. 510–11, 514.

48. *Double Edged Diplomacy*, pp. 155–156.

49. See the essays by Miles Kahler and Ellis Krauss in, *Domestic Bases of Grand Strategy*.

50. John Odell, "International Threats and Internal Politics: Brazil, the European Community and the United States, 1985–87," in ibid., pp. 233–264.

51. Beth Simmons, *Who Adjusts?* (Princeton: Princeton University Press, 1992), the "market" that judges governments turns out to be a handful of major banks.

52. Matthew Evangelista, "Internal and External Constraints on Grand Strategy: the Soviet Case" in, *Domestic Bases of Grand Strategy*, p. 156.
53. Douglas Van Belle, "Domestic Imperatives and Rational Models of Foreign Policy-Making," in *Limits of States Autonomy*, p. 153.
54. Steve Smith, "Introduction," in Smith, ed., *International Relations: British and American Approaches* (London: Basil Blackwell, 1985), pp. x–xi. Also, Herbert Butterfield and Martin Wight, *Diplomatic Investigations* (London: George Allen & Unwin, 1966), p. 1.
55. Smith, "Foreign Policy Analysis," ibid., pp. 50, 54.
56. "The Americans mass-produce strategists while the British remain satisfied with a small number of craftsmen. The Americans are preoccupied with technology while the British have more regard for politics. The Americans continually look to the future while the British never forget the past. Such judgments, while not wholly unfair, do justice neither to the quality nor the variety of much of American strategic writing nor to the extent to which some of its worst features would have been happily copied in Britain if only circumstances permitted." Lawrence Freedman, "Strategic Studies" in Smith, *International Relations: British and American Approaches*, p. 31.
57. *The Empire of Civil Society*, p. 34.
58. These resources may be military, up to and including allied troops; economic, whether from other branches of multinational corporations as an aid to embattled holders of state power; or political, in the form of moral support, treaties, or alliances provided by friendly states." Halliday, *Rethinking*, p. 85.
59. Antonio Gramsci, *Prison Notebooks* (New York: International Publishers, 1971), pp. 176, 240. Carr's "Doctrine of the Harmony of Interests," incidentally, verges very closely on Gramsci's concept of "hegemony." *Twenty Years Crisis*, pp. 44–45, 79–80.
60. Halliday takes care to reject "internalist arguments" that reduce foreign policies to "the product of domestic factors alone; thus interstate relations, changes in the outside world, legitimate national needs, appeals for help from abroad are all submerged in the identification of domestic causes." In "Theory and Ethics in International Relations: The Contribution of C. Wright Mills," *Millennium* 23, 1 (1994), pp. 380–381.
61. Alexander Wendt, "Collective Identity Formation and the International State," *American Political Science Review* 88, 2 (June 1994), pp. 388–389.
62. Halliday cites Tilly, Skocpol, Mann, and Anderson. See Philip Abrams, *Historical Sociology* (Ithaca: Cornell University Press, 1982).
63. Linklater, *Between Marxism and Realism*, pp. 170–171.
64. See Richard Cloward and Frances Fox Piven, *Why Americans Don't Vote* (New York: Pantheon, 1988).
65. Snyder, *Myths of Empire*, p. 310. On "antipolitical" efforts in the financial realm to "move effective decision-making entirely out of the political arena and into the hands of technicians and market 'players'," see Louis W. Pauly, "Capital Mobility, State Autonomy, and Political Legitimacy," *Journal of International Affairs* 48, 2 (Winter 1995).
66. Simmons, *Who Adjusts?*, pp. 4, 281.
67. Ibid., p. 27.
68. John Odell, "International Threats and Internal Politics" in *Double Edged Diplomacy*, pp. 233–234.
69. The peace movement "fed the mounting unease with the conflict by key ad-

ministration officials in late 1967 and 1968 [and] fueled Eugene McCarthy's presidential bid, which shaped official perception in 1968 that the public had turned against the war [and] was the most important manifestation of the domestic antiwar mood that forced the Johnson administration to reverse course in Vietnam in 1968. [It] "exerted a critical influence on Nixon's decision in 1969 not to carry out his threat to Hanoi of a massive military blow. It shaped his determination to prematurely withdraw U.S. Forces in Cambodia in 1970 . . . nourished the deterioration of U.S. troop discipline and morale . . . put pressure on the administration to negotiate a settlement . . . gave impetus to congressional legislation that cut off U.S. funds for the war . . . [and] promoted the Watergate scandal, which ultimately played a pivotal role in ending the war." Tom Wells, *The War Within* (Berkeley: University of California Press, 1994), pp. 5–6. Also, the Clifford Group report in *The Pentagon Papers*, pp. 601–602; Terry Anderson, *The Movement and the Sixties: Protest from Greensboro to Wounded Knee* (New York: Oxford University Press, 1995), pp. 237–238; and Seymour Hersh, *The Price of Power: Kissinger in the White House* (New York: Simon & Schuster, 1983), pp. 129–131, 195. On Nixon countermobilization on the domestic front, see H. R. Haldeman, *The Haldeman Diaries: Inside the Nixon White House* (New York: Putnam, 1994), pp. 126, 164, 172, 326.

70. Tamar Hermann, "Grassroots Activism as a Factor in Foreign Policy-Making," "The Case of the Israeli Peace Movement," in *Limits of State Autonomy*, p. 141.

71. Wells, *The War Within*, pp. 256, 257. Nixon believed he could not "hold the country together" had he escalated fighting. *No More Vietnams* (New York: Arbor House, 1985), p. 102.

72. *The Haldeman Diaries*, p. 225.

73. James William Gibson, *The Perfect War* (New York: Atlantic Monthly Press, 1986), pp. 64, 332. Also, *The Pentagon Papers*, pp. 316, 321, 470, 515. "The best and the brightest" approached the public much as ancient Greek leaders approached the Oracle at Delphi. They "did not ask Apollo to originate or direct their policy," J. B. Bury observed. "They only sought his authority for what they already had determined." Cited in Wight, *Systems of States*, p. 48.

74. Contrast Morgenthau's essays on leaders "blinded by prejudice and paralyzed by pride" in *Truth and Power* (New York: Praeger, 1970), pp. 398–439 with the haughtier views in *Politics Among Nations* (New York: Knopf, rev. 1985), or *The Purpose of American Politics* (New York: Knopf, 1960). He does not appear to have revised earlier writings in light of this disenchantment which of course may have been restricted to a specific group of Americans at a particular time.

75. Sam Adams, *War of Numbers: An Intelligence Memoir* (South Royalton, VT: Steelforth Press, 1994). A correction in Viet Cong strength—from 240,000 to 600,000—was not welcomed by authorities in 1967. The official figure prior to the consequently shocking Tet offensive was lowered to 224,000. See p. 217.

76. Snyder, *Myths of Empire*, p. 300.

77. The Reagan administration pursued destabilization of the Sandinistas, despite a skeptical Congress and adverse public opinion, to the brink of destabilizing itself. On the problem of intellectual conformity among political elites, see Kolko, *Century of War*, pp. 15, 20, 417.

78. See Daniel Hallin, *The "Uncensored" War: The Media and Vietnam* (Berkeley: University of California Press, 1986) and Sheehan, *A Bright Shining Lie*, pp.

342–348. In Britain in the major nineteenth century instances when the public disagreed with government—the American Civil War, the Russo-Turkish War and the Boer War—the public proved correct. In Nincic, *Democracy and Foreign Policy*, p. 16.

79. Theodore Zeldin, *France 1848–1945* (Oxford: Clarendon Press, 1973) Vol. 1, p. 3. On internal divisions in Britain, see Clive Ponting, *1940: Myth and Reality* (London: Hamish Hamilton, 1990). Harold Nicolson wrote in his diaries on 6 June 1938 that the British "governing classes think only of their own fortunes, which means hatred of the Reds. They create a perfectly artificial but at present most effective secret bond between ourselves and Hitler. Our class interests, on both sides, cut across our national interests." Quoted in Ralph Miliband, *Capitalist Democracy in Britain* (Oxford: Oxford University Press, 1982), p. 51. On the role of Chamberlain's ideological antipathy in his passing up an opportunity to forge on uninhibitedly realist grounds an alliance with the USSR, see Rosecrance and Steiner.

80. Gibson, *The Perfect War*, p. 103. Almost 80 percent of U.S. troops in Vietnam came from working-class and poor backgrounds. Christian G. Appy, *Working Class War: American Combat Soldiers and Vietnam* (Chapel Hill: University of North Carolina Press, 1993), p. 5.

81. David H. Edgerton, *England and the Aeroplane: An Essay on a Militant and Technological Nation* (London: Macmillan, 1991), pp. 1–11; Kolko, *Century of War*, pp. 184, 214; on Nazi concern over the public's "war psychosis" in the 1930s see William Sheridan Allen, "The Collapse of Nationalism in Nazi Germany" in Breuilly, *The State in Germany*, pp. 147–149.

82. Richard Rosecrance and Zara Steiner, "British Grand Strategy and the Origins of World War II" in *Domestic Bases of Grand Strategy*, pp. 136, 139, 147–148.

83. Arthur Stein, "Domestic Constraints, Extended Deterrence and the Incoherence of Grand Strategy: The United States, 1938–1950," in ibid., pp. 106, 110.

84. Kenneth Davis, *FDR: Into the Storm, 1937–1940* (New York: Random House, 1993), p. 565.

85. Robert Shogan, *Hard Bargain* (New York: Scribners, 1995), p. 267. In June 1940 85 percent of Americans polled favored aid to Britain and France. See p. 231.

86. See Frank Kofsky, *Harry S. Truman and the War Scare of 1948* (New York: Saint Martin's Press, 1993).

87. John Mueller, "The Impact of Ideas on Grand Strategy," in *Domestic Bases of Grand Strategy*, pp. 52, 57. Indeed "domestic changes that lead to changes in political ideas may be far more important influences on international behavior than changes in the international distribution of military capabilities."

88. Wendt, "Collective Identity Formation and the International State," p. 389.

89. Thomas Skidmore, "The Politics of National Security Policy: Interest Groups, Coalitions, and SALT II Debate" in *Limits of State Autonomy*, pp. 223, 225, n. 9, and Muller and Risse-Kappen, p. 37.

90. Nincic, p. 39.

91. Paul Wapner, "Politics Beyond the State: Environmental Activism and World Civic Politics," *World Politics* 47, 3 (April 1995), p. 314. Ellen Dorsey, "Expanding the Foreign Policy Discourse: Transnational Social Movements and the Globalization of Citizenship," p. 264. These transnational entities form because citizens hope to gain goods or redress that they cannot obtain—or obtain so easily or quickly—in national arenas.

92. Rosenberg, *The Empire of Civil Society*, p. 20.
93. Nincic, p. 107.
94. Evangelista divides domestic structure into descriptive categories (1) political institutions, (2) structure of society, and (3) nature of coalition-building processes. See "The Paradox of State Strength."
95. Almond, "The National-International Connection," p. 26.
96. Note the reliance on a focus on interactions alone as a sufficient explanation in Geoffrey Garret, "Capital Mobility, Trade and the Domestic Politics of Economic Policy," *International Organization*, forthcoming.
97. Robert Putnam, "Diplomacy and Domestic Politics: The Logic of Two-Level Games," in Evans, *Double Edged Diplomacy*, p. 433.
98. "It may indeed be necessary, for the sake of the precise observability of the formal sequence of experiences and values, to discard the concrete contents of experiences and values. It would "constitute a type of scientific fetishism to believe that such a methodological purification actually replaces the original richness of experience. It is even more erroneous to think that scientific extrapolation and abstract accentuation of one aspect of a phenomenon, for the sole reason that it has been thought through in this form, is able to enrich the original life-experience." Karl Mannheim, *Ideology and Utopia* (New York: Harcourt, Brace & World, 1936), pp. 18–19.
99. Gilpin, "The Richness of the Tradition of Political Realism," pp. 302–305, 316; and Waltz, "A Response to My Critics," p. 337, in *Neorealism and Its Critics*.
100. Duncan Snidal and Christopher Achen, "Rational Deterrence Theory and Comparative Case Studies," *World Politics* 41, 2 (January 1989).
101. Abrams, *Historical Sociology*, pp. x, xi.

PART III
POSTSCRIPTS: POLITICIZATION AND POLITICAL IMAGERY

9

Television, Ideology, and the Korean War

Wartime censors, as Philip Knightley's *The First Casualty* reminds us, perform a twofold mission: (1) deny vital data to the enemy and (2) conceal from the citizenry any potentially perturbing news as to how their leaders are conducting all the mayhem at the front.[1] This protective zeal tends to become habit-forming and usually outlasts the formal conclusion of hostilities. Take the recent case of two historians who tried to pry past what one called the "received wisdom and received ignorance" about Western military activities in a gory conflict fought on Third World terrain.

A tyrant launched a lightning invasion into a neighboring southern state over which he claimed to have historical sovereignty. A U.S. diplomat earlier had "signaled" to this avaricious dictator that the target state lay outside the perimeter of vital U.S. interests. It looked like a green light—or was close enough. Nonetheless soon seventeen U.N. nations—though primarily the United States—charged in to repel the invaders with a ferocious aerial campaign and a massive ground assault. The tyrant, alas, survived this onslaught because several hundred thousand—and eventually several million—highly motivated Chinese troops came to the rescue.

"Korea: The Unknown War," a six hour television documentary produced by Britain's Thames television with substantial funding (about 40 percent) from Boston's public television station WGBH, premiered in Britain in the summer of 1988.[2] Judging by reviews there, the series stirred neither wrath nor rapture. But the high jinks behind the scenes during the editing of the series for the U.S. broadcast were very exciting and intriguing indeed.

Say what else you will about U.S. covert operations specialists, Asian intelligence agents, and Reed Irvine's Accuracy in Media (AIM) pitbull watchdogs, they are extremely colorful and provocative subjects. As a result of their collective intrusions, series writer Jon Halliday and principal historian Bruce Cumings complain, their documentary suffered unwarranted changes to make it politically palatable to a middle-of-the-road audience.[3] They are especially, though not exclusively, aggrieved over what they regard as a high-handed

215

and irresponsible editing process at WGBH in Boston. WGBH producer Austin Hoyt, who said his only concern in editing was to improve accuracy, denied the charge.

Jon Halliday and Ian Bruce conceived the idea for the series in the summer of 1982. Archives were opening in Moscow, Pyongyang, and the West, and they wanted to capture this opportunity to reappraise the Korean War. Halliday brought aboard historian Bruce Cumings and sold the project to Octagon Films in London which in turn sold it to Thames in 1986—when WGBH also joined. Halliday's outlines and rough assemblies for scripts were subjected to intense scrutiny in studio-sponsored seminars attended by many other historians (including Rosemary Foot, Callum MacDonald, and Peter Lowe), high-ranking military veterans, South Korean officials, and WGBH's Hoyt who, Halliday and Cumings recall, mostly kept quiet.[4] Hoyt later acknowledged in writing to an aggrieved Cumings that WGBH had been "part of the consensus" reached in London.

These sessions, Thames producer Philip Whitehead recalls, tended to polarize—with Halliday and Cumings on one edge of the spectrum and General Sir Anthony Farrar-Hockley blazing away from the other. Cumings was asked to provide what he judged were North Korean positions on a range of controversial issues and for his troubles was denounced as a commie by rather literal-minded South Korean officials. Tempers frequently flared. "We were re-fighting the Korean War," says Thames producer David Elstein. "It would be a mistake to say it was a noncontroversial production that got perverted in the United States." Elstein also points out basic differences over the treatment of defoliants, brainwashing, and germ warfare as they appeared in the text of the British version and in the accompanying book on the series written by Halliday and Cumings.[5]

Outside the seminar room some shabby B-movie antics were transpiring. "The South Koreans tried to get me fired," Halliday says. "They also were very difficult about granting film permission in South Korea and intercepted faxes and telexes—and all this interference went on." A producer's car was ransacked, items were swiped, and other mischief occurred that bespoke low-grade harassment tactics by spooks hailing from *both* sides of the 38th parallel. The North Koreans, for their part, blocked Whitehead from taking a plane to Pyongyang, swiped Cumings's visa for North Korea while he was in Beijing, and otherwise behaved skittishly about giving the Thames crew filming permission. The FBI later chillingly informed Cumings that the South Korean consulate had accused him of being a North Korean agent. He also underwent his very first IRS audit.

Despite devious deeds and discouraging words a documentary eventually emerged that was deemed fit for British consumption. The documentary was completed in spring 1988 and broadcast that fall and, soon after, in Australia, Japan, and continental Europe. (It was declined in South Korea in a 5–4 vote by a state commission for the Korean television network, MBC.) On reflection Cumings appreciated that scholarly disputes had been worked out more or less in the open and that he and Halliday had gotten about two-thirds of the series the way they wanted: "In the end, on balance, I thought the Thames film was still quite good." Cumings felt they owed this much success to a Thames "committed" programming policy that preferred to proclaim the film makers' views "up front and let viewers pick as they please." Halliday took a far dimmer view of the British round in this saga (see note on p. 222).

Cut to Boston WGBH studios where Austin Hoyt, producer of two episodes of the PBS Vietnam series, takes charge of changing "thick British accents to American ones and of adding five extra minutes of material to fill commercial slots." In all, this amounted to thirty minutes of new footage for the Yank version. His apparently innocuous task was to make the documentary more intelligible and more pertinent to U.S. viewers, which was a reasonable concern. After all, the U.S. role in Korea, gauged by casualties alone, exceeded the British by a factor of fifty to one. The United States had more at stake there and for far longer.

However, Hoyt ominously said he detected an "anti-Western bias" in the Thames version. So he intended to make considerable changes to redress what he judged a distressing imbalance. Hoyt also objected to the tone and content of the voice-over. "I dislike having a narrator express a point of view," Hoyt told me. "It may be a difference between what the British do and what we do but I had to get out of the narrative anything judgmental." Thus Hoyt apparently subscribed to the Solomonic belief that one can create historical narratives free of distortions so long as one didn't disturb the "received wisdoms" (riddled with biases) that the series authors had set out to challenge. What was an example of bias in the Thames version? "I think Halliday and Cumings claim [the war] wasn't a legitimate U.N. effort. It's a legitimate point to raise, but I think they made it by innuendo in their writings."

Was this aversion to "innuendoes" all that motivated the many script changes? At the annual Association for Asian Studies meetings in March 1989, Halliday and Cumings screened their Thames documentary and conducted a discussion. In the audience a member of the U.S. Army Center for Military History rose and announced that a "General Stilwell" already had requested that the controversial documentary be sent to the Center to be checked for "accuracy."

That same month a source in the U.S. government leaked to Halliday a memo, dated 25 January 1989, from General Richard G. Stilwell (retired) to Hoyt regarding "accuracy checks, which you particularly requested" on the series. In the memo Stilwell issued this indignant and peremptory verdict: "The Thames series, in present form, is not appropriate for an American audience. If shown without extensive editing and caveats or both, it would be ill-received by that audience and thus an embarrassment to sponsors and station . . . It simply is not an objective portrayal of the war."[6]

Stilwell was former chief of covert operations (the Office of Policy Coordination) in the Far East during the Korean War and deputy undersecretary of defense (1981–85) in the first Reagan administration.[7] He appeared at least as incensed at British officers—particularly a Major Anderson—who gave the "impression that America bumbled about" in Korea as he was at "an overall pro-North Korean stance." In the memo Stilwell (no relation to "Vinegar Joe") urged twenty-two specific editing changes. An especially noteworthy objection read: "True or not, should be edited out. American audiences will be revolted and irate"—which is not a widely recognized criterion for conducting historical research. The good general, not missing a trick, also remarked that while it "may be out of line. Sponsors deserve to be alerted to a probable rash of complaints."

When did Stilwell actually come onto the scene and what impact did he really have? The Thames producers first approached him. "We interviewed him [for the Thames version] and he didn't say anything interesting enough to be on it," Halliday recalls, "which might have made him sore." Cumings and Halliday learned that the Thames version had an unofficial debut in Hawaii in November 1988 in front of the right-wing council on U.S. Security Studies. When Cumings complained about the unauthorized screening, the organizer of the event mollifyingly replied that "the film was well received, including laudatory comments by General Paik himself" [Paek Sŏnyŏp commanded ROK forces in the war and was an old colleague of Stilwell]. Meanwhile the documentary went through many postponements of its U.S. debut. Stilwell told me that Hoyt, whom he had helped to contact several high echelon U.S. and Korean officials including General James Van Fleet, had invited him to screen the Thames version. Here the sequence of events gets quite murky.

Accuracy in media spokesperson Joseph Goulden told me that Stilwell had informed AIM of his concern that "a pretty far left" documentary would be broadcast in the U.S. Whether Stilwell summoned AIM or vice versa, AIM contacted Hoyt who appeased the media vigilantes by agreeing to consult Stilwell. This should have been a fairly innocuous tactic to fend off AIM. Indeed, Hoyt told Cumings that he dealt with Stilwell only in order to know "where the brickbats would come from the Right." But Cumings believes Hoyt, who endured AIM shot and shell for his PBS Vietnam episodes (which were not among the more provocative in the series), had grown "gun-shy."

"I gave Stilwell half his minor points—about twelve—and we didn't cater to his major concerns at all," Hoyt said. "Stilwell was trying to turn the war, which had a lot of warts on it, into a moral crusade. Cumings was concerned that we were under influence. Absolute nonsense. But the rumor got around that we were whoring to Washington and the South Korean government. I never heard a peep from the Koreans" Hoyt deleted what he believed to be "innuendoes" and then consistently added more footage of figures such as Dean Rusk, Paul Nitze, and other honchos who, Cumings complains, thereby wound up in the cozy position of being "historians of their own actions" even more so than in the British version.

Hoyt allows that the editing stage, from which Cumings and Halliday were completely excluded, "possibly resulted in a tilt toward the American perspective." But there was no question of effective right-wing interference or impact on the finished product. "We spent a lot of time and money checking accuracy. I played researcher personally"—which was no comfort to the originators. Cumings and Halliday, who got hold of the first WGBH script revisions in April 1989, beheld the dismaying spectacle of Hoyt, who "didn't know beans about the war," ruling on what was true and what was not.[8]

At Thames Elstein and Whitehead said that on viewing the WGBH version they detected no troubling changes. Cumings relates that Whitehead and fellow producer Max Whitby privately expressed their dismay over some WGBH changes though not so much so as to lodge protests. "If we had disapproved we could have prevented [a showing]. We do this with nearly all the programs we coproduced—the ones on Stalin and Nixon had a 3 to 5 percent difference [from the U.K. version]," said Elstein. Of course, he reflected, "Korea was more an issue in the United States than in Britain." In interviews, however, it was quite unclear who actually exercised authority over the final cut. Hoyt said that he sent the edited U.S. version to Thames "only as a courtesy."

A flurry of memos between Halliday and all the producers escalated in tone over time and eventuated in a complete break with WGBH. Cumings confirms that Thames declined to step into the fray. Philip Whitehead in October 1989 did ask that WGBH send the revised scripts to Cumings for review. They were never received. Neither author was allowed to view the U.S. version; WGBH refused Cumings's request to see Hoyt's handiwork before its PBS broadcast in Fall 1990. WGBH's reply, drafted by Peter McGhee, portrayed the studio as staunchly defending its pristine production against "outsiders" who would, if they could, act as censors. The series authors were the "outsiders."

Cumings found that all but two of the twenty-two items on Stilwell's list were inaccurate and easily proven so. Nearly all of Hoyt's minor concessions to Stilwell created or reaffirmed errors. Stilwell, for example, said that the South Korean Army in 1949 had not been expanding when, in fact, it doubled in strength. Stilwell said South Korea was not given antitank mines which it indeed possessed but hadn't planted. He also claimed that mammoth 14,000 pound bombs had not been used in 1950 when just such a bomb had dropped on Kim Il-Sung's bunker. The list of incorrect corrections goes on.[9]

"Everyone at PBS was aware of the AIM flak aimed at the Vietnam documentaries, which led to an agreement to show a ridiculous distortion of the war to please Reed Irvine," Cumings observed. Hence the Korean series "was aimed at the complacent middle roader Hoyt took to be the modal U.S. viewer." The editing process in the United States became a contest "between Hoyt's unarticulated premises and the documented text of the film," Cumings charges. "That's a completely fake balance."

What had changed? Halliday and Cumings compiled a lengthy list. These alterations include excisions of vital materials on U.S. contemplation of use of atomic bombs and about threatening nuclear dummy runs by B-29s over the North ("Operation Hudson Harbor"), on the seaminess of the South Korean regime (deleting a "statement that the entire South Korean general staff served the colonial Japanese regime"), dropping references to vigorous guerrilla activity in the South, and sidestepping treatment of the U.S. National Security Council document (NSC 68) that authorized military build-ups and virtually institutionalized the cold war. MacArthur's march to the Yalu was portrayed as a maverick maneuver when it actually had full White House backing.

Deleted, despite increased screen time, was a presmart bomb era Dean Rusk calmly explaining that in North Korea the U.S. bombed "everything that moved, every brick standing on brick" which was why "we didn't need the atomic bomb so far as North Korea was concerned." The United States and South Korea appear far kinder and gentler than the records warrant. Hoyt removed references, based on much evidence, that *both* sides were guilty of killing prisoners in the field. "I found a My Lai—Americans killing villagers as in Vietnam," Halliday said. "It wasn't used. I don't believe Hoyt was a neutral arbiter. I can document cases of non-neutrality." A few improvements admittedly crept in. "Hoyt got the Inchon landing straight, Cumings noted. Also, he "brought in American Blacks in the Armed Services to very good effect." But "overall the score is 20% improvement and 80% detraction from the Thames version."

Cumings cannot help but credit AIM with motivating many snips and inserts although Halliday is not so sure these changes wouldn't have happened anyway for other reasons. Cumings later got word that at a jamboree for former intelligence officers Stilwell, who died in 1991, bragged that he single-handedly dissuaded potential sponsors. Indeed, the project was aired on PBS in November 1990 without sponsorship. "Stilwell also circulated some sort of dossier on Halliday to newspapers," Cumings said. "That's pure McCarthyism. It's an example of their tactics."

Did WGBH fold under pressure? Former WGBH producer Joe Blatt said his experience was that "stirring up controversy was just what [WGBH producers] want to do—though he was not privy to reactions of line producers for the Vietnam and Korea series in the face of AIM assaults. Another source in WGBH mentioned the "consistent stubborn streak" producers exhibit but also alluded to a "schizophrenic corporate culture" that was a volatile blend of "hubris and arrogance" on one hand, and, on the other, "extremely sensitive antennae" regarding public criticism. Sometimes they "go crazy and do back-flips no matter how specious the criticism might be." One strategic way to preempt criticism is the imposition of a "common style" on documentaries, an "encyclopedic drone that appears to say everything while saying nothing."

Bottom line? "I never underestimated the difficulty of doing a documentary on a war that is still going on" [referring to the truce], Cumings reflects.[10] "Despite the PBS stuff I was glad to get as much on screen as we did." Did Hoyt have any regrets? "I think the series can be faulted for not asking, Was the war worth it? Were there any winners, apart from Japan as supply base?"

Since AIM's meddling did not emerge publicly until after the series was screened, the behind-the-scenes controversy was barely noted in the press except for an Associated Press television critic and short articles in *The Village Voice*, *The Philadelphia Inquirer*, *The Guardian* (NY) and *Knight-Ridder* news service. Cumings and Halliday removed their names from the U.S. version but the PBS broadcast rolled both the U.S. and the British credits.

This controversy—after the fact—opens several problems that recur when TV producers attempt to treat disputed accounts of politically charged events. The sincerity of the producers is not really in question. Rather, the problem is that very likely a naive notion of "objectivity" wielded by producers-playing-historians enabled what a Thames producer termed a "bunch of fruitcakes" at AIM to sway the content of a public broadcast carrying the imprimatur of scholarship.

The tricky enterprise of historical research—the more principal characters alive and the more power they have, the trickier—is a grueling one of constant tension between evidence and interpretation, an ongoing debate requiring the most intense methodological reflection and soul-searching.[11] Most producers need not and will not bother with such arcane academic debates. Rather they must cope with influential groups concerned that unsaintly, even unsavory, images of themselves may reach the screen. One must wonder, when a forty-year-old war arouses so much flak, if and when we can expect any better of treatments of the Gulf War, Panama, or Grenada.

The upshot? Hoyt said Stilwell felt "we did not take him very seriously." This is quite true. Stilwell and AIM spokesman Joe Goulden both told me that they still detested the PBS version for "an overemphasis on the British role, a denigration of the U.S. performance, and a pro-North Korean stance." If everybody's unhappy, that's a victory for objectivity, isn't it?

Well, isn't it?

LETTER FROM JON HALLIDAY

I would like to make one clarification to Jacobsen's piece about the TV series that I wrote "Korea: The Unknown War," and to give one specific example of how Hoyt/WGBH dealt with evidence.

Clarification: It is true that Hoyt/WGBH carried out extensive reediting, as Jacobsen describes. They tampered with the agreed consensus—of which they were, by their own admission a full part—and did so from a position of ignorance (for example, rewriting my commentary, introducing factual errors, wrong dates, and so forth in it without consulting me). But I would not like readers to conclude that WGBH inherited a balanced product from Britain. Most of the misrepresentations and imbalances in the U.S. version were in the original assemblies. It was the British version that allowed un-reliable witnesses like Rusk to be "historians of their own actions"; was unbalanced on key issues such as atrocities, the treatment of POWs, and the Armistice talks; and perpetrated the original misrepresentation of evidence in the germ-warfare controversy.

Although Jacobsen's account is brief, there was little room for him to spell out how Hoyt/WGBH handled evidence. May I give one example? The British version contained an interview with an Australian ex-POW in Korea, who some thirty-four years later recounted a conversation with Wilfred Burchett, the Australian journalist who covered the war from the commu-nist side; the ex-POW attributed unsavoury words and deeds to Burchett. Between the completion of the British version and the end of the reediting by WGBH we obtained (thanks to Gavan McCormack) an affidavit sworn by another Australian ex-POW, sworn within weeks of his release in 1953, which proved the alleged conversation could not have taken place—and this was confirmed by a second 1953 affidavit sworn by another Australian ex-POW. I sent these affidavits to Hoyt, and told him it would be dishonest to keep the interview in. Hoyt refused to remove the misrepresentation. Why? In his own words: "We needed a filler . . . and he [the ex-POW] says it with some certainty . . . and I guess we live with it on that basis."

Notes

1. Philip Knightley, *The First Casualty: The War Correspondent as Hero, Propagandist and Myth Maker* (New York: Harcourt, Brace, Jovanovich, 1975).
2. Thames television later lost its license for the private (ITV) television channel in Britain. Many commentators infer that this was deliberately engineered by the Tory government as a punishment for Thames's production of "subversive" documentaries, especially "Death on the Rock" which questioned British Army tactics in an incident in which three unarmed IRA members were killed on Gibralter.
3. Jon Halliday, author of several books on Asia, is a free-lance academic and writer living in London. Bruce Cumings is author of a two volume history of the Korean War and at the time of these events was a historian at the University of Chicago. He now teaches at Northwestern University.
4. Historians Clay Blair and Roger Dingham were also consulted.
5. Jon Halliday and Bruce Cumings, *Korea: The Unknown War* (New York: Pantheon, 1988).
6. Memorandum, General Richard G. Stilwell, ret., to Mr Austin Hoyt, WGBH, Subject: "Comments on Thames's Korean War Series," 25 January 1989.
7. Stilwell was chief of staff to General Paul Harkins and then to William Westmoreland in Vietnam, commanded the U.S. Army in Korea over 1973–76; was a director of the Committee on the Present Danger (which published the infamously biased "Team B" report on the state of U.S. military preparedness in the late 1970s); and president of the Association of Retired Intelligence Officers. In the 1950s Stilwell authored an aggressive counterinsurgency report on strategic doctrine for U.S. Special Forces. On this latter activity see Richard Drimmon, *Facing West* (Minneapolis: University of Minnesota Press, 1982). According to the *Korea Herald* 18 November 1986, Stilwell also was a consultant to the flagship firm of a South Korean conglomerate (Hanil Synthetic Fiber Company). In Vietnam he authored memos denouncing the reporting of David Halberstam and Neil Sheehan.
8. Besides Stilwell, Hoyt consulted army historian Billy Mossman and one other military historian.
9. Memorandum, Bruce Cumings to Bob Sokolove, Subject: "Stilwell's Consultancy with WGBH/Boston," 6 November 1990.
10. Cumings since has published an account of his travails with the documentary. See his, *Television and Politics* (London: Verso, 1993).
11. See, for example, Theda Skocpol, ed., *Vision and Method in Historical Sociology* (Cambridge: Cambridge University Press, 1984), pp. i–xi, and E. H. Carr, *What is History?* (New York: Vintage, 1961).

10

Schindler's List, American Culture, and the Politics of the Holocaust

It is all too tempting to remark that only in a Spielberg film about the holocaust would the showers in Auschwitz really work.[1] Likewise only a Spielberg film would star a Nazi industrialist who changes as if by magic into a soft-hearted savior of *untermenschen*, or would contrive a scene of several SS pistols misfiring to spare the life of a terrified Jew. They seem to be blatant Spielberg touches. Yet all these highly unlikely events occur in Thomas Keneally's book on Schindler, a fact that proves again the terrible cliche that the holocaust encompassed and surpassed all human imaginations from the demonic dementia of Hieronymous Bosch to the benign cinematic impulses of a Disney or Capra.[2]

Given their obvious affinities, Schindler's tale and Spielberg's style seem fated to meet. The graying *wunderkind* embarked on a very personal venture that film financiers had to humor and the result is a film that zeroes in memorably on humanity caught in a whirlpool of howling horrors. Above all, Spielberg's trademark child's-eye view—beneath a bed, beside a trembling parent, chest-deep in a latrine—of methodical Nazi mayhem and murder manages to get under even a jaded audience's skin. Recall the shot of the gentile girl malevolently shouting "Goodbye!" to evicted Jews filing by her on the street and contrast it to the ghetto scene of a Jewish child in a coat the color of a bright bloodstain who meanders the pavement as the Nazi wolves rampage around her.

Spielberg manages to make those infernally abstract numbers—so many numbing millions of deaths—a shivering reality of flesh and blood, bone and tears, and ashes. Even if we must ask at what cost it succeeds, *Schindler's List* is indeed a cinematic accomplishment that reached and touched the mass audiences it sought. The horrors it portrays are vivid and accurate—but is horror alone enough?

224

The same ingredients Spielberg employs to win a wide audience also work to reshape the events depicted in disturbing ways. All commercial filmmakers must refashion the raw material of events to suit dramatic criteria; this frequently requires trade-offs of factual details for scenes geared to action or high emotion. The typical narrative features a single hero molded so as to invite identification, a set of mettle-testing challenges, a fierce opponent and eventually a resolution imposed by the hero. Hence group action is likely to get short shrift, vital nuances go unexplored and little space is allowed to examine how overarching systems of power affect protagonists. The Third Reich is to some degree an exception because it is a vanquished system and was *by definition* evil; so audiences need not consider how Nazism related to capitalism or militarism or any extant system closer to home.

Unlike German audiences who are familiar primarily with the kitschy Holocaust (1979), Americans, at least at the "art house" level, are deeply steeped in holocaust films. So one is more inclined to inquire how *Schindler's List* compares to outstanding documentaries like *Night and Fog, Shoah and the Sorrow,* and *The Pity,* or with feature films like *The Damned, The Garden of the Finzi-Continis, Au Revoir, Les Enfants,* and *Lacombe Lucien*—to name but a few. The *historikerstreit* has no counterpart in the United States except insofar as the German controversy spilled over.[3] Only crackpots deny the holocaust or try to "relativize" it in light of other historical atrocities in order to diminish its enormous horror. Americans themselves obviously feel no guilt, obligatory or otherwise, about their conduct in the Second World War or, for that matter, any war.[4] This is Spielberg's target audience and that poses a problem. What may be useful is a discussion of several nagging problems within the structure of Spielberg's film, especially given the way it has been viewed through—for the most part, uncritical—American eyes. I focus particularly on three themes or, if you like, complaints: (1) Schindler, the "holy entrepreneur" as hero, (2) the Psychotic Nazi approach, and (3) the politics of victimhood.

THE LEGEND OF THE HOLY ENTREPRENEUR

Spielberg packages Schindler as a proto-yuppie with an attractively crooked halo, which is indeed a fairly faithful reflection of the real man. This immensely charming buccaneer who takes care first to get rich quick becomes staunch protector of "his" Jews—almost as if he were scaling Abraham Maslow's self-actualization chart from grubbing for shelter all the way up to hunting for higher values.[5] He is the dreamy stuff that rationalizations are made on: behave as viciously as you like today in order to be able to afford to be virtuous tomorrow. How many stockbrokers, commodities traders, Savings and Loan manipulators, and other makers of nothing but money have promised that just as soon as they amass their fortunes they will retire and make documentaries about Mother Teresa or run dude ranches for under-privileged kids?

If the rascal Schindler can be a hero then everyone can, or so the movie implies. Skirted over by American critics is the smooth way the film affirms the division of ethical action into a hermetically sealed private sphere (where Schindler does as he pleases) and a public sphere (where out of the blue he behaves with stunning moral courage). The average corporate cutthroat or financier certainly would welcome this conveniently compartmentalized view. But is there really no connection? Although Spielberg may be taking a jab at moral majority maniacs, we hardly need him to demonstrate that pious people aren't always moral paragons nor are shady characters always heartless.

Schindler goes on to pull off the ultimate confidence trick by managing a munitions factory that contrives to manufacture nothing at all. One can't help but suspect that Oskar is deeply addicted to the thrill of dangerous gambles; of course, he looks even more attractive because of the intriguing ambiguity of his motives. The conventional commercial screenplay demands an easily understood and extremely urgent motive—money, love, revenge—because audiences are assumed to believe that no one who is sane would undergo risks for any other reasons. Hence all the dapper Schindler initially wants is a profitable factory which, cast against a bloody background of racialist terror, seems like an almost wholesome activity. Although the abominable records of I. G. Farben, Krupp, and other firms feasting on slave labor attest otherwise, the profit motive in this gruesome context subtly takes on all the trappings of a life force. (Recall the ecstatic workers who thank Schindler for giving them jobs that pay virtually nothing.) Indeed, this is a film that market ideologues everywhere can adore.

However, profit is not enough for Schindler (here the film gets a tad subversive); this most paternalist of employers eventually falls in something like love with his mortally endangered workers. Nonetheless, for Schindler to act as classic Hollywood hero the Jews must be reduced to a hapless mass, undifferentiated except for a Rabbi here, a *Judenrat* policeman there, and—that ethnic aide traditionally so prized by rich American WASPs—a Jewish accountant. But Keneally's book demonstrates that the *Schindlerjuden* were anything but a passive lot. Within the shrinking arena of existence imposed by the Nazis (who weren't the only antisemites in Poland), his workers struggled fiercely to seize whatever evanescent wisps of control were possible over their fate. These "employees" included former army officers, business people, craftsmen, and many less exalted people who were tough and wily enough to have survived over generations the pogroms of the past.

These desperate and ingenious people kept the Cracow factory running through their resourceful black marketeering and later rigged the Brinnlitz munitions factory to deceive inspectors.[6] In the last days of the war they were armed—unlike the movie scene—and awaiting the Soviet Army liberators. So Keneally suggests that even in these dire circumstances the Jews "chose" Schindler. Keneally also emphasizes that Schindler related to the scholarly accountant Itzhak Stern as a father figure. Schindler was a man who was emotionally susceptible to humane concerns, if not to abstract moral appeals. (Indeed, the vile predicament Schindler copes with might not have arisen if only he, and many people like him, had acted upon abstract moral appeals at an earlier point when the Nazi's rise to power might have been halted.) Schindler ultimately was seduced by the people he went on to save. In this act, however, he was almost unique among entrepreneurs for whom, if the "bottom line" was six feet deep, so be it.

The most haunting holocaust films not only suggest that "it can happen here"; they reveal in subtle ways how one, or one's neighbors, might accommodate or even come to collaborate in an evil regime. (Consider *Au Revoir, Les Enfants, Lacombe Lucien, The Damned, Mephisto, The Conformist*, or most controversial for its grand guignol antics, *Seven Beauties*.)[7] Unfortunately Spielberg reinforces the disinclination by contemporary audiences to imagine how Nazi crimes might relate to issues in their daily lives. Heroes like Schindler are exceptions and, in any fight against fascistic forces, by the time heroes show up it's already too late. An acute appreciation of this truth might encourage nervous citizens to move against authoritarian trends in early stages—long before there is nothing between oneself and the Gestapo's basement.

THE PSYCHOTIC NAZI SYNDROME

From his sundeck the sybaritic and sadistic work camp commandant Amon Goeth calmly picks off inmates randomly with a sniper rifle. His pastime is a powerful cinematic moment and a distancing mechanism. So far as the audience is concerned the swollen-bellied Goeth might as well wear a Halloween hockey mask as a death's head insignia for he is certainly a cold-blooded psychopath as are virtually all other Nazis we see.

Spielberg plunges us reelingly into the brutal clearances of the Cracow ghetto where when night falls Schmeissers flash like murderous sparklers as storm troopers flush out Jews in hiding. The delirious sequence of the burning of corpses is enacted like a *walpurgisnacht* in broad daylight climaxed when an SS officer, rabid and insatiable, shrieks and shoots into the flames. Ghastly ashes float like a snowfall from hell upon a nearby town. There seems nothing more to say about German fascism. Isn't all this butchery the work of psychos? The trouble, of course, is that it was not. Psychotic killers and calm technocrats worked hand in hand: the former stained with blood, the latter with ink. Both were absolutely necessary in the final solution.

Spielberg does give us the key clue when Goeth insists upon construing Schindler's hosing of the packed freight cars as an eccentric act, even a prank. ("That's really cruel, Oskar. You are giving them hope.") So far as Goeth and his ilk can see, Schindler is agitated over a waste of exploitable labor. Many indignant Nazi industrialists lodged similar complaints: human capital was being squandered by SS oafs before being wrung of every trace of surplus value.

Goeth can be so confident Schindler has an acquisitive angle—even if he "can't work it out"—because there is only one brute reality and one logic within it. In this blinding conceit Goeth is no more irrational than any conventional economist dictating plant shut-downs or "austerity programs" based on short-run market calculations. The holocaust is not just a mass homicidal psychosis at work but a system of power in operation. Inside this system people who were otherwise sane accepted bureaucratized mass murder as normal behavior. (Perhaps *Shoah*'s hypnotic shot of a train creeping toward Auschwitz again and again best conveyed this routinization of murder.) Punctilious legality and arbitrary rule commingled within a criminal regime intent on employing legal devices and rational organization for inhuman ends. (Goeth, was arrested later by the SS not for murder but for embezzling the Third Reich.) Is this mentality just a relic of the past?

Apart from the outright "ethnic cleansing" bloodbaths in Rwanda or Bosnia, one observes how many Western regimes select plausible scapegoats—usually recent migrants—for their own policy failures and inequities. A new Act in Britain repeals the right to silence and gives police the power to criminalize public protest. In 1992 many U.S. voters mistook a petulant billionaire for a populist guru. Italy elected a media billionaire who had nothing against Mussolini. Economic elites in the affluent OECD states evidently are intent on abolishing not only full employment but job security, which provides a fertile milieu for bootboys and demagogues. It's all enough to give vulgar marxism a good name. One even gets a whiff of Nazi biology in the many extravagant claims made by contemporary genetic research; the notion of "lebensunwertes leben" is likely to surface again.[8] The holocaust is certainly not a closed book.

Spielberg resists hinting that ordinary men became not only bureaucratic accomplices but mass killers themselves. A study of one Police Battalion of middle-aged men, who killed 38,000 Jews and shipped 45,000 more to Treblinka, found that they were motivated neither by fanaticism nor the heat of battle.[9] (Indeed, the first shot that they heard fired in anger was their own pistols blasting off the back of a victim's head.) Instead, they were "political and moral eunuchs" who "accommodated to each successive regime."[10] Conformity smothered sanity and fed a persistent human temptation to evade moral and social responsibility, whether by invoking astrology or a "free market" or der fuhrer. There's food for thought here but Spielberg tells us that only Nazis are, well, Nazis.[11]

Lust for success *at any cost*—a value so tirelessly celebrated in our popular culture—renders one completely manipulable whether as an ambitious henchmen like Eichmann, who was inconsolable because he failed to advance beyond the rank of lieutenant colonel, or as cultural baubles for noxious regimes such as the unscrupulous actor in Istvan Szabo's *Mephisto*. We know the professions in Germany and Austria adapted to Nazism with alacrity.[12] When the "central legitimizing norms have been perverted and made criminal," Maier writes, "the average functionary's zeal [led] to genocide"[13] Within this legal milieu Schindler mysteriously succumbed to humane impulses and somehow became an immensely courageous "traitor." But Spielberg has shielded audiences from confronting the question of where they would draw the line. How many other people in Germany and in occupied lands, however troubled, found it "realistic" to adapt? Indeed, how many profited from looted Jewish property or job dismissals? An accommodating attitude is hardly a unique Teutonic trait. "To get along, go along," one must note, is an American expression.

THE POLITICS OF VICTIMHOOD

Not even Jews were wholly immune to the orchestrated emotive power of National Socialism. When the *wehrmacht* was welcomed in Vienna after the *anschluss* George Clare recalls as a Jewish youth how terribly he was tempted to cheer.[14] In the documentary *We Were So Beloved* a Jewish editor at the *New York Times* relates how as a child in Hamburg he craved to join the glamorous Hitler Youth—but for one small technical difficulty. The ironies can be multiplied. If the Nazis had selected another scapegoat some Jews would have joined in the Party's other adventures.[15] Indeed, some Jews joined the Italian Fascist Party. Even some concentration camp prisoners, prior to the Final Solution, still believed in the "superiority of the German race" and were utterly bewildered as to why they wound up in Dachau or Buchenwald.[16]

The Jews were marked for death and as a group they suffered the most horrific losses. Yet they were not the Nazi's sole target although it appears in Spielberg's film as though they were, which may be a disservice to Jewish and non-Jewish victims alike. It appears to be a highly delicate matter in certain quarters to recognize the millions of murders of political dissenters, Gypsies, Russian POWs, gays, and all others deemed "life unworthy of life," as if this would diminish the uniqueness of Jewish suffering. This attitude has been carried to obscenely ironic extremes: witness the protest at Yad

Vashem by Orthodox Jews against granting ceremonial recognition to gays and gay Jews in the camps.[17] In a milder fashion Spielberg invites audiences to experience the holocaust as a kind of tribal tragedy, which it is, but it is also far more than that.

In hard times rulers concoct, and frightened people grasp at, marginal figures to blame for economic inequities, corruption, and adversities—and, especially in Europe, Jews filled the bill. Yet the susceptibility to being scapegoated is not due to anything intrinsic in Jewishness itself but rather stems from their status as a vulnerable and visible minority. A scapegoat is a political creation, and other groups fill that role elsewhere. The best (though not the only) defense is a political defense based both on forming progressive alliances and educating the wider populace so that they are not easy prey for racist slander and demagogic cant. After all, to get at the Jews the Nazis and their allies had to destroy all political opposition first. Portraying the holocaust as an exclusively Jewish experience is dangerously isolating and it mistakenly treats racism as if it were a free-floating plague rather than a political phenomenon.

Regarding education: Auschwitz certainly is not the equivalent of Dresden, Hiroshima, or Cambodia under illegal U.S. bombing or consequent Khmer Rouge rule. But "does not a denial of comparability also lead to evasive moral judgement?"[18] The purpose of the comparisons is what is at stake. The *historikerstreit* debate ultimately centers on the issue of exculpation and the many forms it takes. It is odious to equate Israeli oppression in the formerly occupied lands with Nazism but we cannot let disproportions in suffering, however vast, license anyone to deny the essential injustice undergone in either case.

Finally, the volatile question of complicity arises. Hannah Arendt notoriously accused ghetto authorities of foolishly cooperating with Nazis—a cooperation, however tactical, that only speeded the pace of murder.[19] Spielberg, one must note, sidestepped the similarly harsh judgment Thomas Keneally makes of the Judenrat in Cracow. Arendt attracted enormous vilification, as did Bruno Bettelheim for denouncing "ghetto thinking" that he argues only made Jews more vulnerable. Enraged critics claimed that they simply blamed helpless victims.[20] And, it would have been horrible if that was indeed their aim, which it was not. No one has a right to judge the victims and survivors (as if any of us would behave better). Bettelheim and Arendt instead concentrated on lessons for the present, on showing complacent contemporary readers that they are not exempt from history and must always be vigilant and sensitive to assaults on *any* scapegoat anywhere. When critics say that by the time the Nazis seized power no latitude for resistance remained, they are in an odd way only affirming Bettelheim and Arendt. All the more reason to heed such warnings while we can.

CONCLUSION

Niemals vergessen, yes. What exactly is it about the holocaust that is not to be forgotten? History is so easily forgotten or rewritten that we badly need spurs like Spielberg's film and the debates it engenders. Reality today seems patently the plaything of "spin doctors"; at the same time it is countered by a pervasive but unfocused public skepticism so that one is almost paralyzed over what to deem credible. Yet there is no exaggerating the holocaust.

Nonetheless, the abiding flaw in *Schindler's List* is that it must flatter and exculpate non-German audiences, treating them as if they have some sort of an immune system to the fascist bacillus which Germans singularly lack. This may very well be a small price to pay for winning a huge and well-deserved attendance. But it is always worth recalling Yale psychologist Stanley Milgram's so-called "Eichmann experiments" to detect and sift out authoritarian personality traits.[21] He originally intended to go to Hamburg to test German national character, but soon discovered that he needn't leave New Haven, Connecticut to find all the potential Nazis he needed.

Notes

1. This piece originally was intended for a German audience. It was commissioned and accepted by the German journal *Asthetik & Kommunikation*. Due to changes in the editorial board and the attendant elapsing of time and topicality, it ultimately was not published.
2. Recent biographers reveal that Frank Capra and Walt Disney had dark sides. See, for example, Marc Elliot, *Walt Disney* (London: Andre Deutsch, 1994).
3. See Charles S. Maier, *The Unmasterable Past* (Cambridge: Harvard University Press, 1988).
4. While Ronald Reagan did not quite succeed in peddling his interpretation of the Vietnam War as a "noble cause," only a minority of Americans see it as anything worse than a "mistake."
5. See Abraham Maslow, *Toward a Psychology of Being* (New York: Von Norstrand, 1968).
6. Keneally, *Schindler's Ark* (New York: Vintage), pp. 224, 324.
7. See Bettelheim's essay savaging "Seven Beauties" in his *Surviving and Other Essays* (New York: Vintage Books, 1980) and the counterattack by Eli Pfefferkorn, "The Case of Bruno Bettelheim and Lina Wertmuller's Seven Beauties" in *The Nazi Concentration Camps: Structure and Aims*. Proceedings of the Fourth Yad Vashem Historical Conference (Jerusalem: Yad vashem, 1984). Bettelheim's analysis turns on his perception of Wertmuller's apparent approval of the "hero" (which he misunderstood) although his main concern was what audiences believed.
8. See Ruth Hubbard and Elijah Wild, *Exploding The Gene Myth* (New York: Norton, 1993) and R. C. Lewontin, Steven Rose, and Leon J. Kamin, *Not in Our Genes; Biology, Ideology and Human Nature* (New York: Pantheon, 1984).

9. Christopher R. Browning, *Ordinary Men: Reserve Police Battalion 101 and The Final Solution in Poland* (New York: Harper Perennial, 1992).

10. Ibid. A touring entertainment unit begged to join "Jew Hunts" in the countryside, which would be akin to a Bob Hope USO tour volunteering to napalm Vietnamese or Iraqis.

11. Some U.S. soldiers who liberated concentration camps in 1945 testify that upon viewing the helpless inmates they felt not only pity but a terrible contempt involuntarily welling up. They were horrified and ashamed at their own feelings— feelings which in its own members the SS obviously put to use.

12. Robert J. Lifton, *The Nazi Doctors* (New York: Basic Books, 1986).

13. Maier, *Unmasterable Past*, p. 93.

14. "So caught was I, the seventeen year old Jew in my Austro-German conditioning from childhood, that I could not see these clean-limbed young men as my enemies. The Nazis, the SS and SA, they were my enemies but not the young and handsome soldiers of the wehrmacht. If I had not been born a Jew, could I have been a Nazi at Seventeen?" George Clare, *Last Waltz in Vienna* (London: Macmillan, 1980), p. 19.

15. Obviously this scenario is as far-fetched as polls revealing that a minority of Germans would approve of Hitler as a national leader if only there had been no war and no holocaust, which is like approving of great white sharks if only they were vegetarians.

16. Bettelheim, *Surviving and Other Essays*, p. 81.

17. "Gay Jews Hit, Scorned During Holocaust Rite," *Chicago Tribune*, 31 May 1994.

18. Maier, p. 54.

19. Hannah Arendt, *Eichmann in Jerusalem: A Report on the Banality of Evil* (New York: Viking, 1963); and see Bruno Bettelheim, "Freedom from Ghetto Thinking," *Midstream* Spring 1962, "The Ignored Lesson of Anne Frank," in *Surviving and Other Essays*, and *The Informed Heart* (New York: Free Press, 1960).

20. See Isaiah Trunk, *Judenrat* (Manchester: Manchester University Press, 1972).

21. Stanley Milgram, *Obedience to Authority* (London: Tavistock, 1974).

Index

Abraham, David, 59, 78
Acheson, Dean, 201; and Acheson-Lilenthal Report, 60
Accuracy in Media (AIM), 215, 218, 220, 221
Adams, Gerry, 166–67, 170, 179, 180
Adler, Emanuel, 29, 36–39, 45, 46, 49
Adorno, Theodor, 11, 12, 23
Afghanistan, 69, 72
Alexander, Alba, 79
Algeria, 91
Almond, Gabriel, 190, 191, 193, 212
Alquie, Ferdinand, 10
Alt, James, 158
Althusser, Louis, 8
Alvey (UK), 126, 128
American Enterprise Institute, 65
Anglo-Irish agreement, 178, 180
Anglo-Irish War, 92
anti-war movement (Vietnam), 199–200, 209–10
Archer, Margaret, 50, 171, 184
Arendt, Hannah, xiv, 230, 232
Argentina, 39, 41, 46, 73, 96, 107, 116
Association for Asian Studies, 217
Atomic Energy Commission (AEC), 61–65
Atomic Industrial Forum, 63
Auschwitz, 224, 228, 230
Austria, 138, 152, 229
autarchy, 93, 173
automation, 99, 109, 123, 124, 136–37, 155–57, 163

Bakunin, Mikhail, 16, 24
Baran, Paul, 83
Barbour, Ian, 6, 21
Baruch plan, 60
Begin, Menachem, 199
Belgium, 64, 97, 102, 114, 139
Bell, Bowyer, 184, 185
Bell Curve, The, 14, 23
Ben-David, Joseph, 20, 23, 24

Bettelheim, Bruno, 230, 231, 232
Bew, Paul, 185, 186
Blair, Tony, 183
Block, Fred, 58, 78, 161, 164
Blum, Leon, 200
Bohr, Neils, 6, 7, 8
Bolivia, 108, 116
"bonanza" development, 104
Bosnia, 228
Brazil, 39, 40, 41, 107, 109, 116, 195
Brenner, Michael, 71–72
Breton, Andre, 10
Bretton Woods, 38, 39
Britain, Great. *See* United Kingdom
Bronner, Stephen E., 20, 24, 208
Brook, Peter, 168
Browning, Christopher, 232
Bundy, McGeorge, 199
Burchett, Wilfred, 222
bureaucratic-authoritarianism, 83, 89
"bureaucratic rings," 41
Burnham, Walter Dean, 88
Burtt, E. A., 6, 22

Cambodia, 210, 230
Campbell, John L., 60, 75, 78, 79, 81
Canada, 60, 61, 70
Cardoso, Fernando, 83, 84, 86, 102
Carnoy, Martin, 163, 164
Carr, Edward Hallett, 206, 209, 223
Carroll, Lewis, 28
Carter, Jimmy, 55, 66, 69, 70, 71, 72, 130, 199
Catholic Church, 7, 92, 111, 182
Central Intelligence Agency (CIA), 37, 167
Charcot, Jean Martin, 188
Chernobyl, 73
Chile, 53, 77, 96, 109
China, 3, 31, 34, 35, 63, 82, 155, 159, 215
Chomsky, Noam, 14, 23, 43
Clare, George, 229, 232

233

Clinton, Bill, 148, 152, 154, 159, 166, 167
Cohen, Stephen, 154, 161, 163
Comte, Auguste, 11
corporatism, 96, 97, 139, 153
Council on Foreign Relations, 43
counterinduction, 8, 11, 15
Crozier, Michel, 23
Cuba, 72
Cumings, Bruce, 215–23
Cyert, Richard, 124
Czech Republic, 154

dadaism, 4, 10, 14, 15, 19, 20
Daley, Richard, Sr., 38
Dead Reckonings, definitions of, x, xi
debt, 107–8, 115
Defense, Department of (US), 126
deference (propensity to defer), 88, 92, 101, 105, 107, 108
Democratic Leadership Council, 159
Democratic Left, 180. See also Workers Party
Democratic Unionist Party (DUP), 167, 177
Denmark, 113
dependency (dependencia), 83–85, 89, 102, 107
Derian, Jean Claude, 124, 127, 128
DeSade, Marquis, 12
dialectical materialism, 13, 19
dialectics, 4, 6, 8, 36
domestic structure, 203, 204
Dosi, Giovanni, 124, 129–33, 143–46
Doyle, Michael, 190, 193, 204
Duchamp, Marcel, 14, 15
Duvall, Raymond, 85, 91, 98

Eichmann, Adolf, 229
Einstein, Albert, 6
Eisenhower, Dwight, 61, 71, 208
Ellis, P. Bereford, 119
Ellsberg, Daniel, 46
Ellul, Jacques, 150, 161
Elsenhans, Hartmut, 102
Elstein, David, 216, 219
Elster, Jon, 46
Enlightenment, 11
epistemic communities, 28, 94, 97, 100, 101, 103, 109, 111, 113–15, 152, 167

European Economic Community (EEC) or European Union (EU), 94, 97, 100, 101, 103, 109, 111, 113, 114, 115, 139, 152, 167, 181
European monetary system, 157
Evangelista, Matthew, 195, 202, 212
Evans, Peter, 89, 162, 192, 194

Faletto, Enzo, 83, 84, 86
famine, 92
Farrar-Hockley, Anthony, 216
Federal Bureau of Investigation (FBI), 167, 216
Feyerabend, Paul, i–ii, xiv, 1–24, 47
Fianna Fail, 93, 94, 97, 98, 103, 110, 111, 112, 115, 169, 187
Fifth Generation project (Japan), 134
Fine Gael, 98, 103, 104, 110, 111, 112, 115, 180
Finland, 152
Fitzgerald, Garret, 113, 177, 179, 181, 186, 187
Ford, Gerald, 65
Fordism, 132, 139, 141, 142
Foucault, Michel, 22
France, xiii, 5, 64, 73, 74, 76, 126, 127, 130, 136, 162, 190, 200
Frank, Andre Gundar, 83, 102
Frankfurt School, xiv, 3, 6, 7, 20, 54
Franklin, H. Bruce, 46, 207, 208
free trade, 35, 38, 93–94, 148, 151–52
Freeman, Christopher, 124, 129–34, 143–46
Freeman, John, 50, 85, 91, 98
Freiden, Jeff, 43, 120
Friedman, David, 124, 125, 136
Friedman, Milton, 37

Galbraith, John Kenneth, 110, 160, 164
Galileo, 7, 8, 20
game theory, 17, 29
Garret, Geoffrey, 34, 35, 39, 42, 46, 212
Gates, Robert, 37
Gay, Peter, 207
Geertz, Clifford, 47, 49
General Agreement on Tariffs and Trade (GATT), 149, 157, 159
General Electric, 69, 138
Germany (West), 63, 67, 74, 97, 114, 127, 134, 138, 166, 190–91, 200, 207, 225–31

Gerschenkron, Alexander, 84, 93
Gibraltar, 166
Gibson, William James, 184, 211
Gilder, George, 150
Gilman, Roger, xii
Gilpin, Robert, 205, 212
Gingrich, Newt, 159
Goldstein, Judith, 26, 28, 29, 32–33
Goodman International, 114–15
Goodman, Paul, 48, 110
Goulden, Joseph, 218, 222
Gouldner, Alvin, 4, 15, 20, 21
Gourevitch, Peter, 45, 47, 49, 105
Gramsci, Antonio, xi, xiii, 39–40, 42, 49, 54, 77, 82, 87–88, 197, 209
Greece, 90, 101
Grenada, 208, 221
Grossberg, Lawrence, 50
Gulf War, 73, 128
Guardian, The (London), 144, 184

Haas, Peter, 26, 36, 46, 49
Habermas, Jürgen, 4, 16, 17–19, 24, 46, 77, 78, 161, 184
Hacking, Ian, 21
Haggard, Stephen, 45, 85, 162, 164
Halberstam, David, 223
Halderman, H. R., 199
Hall, John, 28, 44
Hall, Stuart, 50
Hall, Peter, 31, 32
Halliday, Fred, 48, 191, 196–98, 202, 207, 209
Halliday, Jon, 215–23
Halpern, Nina, 27, 34, 45, 49
Haughey, Charles, 114, 115
Heisenberg, Werner, 21
Helms, Richard, 199
Hersh, Seymour, 77, 79
Hintze, Otto, 190
Hirschmann, Albert, 25, 32, 39, 44, 47, 49, 88, 230
Historical sociology, xiv, 198, 203
Hitler, Adolf, 200
Holocaust, 224–31
Hong Kong, 82
Horkheimer, Max, 3, 6, 7, 11, 12, 17, 21, 23
Hoyt, Austin, 216–23
Hume, John, 167, 169, 170, 184, 186

Hungary, 154
Husserl, Edmund, 21

ideology, 6, 12, 29, 35, 40, 53, 54, 88, 150, 171
I. G. Farben, 226
Ikenberry, John, 38, 48
import substitution, 93–94
India, 65, 68, 73, 82, 155
Industrial Development Authority, 96, 97–100, 112–15
International Monetary Fund (IMF), 40, 107–8
International Telephone & Telegraph (ITT), 53
Iran, 53
Iraq, 73, 114, 115
Ireland, Republic of, 84–89, 91–107, 171, 178, 179
Irish Congress of Trade Unions (ICTU), 97, 98, 181
Irish Free State, 92
Irish National Liberation Army, 177
Irish People's Liberation Organisation, 177
Irish Republican Army (Official IRA), 111, 174, 175, 185
Irish Republican Army (Provisional IRA), 165, 175, 176, 177, 179, 180, 181, 182, 185, 186
Irvine, Reed, 215
Israel, 73, 107, 199; and Israeli peace movement, 199
Italy, 114, 229

Jamaica, 106
Janus, 193
Japan, xiii, 63, 71, 109, 124, 125, 126, 127, 130, 131, 132, 134–35, 137, 142, 151, 195, 217, 220, 221
Johnson, Lyndon, 194, 199, 208
Joravsky, David, 24
Joseph, Paul, 58, 72, 78

Kantor, Mickey, 159
Katzenstein, Peter, 152, 161, 162, 163
Katznelson, Ira, 24
Kaufman, Robert, 96
Kehr, Eckart, 191, 207
Keneally, Thomas, 224, 225, 227, 231
Kennedy, John F., 200, 208

Kennedy, Paul, 191, 207, 208
Kennedy, Ted, 178
Keohane, Robert, 26, 28, 29, 188, 205
Keynes, John Maynard, 26, 44, 136
Keynesianism, 28, 31, 32, 33, 123, 129, 130, 133, 152, 157
Khmer Rouge, 230
Kinnock, Neil, 115
Knightley, Philip, 215, 223
Kohl, Helmut, 190
Kolko, Gabriel, 209, 210, 211
Kondratiev waves, 127
Korea, North, 73, 216, 220
Korea, South, 82, 85, 90, 109, 215, 217, 219, 220
Korean War, xiv, 215–23
Krasner, Stephen, xiii, 44, 53–55, 57, 60, 64, 70–71, 74, 77, 78
Krupp, 226
Kuhn, Thomas, 30, 47
Kuttner, Robert, 144, 153, 164

Labour Party (British), 131, 152, 162
Labour Party (Irish), 95, 97, 98, 105, 110, 111, 112, 115, 169
Laos, 194
Latin American Commission for Economic Development (ECLA), 40
legitimacy, 26, 31, 43
Lemass, Sean, 95
Lenin, Vladimir, 13, 15, 19, 23, 48, 162
Libya, 73
Lifton, Robert J., 232
Linberg, Leon, 77, 81
Lindblom, Charles, 88
Lippman, Walter, 192
Lipson, Charles H., 77
List, Freidrich, 93, 153
living standards (Ireland), 101, 102
Lockean liberalism, 55
Loyalists, 166–87
Lukacs, Georg, 21
Lysenkoism, 24

Maastricht Treaty, 113, 114
Maier, Charles, 33, 41, 47, 48, 207, 229, 231, 232
Major, John, 169, 180, 181, 182, 183
Malthus, Thomas, 92
Mannheim, Karl, 6, 7, 37, 204, 212
Marcuse, Herbert, 8–9, 11, 12, 16, 24

Martians, 194
Marx, Karl, 5, 18, 19, 26, 27, 37, 49, 56, 91
marxism and neo-marxism, 3–4, 8, 11, 15–16, 17, 18, 24–26, 44, 56–59, 64, 136, 138
"marxist outlaw," 3–4
Maslow, Abraham, 225, 231
Matthews, John, 124, 125, 132
Mayhew, Patrick, 170, 181
McCarthyism, 201, 220
McGuinness, Martin, 179
McNamara, Robert, 208
Merton, Robert, 4, 21
Mexico, 85, 108, 109, 155
microelectronics, 109, 124, 126, 127, 137, 141, 160, 190
Milgram, Stanley, 231, 232
military Keynesianism, 126
Mill, John Stuart, 11, 13, 14, 16, 24
Moore, Barrington, Jr., 88
Moravscik, Andrew, 194–95
Morgenthau, Hans J., 49, 200, 210
Morrison, Bruce, 111, 167
Mowery, David, 124
Moynihan, Senator Daniel Patrick, 176, 177, 178
Muller, Herbert, 191, 199
multinational corporations, 97, 98, 99, 103, 109, 151, 155, 157, 159, 162, 174
Mumford, Lewis, 5, 21

Nazism, 200, 211, 225–32
Neikirk, William, 148
Nelson, Richard, 124
Netherlands, 114, 136
new industrializing countries (NICs), 82, 102, 141, 153, 155
New Ireland Forum, 186
Newton, Isaac, 4, 6, 8
Nincic, Miroslav, 192, 208
Nitze, Paul, 219
Nixon, Richard, 64, 65, 66, 71, 210, 219
Noble, David, 48, 140
Nora Report, 124, 135, 141, 143, 149, 161
North American Free Trade Agreement (NAFTA), 34, 151, 152, 155, 157, 158, 162

Northern Ireland (British Ulster), xiv, 111, 165–83
Northern Ireland Civil Rights Association, 174
Norway, 138
nuclear freeze movement, 199, 201
Nuclear Non-Proliferation Act of 1978 (NNPA), xiii, 54, 60, 63, 66–73, 79
nuclear weapons, 66

Oakley, Brian, 124, 125
Odell, John, 50, 87, 209
Office of Technology Assessment (OTA), 66, 157, 163
O'Leary, Brendan, 183
O'Neill, Terence, 173, 175
O'Neill, Tip, 167, 178, 204
Operation Hudson Harbor, 220
Oppenheimer, Robert, 5, 60
Orange Order, 173
Organization for Economic Cooperation and Development (OECD), 90, 102, 124, 141, 228
Owen, Kenneth, 124, 125

Paisley, Ian, 167, 170, 179
Pakistan, 69, 73
Parnell, Charles Stewart, 173
Patriot missile, 127
Pentagon Papers, 37, 208
"peripheral postindustrialization," 84, 102, 106
Perot, Ross, 228
Peru, 104, 109
Pierson, Paul, 45, 162
Piore, Michael, 132, 139
Poland, 116, 154, 192, 226
Polanyi, Karl, 48, 125, 142
Polanyi, Michael, 6, 23
policy concordance, 64, 75
policy crisis, xiii, 56–58, 60, 89
policy entrepreneurs, 33, 35, 47, 86
Popper, Karl, 6, 7, 22
Portugal, 90
Poulantzas, Nicos, 57, 59, 77
poverty (Irish), 111
privatization, 112, 115
product cycles, 82
Progressive Democrats, 110, 112, 113, 114
Przeworski, Adam, 46, 77

Public Broadcasting Service (PBS), 217, 219, 220, 221, 222
Puerto Rico, 100, 101

rational choice models, 26, 28–29, 166–67
Reagan, Ronald, 71, 72, 73, 76, 154, 208, 231
Reaganomics, 29, 133
realism, 57, 188–204
recombinant DNA, 38
Reich, Robert, 45, 160
research and development, 61, 62, 90, 99, 127, 128, 130, 131
Reynolds, Albert, 113–15
Richter, Hans, 10, 23
Rickover, Hyman, 61
Risse-Kappen, Thomas, 191, 199
Robinson, Mary, 114
Roosevelt, Franklin Delano, 56, 149, 200, 201
Rosecrance, Richard, 159, 164, 202, 211
Rosenberg, Nathan, 109, 125, 126
Rosenberg, Justin, 196, 197, 202, 212
Royal Ulster Constabulary (RUC), 176, 178, 182
Ruggie, John Gerard, 36, 46, 78, 82
Rusk, Dean, 219, 220, 222
Rwanda, 228

Sabel, Charles, 132, 139
Scharpf, Fritz, 155
Schumpeter, Joseph, 88, 123, 131, 144
Science Policy Research Unit, 129
scientism, 18
Scotland, 90, 100, 101
Seeley, Sir John, 191
Sheehan, Neil, 208, 210, 223
Shoah, 228
Sikkink, Kathryn, 27, 28, 39–43, 46
Silverberg, Gerald, 124
Simmons, Beth, 198, 199, 208, 209
Singapore, 82, 101, 159
Single European Act, 34
Sinn Fein—The Workers Party. *See* Workers Party
Sinn Fein (Provisional), 167, 168, 169, 170, 177, 180, 181
Skocpol, Theda, 77, 161, 223
Smith, Adam, 31, 150

Smith, Steve, 195, 209
Snidal, Duncan, 212
Snyder, Jack, 43, 202, 208, 209
Social Democratic and Labour Party (SDLP), 175, 177, 179
"social structure of accumulation," 133–34
Soete, Luc, 124, 129–33
Somalia, 195
South Africa, 166
South Korea. See Korea, South
Soviet Union, 25, 31, 35, 60, 61, 69, 72, 201, 211, 227
Spain, 64, 114
Spielberg, Stephen, x, xiv, 224–31
Spring, Dick, 111, 115
Stalinism, 31, 34, 219
state-sponsored bodies (Ireland), 103
Stein, Judith Gross, 208
Stephens, Evelyn and John, 106
Stilwell, Richard G., 217, 218, 219, 221, 223
Stormont, 173, 175, 178, 180
Strategic Defense Initiative, 37, 126
surrealism, 101, 159
Sussex School, 129–33, 135, 140
Sweden, 106, 136, 138, 140, 152

Taiwan, 82, 85, 90, 109
"Team B" report, 223
"technobureaucrats," 86, 106
technocratic modes, 17, 41, 161
Telesis report, 100, 101, 106
Teller, Edward, 37
Thames television, 215, 216, 217, 218, 219, 221, 223
Thatcher, Margaret, 29, 131, 154, 176, 177, 184
Thomas, W. I., 32
Tito, 27
Tory Party (British Conservative Party), 105, 166, 173, 175, 182, 223, 231
Toulmin, Stephen, 43
Treblinka, 228
Trotsky, Leon, 13, 19, 24
Tzara, Tristan, 14, 20

Ulster. See Northern Ireland
Ulster Defence Association (UDA), 178
Ulster Volunteer Force (UVF), 178

Unionist Party, 169, 170, 173, 175, 179, 180, 182
United Kingdom, xiii, 38, 60, 91–94, 96–97, 105, 165–87, 190, 191, 195–97, 200, 202, 204, 211
United Irishmen, 172
United Nations, 60, 70, 215
United States of America, xiii, xiv, 14, 28, 32, 34, 37, 53–58, 60–64, 68–75, 126, 128–35, 139, 141, 142, 148–64, 167, 168, 170, 178, 182, 215–23
Uranium Enrichment Corporation (URENCO), 64

Vandenberg, Arthur, 201
Venezuela, 107
Verdier, Daniel, 48, 198, 199
Vietnam War, 28, 37, 57, 123, 192, 194, 199, 200, 201, 208, 210, 211, 220, 223
Volksmuseum (Berlin), 206
Volkswagen, 139
Volvo, 139

Wallerstein, Michael, 46
Wallerstein, Robert, 47
Waltz, Kenneth, 188, 189, 196, 203, 204, 212
Weber, Max, 26, 44, 58, 151
Weingast, Barry, 34, 35, 39, 42, 46
Weir, Margaret, 47–48
Wellmar, Albrecht, 17, 24
Wendt, Alexander, 28, 44, 197, 201, 211
Wertmuller, Lina, 231
Westinghouse, 61, 64, 72
Westmoreland, William, 223
WGBH (Boston), 215, 217, 219, 221, 222, 223
Whitaker, T. K., 95
Whitby, Max, 219
Whitehead, Philip, 219
Wilson, Harold, 178
Winner, Langdon, 150, 161
Workers Party, 111, 175
World Trade Organization, 148, 159

Yad Vashem, 229–30, 231
Yugoslavia, 34

Zuboff, Shoshanna, 124, 125, 138–39
Zysman, John, 161, 163